PRAISE FOR *SACRED TENSION*

"In our time, when society and the church are polarized, we know that dialogue mends division. In *Sacred Tension*, Bill Brown invites us into an ancient conversation among the many voices in scripture. This book shows us a future in which our many voices, in sustained and faithful dialogue, are essential to our life with God."

—Rev. David Lewicki, pastor, North Decatur Presbyterian Church

"Who but Bill Brown could write this book? And what a gift he has! Here, Brown offers an accessible and engaging introduction to reading dialogically across a wide range of topics (including hot button ones) and many different texts from what he calls the biblical multiverse. Brown is, per usual, wise and winsome, bold and brave. The path Brown points us down is one with more, not less Bible, with the end goal of canonical comprehensiveness always out ahead of us. I can't wait to use *Sacred Tension* in various classroom settings and I will be referring students, friends, family—anybody and everybody! —to this fantastic book."

—Brent A. Strawn, D. Moody Smith Distinguished Professor of Old Testament and Professor of Law, Duke University

"The Bible is full of different voices—voices often in tension with one another. Usually, this tension feels like a problem: professors are unsure how to teach it, many students fear and resist it, and pastors leave seminary convinced that they should hide it from their congregations. The gift of Brown's *Sacred Tension* is an intellectually honest embrace of difference and disagreements in scripture as valuable and not as a problem. *Sacred Tension* is an invitation to think through the ethical implications, big theological themes, and questions of divine inspiration and biblical authority we encounter when reading scripture. For anyone interested in honesty about what is in the Bible combined with sensitivity to how faith communities can benefit from it, this is the book that we have been waiting for."

—Justin Reed, Associate Professor of Old Testament/Hebrew Bible, Louisville Presbyterian Theological Seminary

SACRED TENSION

SACRED TENSION

EMBRACING DISSONANCE AND DIALOGUE IN THE OLD TESTAMENT

WILLIAM P. BROWN

SACRED TENSION: Embracing Dissonance and Dialogue in the Old Testament

Upper Room Books® website: upperroombooks.com

ISBN: 978-0-8358-2080-6

Epub ISBN: 978-0-8358-2081-3

Cover design: Emma Elzinga, Inksplatter Design

Interior design: PerfecType, Nashville, TN

Printed in the United States of America

To Gail,

with deep gratitude for our partnership of thirty-four years

TABLE OF CONTENTS

CHAPTER 1

The Bible as Dialogue

As I worked on this book, I found inspiration in a monumental work by acclaimed historian Allen Dwight Callahan. In his eye-opening historical review, *The Talking Book: African Americans and the Bible*, Callahan traces the journey of the Bible among Black people in America, from the era of slavery to the time of Howard Thurman and the Civil Rights Movement. The phrase "talking book" is a reference to how many enslaved Africans first encountered the Bible, including James Albert Ukawsaw Gronniosaw, a formerly enslaved man who published an account of his experiences in 1772:

> [My master] used to read prayers in public to the ship's crew every Sabbath day; and when I first saw him read, I was never so surprised in my life, as when I saw the book talk to my master, for I thought it did, as I observed him to look upon it, and move his lips. I wished it would do so with me. As soon as my master was done reading, I followed him to the place where he put the book, being mightily delighted with it, and when nobody saw me, I opened it, and put my ear down close upon it, in great hopes that it would say something to me; but I was very sorry, and greatly disappointed, when I found that it would not speak. This thought

> immediately presented itself to me, that every body and every thing despised me because I was black.[1]

Another convert, John Jea, expressed his disappointment when he held the book up to his ear, lamenting, "The book would not talk to me."[2] For enslaved Africans in America, the Bible was at first a silent book, one that seemed to speak only to their white enslavers.

However, the Bible did talk eventually. As more and more people who were enslaved learned to read, often covertly, the words of the Bible offered a taste of freedom, speaking no longer just to white enslavers. According to Callahan, reading the Bible was "the chief goal of literacy for African Americans."[3] What they found was a book full of contradictions, which resonated deeply with their unbearable condition, "African Americans themselves incarnated America's greatest contradiction. They were slaves in the land of the free."[4] On one hand, the Bible echoed the language of their oppressors—it was a "poison book."[5] On the other, it spoke of freedom and dignity—it was a "good book." While the Bible was toxic in so many ways, it also contained its own "antidote," its own "balm in Gilead, to make the wounded whole."[6] In other words, for African Americans, "the antidote to hostile texts of the Bible was more Bible, homeopathically administered to counteract the toxins of the text."[7]

---

1. Quoted from Henry Louis Gates, Jr., and William L. Andrews, eds., *Pioneers of the Black Atlantic: Five Slave Narratives from the Enlightenment, 1772–1815* (Washington, DC: Civitas, 1998), 40–41.
2. Gates and Andrews, *Pioneers of the Black Atlantic*, 392.
3. Allen Dwight Callahan, *The Talking Book: African Americans and the Bible* (New Haven: Yale University Press, 2006), 19.
4. Callahan, *The Talking Book*, 25.
5. Ibid.
6. Callahan, *The Talking Book*, 39.
7. Callahan, *The Talking Book*, 40.

CANONICAL COMPREHENSIVENESS[8]

This study delves into the sacred concept of "more Bible," focusing specifically on the Bible's extensive and wide-ranging dialogue with itself and with readers from diverse backgrounds and life experiences. Taken as a whole, the Bible is indeed the quintessential "talking book" because it often has a habit of talking to itself, setting a precedent that invites readers to "talk back" to it and talk with each other. Among all the sacred texts of the ancient world, the Bible stands out as the most diverse, both literarily and theologically. It's a vast library in itself, consisting of sixty-six books (in the Protestant canon) that span over a millennium of diverse testimonies about God, humanity, and the world. As I often remind my students, the Bible was not dropped from heaven fully-formed on golden plates, nor was it dictated in whole to a single individual. Instead, the Bible grew from small, oral beginnings passed down over centuries, with each generation contributing its own stories and understandings in a common struggle to discern God's presence and work in their lives.

In other words, the Bible is no echo chamber, endlessly repeating the same thing over and over again. Rather, it's a canonical cornucopia—a "horn of plenty" filled with diverse perspectives, all tied together by a common affirmation that God is God, expressed in different ways. The Bible is deeply rooted in the specific contexts and concerns of ancient communities across a vast stretch of history. It revels in its cultural and theological particularities while addressing fundamental, timeless questions about human purpose and divine character. This diversity is evident in how the Bible preserves and interweaves its traditions, creating a vibrant, rich, and textured tapestry. It presents a dizzying array of material, from legal codes to love poetry, from family sagas to battlefield accounts. There are prophetic judgments and salvation oracles. Words of lament are followed by

8. For a more detailed and extensive discussion of the Bible's canonical diversity, see William P. Brown, *Deep Calls to Deep: The Psalms in Dialogue amid Disruption* (Nashville, TN: Abingdon, 2021), 11-17.

words of praise and back again. If the Bible were an anthem, it would be filled with soaring harmonies and lilting melodies, alongside jarring dissonances and "sour" notes. Not every voice in the Bible is pitch-perfect; not every voice sings the same tune, and this is intentional. Harmony here, dissonance there—is that a problem?

For some readers, it is. The Bible's diversity can pose difficult challenges for those who seek simplistic answers to complex issues or desire absolute certainty about every matter under heaven. It's an issue for those who expect complete consensus and the elimination of ambiguity, for those who want wisdom hand-delivered to them without any need for discernment. But the Bible wasn't written for passive readers or lazy listeners. It's meant for active engagement, deliberation, dialogue, and debate because the Bible itself is inherently a conversation. Scripture embodies its own version of America's traditional motto *e pluribus unum*—"one out of many."[9]

Among ancient religious texts, the Bible stands out for preserving diverse and sometimes conflicting viewpoints. Biblical scholar Seth Sanders notes that the Pentateuch (the first five books of the Bible) is unique in the ancient world for its deliberate avoidance of uniformity. Genesis and Exodus, for instance, are filled with parallel narratives that are often "glaringly inconsistent," resulting in an "incoherent interwoven source."[10] Sanders points out that the Pentateuch's "most problematic and important feature" is its choice to weave together "parallel variants of the same event" without any attempt to harmonize them.[11]

---

9. The motto, coupled with its converse, draws from Heraclitus' tenth fragment, "The one out of all things, and all things out of the one" (*ek pantōn hen ex henos panta*).

10. Seth L. Sanders, "What If There Aren't Any Empirical Models for Pentateuchal Criticism?" in *Contextualizing Israel's Sacred Writings: Ancient Literacy, Orality, and Literary Production*, ed. Brian B. Schmidt (Ancient Israel and Its Literature 22; Atlanta: SBL Press, 2015), 299-300.

11. Sanders, "What If There Aren't Any Empirical Models," 282.

Although Sanders is not using the term "problematic" pejoratively, I'd prefer the word "unprecedented." The Pentateuch's so-called "problem" of unharmonized differences actually proves to be its badge of honor. Sanders argues that these preserved inconsistencies create a biblical text that is "radically incoherent, yet still strangely readable."[12] I would add that this "strange" readability is precisely what makes scripture so compelling. What Sanders labels "problematic" is one of the Bible's most compelling features for readers today. For example, he notes that between the conflicting flood stories in Genesis 6-9 and the divergent creation accounts in Genesis 1-3, we see that "comprehensiveness trumps cohesion."[13] The Pentateuch's authors and editors found greater value in bringing together divergent accounts of the same events rather than forcing them into a single, consistent narrative. The same can be said for the four gospel accounts in the New Testament, each offering its unique perspective on Jesus. Our biblical editors recognized "the danger of a single story,"[14] the risk of silencing one account in favor of another. For them, it was crucial to present conflicting stories, even of the same event, whether it was the exodus through the Red Sea or the ministry of Jesus.

But the Bible's "problematic" diversity extends beyond just recounting events in different ways; it also encompasses major thematic issues central to the life of faith, like wisdom and law, God's presence and humanity's place in creation, or the problem of evil and the idea of election. Is wisdom a gift from God or something to be sought and discovered through human striving? Is God primarily a God of justice or mercy? Can God change, or is God immutable? Is humanity the crown of creation or simply one

---

12. Seth L. Sanders, "What If There Aren't Any Empirical Models for Pentateuchal Criticism?" in *Contextualizing Israel's Sacred Writings: Ancient Literacy, Orality, and Literary Production*, ed. Brian B. Schmidt (Ancient Israel and Its Literature 22; Atlanta: SBL Press, 2015), 282.

13. Sanders, "What If There Aren't Any Empirical Models," 301.

14. To borrow from Nigerian author and speaker Chimamanda Ngozi Adichie, *Ted Talk* (October 7, 2009) at https://www.youtube.com/watch?v=D9Ihs241zeg&t=47s.

species among many? Is being chosen by God a privilege or a responsibility? Is Israel's election primarily a covenantal privilege or a moral responsibility? The answer to all of these questions is: yes! It's complicated—and that complexity can be a good thing.

Why is scripture so uniquely inclusive and complex? That's open to interpretation. In some cases, there's a canonical irony where later traditions meant to replace earlier ones ended up being placed together, almost side by side, as seen with the Bible's various law codes (see Chapter 3). Even if "comprehensiveness" was a goal for these ancient editors, the question remains: why? What motivated such inclusivity? My hunch is that fostering dialogue was a key aim, at least partly because dialogue naturally arises when differing perspectives are presented without an immediate resolution. With diversity as its defining characteristic—whether seen as "problematic" or appealing—the Bible functions like a library where no books are banned (although some came close to being excluded from the canon) but are all available for thoughtful deliberation. This is especially true considering that at least five books—Ezekiel, Proverbs, Ecclesiastes, Song of Songs, and Esther—were controversial either before or after their inclusion in the canon. Martin Luther even argued for the removal of Hebrews, James, Jude, and Revelation from the New Testament canon. Despite these controversies, there they all are, fully controversial *and* fully canonical. Ironically, the Bible itself has occasionally faced book bans in America, most recently in a Utah school district for containing "vulgarity or violence."[15] Guilty as charged.

A SCRIPTURAL CONTRADICTION

As we begin to scratch the surface of the Bible's dialogical diversity, let's consider a glaring example of a scriptural contradiction—one that doesn't

15. See Tilda Wilson, "A Utah School District Has Removed the Bible from Some Schools' Shelves" (June 2, 2023), NPR, https://www.npr.org/2023/06/02/1179906120/utah-bible-book-challenge.

try to hide itself but instead broadcasts itself like a blinking neon sign. Take the "dueling" proverbs found in Proverbs 26:4-5, which rabbis highlighted as a point of controversy (*b Shabbat* 30b):

> Do not answer a fool according to his folly,
> or you yourself will be just like him.
> Answer a fool according to his folly,
> or he will be wise in his own eyes. (Proverbs 26:4-5)

Two contradictory proverbs are set side by side, each suggesting a different course of action with distinct reasons and motivations. If you avoid engaging with fools, they will see themselves as wise—a cardinal sin in the Wisdom Literature (Prov. 26:12). But if you do respond to them, you risk being drawn into their folly. So, what should readers—who presumably aren't fools—do? Rather than being paralyzed by indecision, they must figure out the answer for themselves. They must weigh the pros and cons of responding to fools in any given situation and make a decision. This process of discerning, deciding, acting with informed judgment, and then dealing with the consequences fosters a critical consciousness—which is a good thing!

How might one navigate such opposing admonitions? By making a distinction between engaging in genuine dialogue—where participants are open to learning from one another—and a shouting match, where there's no hope for mutual growth or compromise. Take the topic of race in America, a perennially challenging subject for many white Americans. My African American colleagues have commented that while they are eager to engage in dialogue and share their struggles with discrimination, prejudice, and socioeconomic inequities, they also expect their white dialogue partners to do the work necessary to educate themselves about the enduring realities of racism in America. On the other hand, trying to engage with and open the eyes of avowed white supremacists rarely leads to progress and often leads to something far worse. In such cases, it's best to walk away—not out of fear of succumbing to their racist ideology, but to avoid retraumatization. I have come to learn that it is not the victim's responsibility to enlighten others, including me. As the saying goes, "We can disagree and still love each other, unless your disagreement is rooted in my oppression and denial of my humanity and right to exist."[16]

A BIBLICAL CASE OF INNER DIALOGUE

Have you ever felt yourself torn between two conflicting perspectives, struggling with your own inner conflict? If so, you're in good company—the psalmists often expressed this very struggle, sometimes even creating a dialogue between the speaking subject ("I") and their "soul," or innermost being. For example, Psalm 42 begins with the speaker's soul yearning for God, much like a doe longing for flowing streams. In the following passage, I've italicized the parts of the psalm that give voice to the soul and bolded the sections where the speaking subject addresses or comments on the soul.

> **As a doe groans for water-filled ravines,**
> **so my soul groans for you, O God.**
> **My soul thirsts for God, the living God.**
> *When shall I come and see the face of God?*
> *My tears have been my food day and night,*
> *while it is said to me all day long, "Where is your God?"*
>
> **These things I remember as I pour out my soul within me:**
> *Oh how I passed through to the abode of the Mighty One.*
> *to the house of God,*
> *with cries of joy and praise, a crowded festival.*
> **Why are you so downcast, O my soul,**
> **and so stirred up inside me?**

---

16. This quote is often attributed to James Baldwin but actually comes from the novelist Robert Jones, Jr., who wrote the blog Son of Baldwin and posted this quote to his now-deactivated Twitter account *@SonofBaldwin*. See "Resistance and the Rebirth of Inclusion" (November 28, 2016), UC Berkeley News, https://news.berkeley.edu/2016/11/28/resistance-and-the-rebirth-of-inclusion.

Hope in God; for I still praise him,
my saving presence and my God.

(Yet) my soul remains downcast within me.
That's why I remember you from the land of Jordan and Hermon, from Mount Mizar.
Deep calls to deep at the noise of your cataracts,
as all your breakers and your billows passed over me.
By day YHWH commands his faithful benevolence,
and by night his song is with me, praise to the God of my life.

I say to God, my solid rock,
"Why have you forgotten me?
Why must I walk in gloom, oppressed by the enemy?"
Breaking my bones, my adversaries taunt me,
saying to me all day long, "Where is your God?"
Why are you so downcast, O my soul,
and why so stirred up within me?
Hope in God, for I still praise him,
my saving presence and my God. (Psalm 42)

Psalm 42 famously opens with the evocative image of a thirsty doe, symbolizing the yearning, "groaning" soul that wonders when it will once again see God's face amid deep anguish and social alienation (Ps. 42:2b-3). The speaker also professes to "pour out" her soul (Ps. 42:4a), recalling two sustaining memories: one of the rapturous joy of Temple worship (Ps. 42:4), and the other of the sublime experience of the watery depths at the headwaters of the Jordan River (Ps. 42:6b-8). Between these intertwined memories, the speaker admonishes her soul for being downcast, demanding hope in anticipation of praising God once again (Ps. 42:5), a plea repeated in verse 11. Nevertheless, the soul remains downcast (Ps. 42:6a). The speaker's inner dialogue unfolds between a posture of hope, on the one hand, and that of despair, on the other: the soul laments while the speaker resolves to embody hope and give praise, all happening dialogically. Interestingly, the dialogue is not just internal; even the watery depths are engaged in conversation: "Deep calls to deep" amid the roar of cascading waters (Ps. 42:7), a dialogue that testifies to the mystery of God's benevolence (Ps. 42:8).

Psalm 42 captures an inner dialogue between the speaker and her "soul," which should not be mistaken for some disembodied spirit waiting to be released at death. In ancient Hebrew thought, the soul wasn't seen as pure spirit but as the psychological and physical core of a person's identity and vitality. It was the locus of one's desires and goals, as well as the animating force of one's life. Indeed, in certain cases, the Hebrew word for "soul" (*nefesh*) even refers to the throat or appetite (see Isa. 5:14, Hab. 2:5, Ps. 107:9).

In Psalm 42, the dialogue between the psalmist and her soul reflects an inner conversation between outward and inward identities—between the public self and the most vulnerable, honest self. This inner self is akin to what Howard Thurman described as the "sound of the genuine" in his 1980 Baccalaureate address at Spelman College: "the active presence of my own idiom in me."[17] For the psalmist, it's a conflict between the deepest, most troubled self—the soul, the voice of the genuine—and the outwardly defined self, which chastises the soul for being downcast and urges hope and praise. This dialogue remains unresolved in the psalm (see Ps. 43).

A DIALOGICAL APPROACH TO SCRIPTURE[18]

Dialogue isn't just any conversation; it's a specific kind of exchange rooted in mutual respect and characterized by intentional "listening and

---

17. The full transcript of Thurman's address can be accessed at https://thurman.pitts.emory.edu/items/show/838.

18. For a more detailed description of the "hermeneutics of dialogue," see William P. Brown, *Deep Calls to Deep*, 30-35.

learning,"[19] often tackling difficult subjects. True dialogue embraces the "otherness" of those participating in the conversation. The enemy of dialogue is prejudice—judgment made without knowledge.[20] Contrary to popular belief, the "dia" in "dialogue" does not mean "two." Stemming from Greek, it means "through" or "across." So, dialogue literally translates to "across word(s)." David Bohm compares the dynamics of dialogue to a "stream of meaning flowing among and through us and between us," out of which "may emerge some new understanding."[21]

Dialogue also does not always need to seek common ground or consensus. Psalm 42 (and Psalm 43) does not end with a tidy resolution, which proves that dialogue can embrace conflict and tension for the lessons they offer. True dialogue begins with listening and moves toward mutual understanding.[22] By listening without the pressure to find *common* ground, we can break *new* ground, overcome misunderstandings born of ignorance, and pave the way for transformation. Different does not mean defective, and genuine dialogue across (*dia*) differing perspectives holds the promise of transformation, even if it may not result in mutual agreement. My mantra is, "There is no shame in change"—that is, in changing one's mind. At the very least, genuine dialogue begins to counter the hurtful "othering" of others. True dialogues are courageous, "fearless dialogues,"[23] grounded in hospitality and honesty, particularly as they tackle difficult subjects.

What does dialogue have to do with the Bible? Just about everything, because the Bible itself is a book filled with dialogues. Lamentably, we can't go back in time to converse with the biblical authors directly. We can only

19. S. Wesley Ariarajah, "Creation of a 'Culture of Dialogue' in a Multicultural and Pluralist Society," in *Communication and Reconciliation: Challenges Facing the 21st Century*, ed. Philip Lee (Geneva, Switzerland: WCC Publications, 2001), 5.
20. Ariarjah, "Creation of a 'Culture of Dialogue,'" 6.
21. David Bohm, *On Dialogue* (London: Routledge Classics, 2004), 7.
22. Lisa Schirsch and David Campt, *The Little Book of Dialogue for Difficult Subjects: A Practical, Hands-On Guide* (The Little Books of Justice and Peacebuilding; New York: Good Books, 2007), 5-8.
23. See Gregory Ellison III, *Fearless Dialogues* (Louisville, KY: Westminster John Knox, 2017), 13-23.

engage with these voices of the ancient past through the words they have left us and by partially reconstructing their cultural and historical contexts. When we place these words alongside the words of others, we are invited into a conversation spanning centuries of reception and interpretation. Within these preserved words, the ancients still speak in the living voice of scripture. They call out to be heard, expressing themselves in diverse ways, all woven together into a canonical unity that still honors their plurality.

To hear and interpret the many voices of scripture in all their dialogical richness, I propose a "hermeneutics of dialogue" that honors the dissonance and diversity of the sacred scriptures. This approach engages with differences across (*dia*) texts, exploring the meaningful variations between them and treating various themes as "fraught with background,"[24] that is, full of latent meaning. Dialogical reading attunes the ear to hear the distinct voices within and behind the texts, imagining them on a level playing field, all engaged in conversation. I refer to this as "reading for reciprocity."

Over many years of teaching, I've observed a strong tendency among students to read the Bible in search of harmony and agreement within and across its texts. These readings avoid conflict, often resulting in a lowest-common-denominator approach to theology that invariably reduces the Bible's rich diversity to lazy generalizations. Instead, we should allow scripture's diversity to inspire and spark engaging—often troubling—dialogue. For some faith communities, theological uniformity in interpreting scripture is crucial, and acknowledging diverse views can be seen as a weakness, if not a threat. However, in biblical scholarship, identifying divisions, fractures, and tensions within and between texts is a staple of research. A dialogical approach bridges this gap by recognizing and appreciating the Bible's diversity within its canonical unity, while also finding shared meaning within that diversity. In this approach, *e pluribus unum*

---

24. This phrase comes from Erich Auerbach's *Mimesis: The Representation of Reality in Western Literature*, trans. Willard R. Trask (Princeton, NJ: Princeton University, 1974[1953]), 12-15.

("out of many, one") meets *ex uno plura* ("out of one, many"). This dynamic mirrors the dialectic between Babel and Pentecost: out of one common language, God brought forth many languages and cultures (Gen. 11:1-9), and across those many languages and cultures, God's Spirit enabled the common communication of "God's deeds of power" (Acts 2:1-13). At Pentecost, the people asked, "What does this mean?" (Acts 2:12).

So, what does this mean? What does engaging differing stories and perspectives mean for you and me? It means changing the way we think about one another, seeing one another as partners in dialogue rather than as opponents in debate. We are all human beings, equally created in God's image (Gen. 1:26), each "wonderfully and fearfully made" (Ps. 139:14). It means overcoming implicit biases that see "differences" as defects rather than opportunities for learning and growth. It means striving for mutual understanding and transformation, even if we don't reach full agreement. It requires us to check our privilege at the door, be open to changing long-held views, and practice empathy. It involves engaging both our hearts and minds, being patient with others and ourselves, and connecting with the struggles of those in different contexts. Ultimately, it means living into a world where God's *shalom* reigns—the wholeness that comes when justice and peace finally embrace (Ps. 85:10). The Bible talks to us and is meant to get us talking *with* each other, not *at*, *to*, or *against* each other. This kind of conversation is what cultivates true community.

Let the conversations begin!

DISCUSSION QUESTIONS

1. How can the diversity within scripture, including its tensions and disagreements, be seen as a strength rather than a weakness?
2. Watch Chimamanda Ngozi Adichie's 20-minute TED Talk, "The Danger of a Single Story," https://www.youtube.com/watch?v=D9Ihs241zeg&t=47s. Does she make a compelling case that relying on a single story can be dangerous? Can you think of other examples where multiple stories or viewpoints are crucial?
3. Considering that the Bible was shaped by the specific contexts and concerns of ancient communities, how do you, living thousands of years later, relate to and benefit from it?
4. Is cultivating a "critical consciousness" important for people of faith? Should it be?
5. With the psalms of lament as examples, have you ever been brutally honest to God? Can you relate to the depression and inner dialogue expressed in Psalm 42?
6. What's the difference between dialogue and conversation? What steps are necessary for genuine dialogue to take place?
7. Can you recount a time when dialogue about a difficult subject or differing opinions turned out to be transformative?
8. How does awareness of the Bible's diversity affect your view of biblical authority?

CHAPTER 2

In the Beginning

"In the beginning, God created the heavens and the earth" . . . and started a dialogue. The first two chapters of Genesis set the stage for the Bible's very first conversation, one that explores the identity, role, and place of both God and humanity in relation to creation. These chapters present two distinct depictions of God and creation, with different views on everything from the way God creates to humankind's role in God's creation. And that's just the beginning—beyond Genesis, the Bible offers numerous other accounts of creation, each with its own unique perspective on God's role and humanity's place in the world.[1] It's best that we go in order, so let's start "in the beginning."

IN THE BEGINNING

In Genesis 1:1-2:3, God creates the world through a series of deliberate steps, each one set in motion by God's command. It starts with "Let there be light" (Gen. 1:3) and concludes with "Let us make humankind in our image" (Gen. 1:26), followed by a blessing. After each step, God evaluates

1. For detailed comparisons of the various creation accounts in the Old Testament, see William P. Brown, *The Seven Pillars of Creation: The Bible, Science, and the Ecology of Wonder* (New York: Oxford University Press, 2010).

the work, approving it through visual assessment ("And God saw that . . . was good."), before culminating with a summary approval of the entire effort ("very good") in verse 31. On the seventh day, with creation complete, God stops creating and rests (Gen 2:1-3). In Genesis 1, creation is carried out methodically with order, precision, and care.

Humanity arrives late on the cosmic scene, only after God has created everything else—from plants to sea monsters to wild animals. But humanity holds the unique distinction of being "made in God's image."

> Then God said, "Let us make humankind in our image, according to our likeness, so that they may exercise dominion over the fish of the sea, and over the birds of the air, and over the cattle, and over all the wild animals of the earth, and over every creeping thing that creeps upon the earth." So, God created humankind in [God's] image, in the divine image [God] created them; male and female [God] created them. (Gen. 1:26-27)

Humanity is described as being created "in God's image" for the purpose of exercising "dominion" over all other creatures, both domestic and wild. Over the centuries, there has been much debate about what it is about humanity exactly that embodies or points to God's "image." Is it a particular trait or characteristic of human nature, like rationality or consciousness? Is it a spiritual likeness? Or is it something more physical, or perhaps functional? The passage does not answer this question. However, it's clear that God's image is closely tied to the idea of "dominion," as the syntax suggests ("*so that* they may exercise dominion . . ."). To put it bluntly, the concept of image found here fits hand in glove with the idea of imperial rule. All of humanity—both male and female—is elevated to fulfill the role of the monarch in creation, representing God, the cosmic king. In Genesis, being made in God's "image" has a distinctly royal flavor; it is a privilege reserved for humans alone.

This idea is reinforced in the following verse, which takes the form of a blessing that begins with procreation:

> God blessed them, and God said to them, "Be fruitful and multiply; fill the earth and subdue it. Exercise dominion over the fish of the sea and over the birds of the air and over every living thing that crawls upon the earth." (Genesis 1:28)

God's blessing intensifies the language of dominion by adding the word "subdue" (in Hebrew, *kābaš*). God commands humanity to *kābaš* the earth! The word sounds harsh, and it is—it resembles the English slang "kibosh," though with a slightly different twist.[2] Outside of Genesis, *kābaš* often implies military conquest, as seen in Zechariah 9:15 and Numbers 32:29. In Jeremiah 34:11, the word refers to forcing others into slavery. It is difficult to soften its tone, even here in Genesis. Taken together, the verbs "exercise dominion" and "subdue" seem to give humanity license to subjugate creation. And that's a problem.

In this time of unprecedented ecological destruction, the blurred line between dominion and domination can easily be crossed to justify humanity's exploitation of the earth's resources and its disregard for the welfare of other creatures, driving many species to extinction. Over fifty years ago, Lynn White, Jr. highlighted this issue in his famous article, "The Historical Roots of Our Ecological Crisis,"[3] where he observed:

> Especially in its Western form, Christianity is the most anthropocentric religion the world has seen. . . . Man shares, in great measure, God's transcendence of nature. Christianity, in absolute contrast to ancient paganism and Asia's religions . . . not only established a dualism of man and nature but also insisted that it is God's will that man exploit nature for his proper ends.[4]

White blames the environmental crisis on the "Judeo-Christian dogma of creation" rooted in Genesis 1, which emphasizes humanity's

---

2. To "put the kibosh on" something is to reject, annul, or check it.
3. Published in *Science* 155, 3767 (10 March 1967): 1203-1207.
4. White, "Historical Roots," 1205.

God-given right to rule over creation.[5] The response to White's article was considerable, to put it mildly. The first rebuttal came in the very next issue of *Science* from Ernest S. Feenstra, who argued that White was confusing biblical teachings with the conduct of Christians throughout history, many of whom have strayed into "heresy" with their exploitative practices. Feenstra interprets "dominion" in Genesis 1 as "stewardship" instead:

> The cultural mandate [in Gen. 1:26, 28] makes man the responsible steward of the universe, not its spoiler and looter. Responsible stewardship, not exploitation, is the keynote. . . . Such Christian stewardship of natural resources does not include exploitation for selfish gain at the expense of society, nor pollution of land, air, or water.[6]

White responded by arguing that:

> The historical impact of Christianity upon ecology has depended not on what we, individually, at present, may think that Christianity should have been, but rather upon what the vast "orthodox" majority of people who called themselves Christians have in fact thought it was.

White considered Feenstra's critique as an attempt to "reform Christianity" rather than retrieve its cultural and ecological implications. Even in trying to reform Christianity, White felt Feenstra didn't go far enough. The idea of "enlightened despotism . . . over the rest of creation," White argued, falls woefully short of treating creation as a "democracy of all creatures," as envisioned by St. Francis of Assisi, the "patron saint for ecologists."[7] So, the question remains: does dominion, democracy, or

5. White, 'Historical Roots," 1206.
6. Feenstra, "Christian Impact on Ecology," *Science* 156, 3776 (May 1967): 737.
7. See Lynn White's response in *Science* 156, 3776 (May 1967): 737-38. His discussion of Francis of Assisi can be found at the conclusion of his article, "Historical Roots," 1207.

stewardship best capture the message of Genesis 1? Such dialogue, defined broadly by this exchange, continues to this day.

It's worth noting that Genesis 1 contains its own internal dialogue. While humanity is granted the royal authority by God to subdue creation, this elevated status is tempered by the fact that humanity is made in God's image. Like God, like humanity. The mandate to exercise dominion is held in tension with God's peaceful work in creation, thus pressing the question: How should we act "royally" toward the rest of creation? The God depicted in Genesis 1 is not a violent, conquering, or exploitative deity, in contrast to other ancient portrayals of a high god in relation to creation. The God of Genesis 1 does not slay the primordial waters of creation; instead, the "great sea monsters" are created as "good," not condemned to destruction (Gen 1:21, cf. Isa. 27:1). In short, God has no enemies in creation. If humanity, made in God's image, is to represent God in creation, then we must take our cue from God's way of working—peacefully and nonviolently. A peaceful God should be reflected by a peaceful humanity. So, why does Genesis 1:28 talk about "subduing" the earth? Lynn White saw this as a problem, and given other biblical accounts of creation, he may be right. Moreover, the language of "image" suggests a closer connection between God and humanity than between humanity and the rest of creation, similar to the bond between Adam and his son Seth, who was begotten "according to his image" (Gen. 5:3). To further explore these issues dialogically, we turn to the second account of creation.

IN THE GARDEN

The Garden of Eden story offers a very different perspective. Instead of starting with cosmic primordial soup, the scene opens on a dry, barren landscape, lacking both water and vegetation (Gen 2:4b-5). But then, a stream emerges from underground to water the earth, and "YHWH God" (the name of the deity in this account) creates a human being (Hebrew *'ādām*).

> Then YHWH God formed the *ʾādām* from the dust of the ground (*ădāmâ*) and breathed into its nostrils the breath of life; and the *ʾādām* became a living being (Genesis 2:7).

In Genesis 2, the creation of the first human being highlights a fundamental aspect of humanity's identity, revealed through clever wordplay in Hebrew: the *ʾādām* (human) is formed from the *ʾădāmâ* (ground). To capture this in English, though it doesn't appear in any standard translation, you might say the human is a "groundling," created from the "ground." This emphasizes that humanity is a "grounded" creature, deeply rooted in the fertile soil of creation. The "groundling" carries the essence of its own origin. Just as humanity is made in God's "image" in Genesis 1, in Genesis 2, humanity is formed out of the earth, reflecting the richness and fertility of the soil. In this sense, humanity in Genesis 2 is a "groundling," while in Genesis 1, it could be seen as a "godling." The "groundling" and the "godling" are two aspects of the same identity, or perhaps two identities that are inextricably linked.

In Genesis 1, humanity made in God's image is given the mandate to rule over creation. In contrast, the human "groundling" in Genesis 2 is tasked to "serve" the ground and the garden: "YHWH God took the groundling and put [the groundling] in the garden of Eden to serve it and to preserve it" (Gen 2:15). This dual role complicates humanity's place and function in creation—dominion and service are now two sides of the same human vocation. Equally complicated is another aspect of human identity: gender. In Genesis 1, humanity is clearly differentiated in binary form: "male and female" are both considered part of God's "image" (Gen. 1:27). However, in the Garden, the primal human is distinctly nonbinary. The *ʾādām* at this point is neither man nor woman. The language of binary identity only emerges in Genesis 2:23, when the "woman" (*'îššâ*) is created out of the "man" (*'îš*). Up until this point, the only human being is the genderless "groundling" (*ʾādām*). Between the time when they were formed from the ground and their unsuccessful search for a mate, the *ʾādām* remains a "groundling." But with the creation of the "woman," who is separated out from what is now a "man," the *'ădām* takes on a new identity—the masculine gender. Paradoxically, the splitting of the "*ădām*" results in two fully gendered individuals: a man and a woman. Two from one; binary from unity. As if this weren't enough, Genesis 2:24 suggests that sexual desire is a yearning to return to that original nonbinary state of "one flesh" (*bāśār 'eḥād*). Binary back to unity; two into one. In union, "man" and "woman" become *ădām*, the primordial "groundling." The "man" confirms this in his joyful proclamation:

> Then the groundling said, "This at last is bone of my bones and flesh of my flesh. This one shall be called 'woman,' for out of 'man' she was taken." (Genesis 2:23)

Notice that the newly formed "man" doesn't comment on what makes the woman different from him. Instead, his joy comes from their similarities—they are made of the same stuff: bone, flesh, and everything else that humans share. The expression "bone of my bone and flesh of my flesh" is used elsewhere to acknowledge unbreakable family ties (Gen. 29:14). In other words, the man's jubilant recognition of the woman is expressed primarily from the perspective of the "groundling" (*'ădām*) rather than that of the "man." Compared to Genesis 1, the Garden story presents a more nuanced and complex view of gender, one that goes beyond—or perhaps, behind—the conventional male-female binary to reveal that humanity's origin is fundamentally nonbinary, from the ground up in fact.

To sum up so far: the two creation accounts in Genesis initiate a dialogue concerning humanity's identity and place in creation. In the first account, humanity is elevated to the point of near divine status, "made in God's image" no less. In the second, humanity's origin comes from below, a position of humility derived from the humus, the rich topsoil that is the "ground" of humanity's origin. Is the human being a "godling" (Gen. 1) or a "groundling" (Gen. 2)? Humanity's identity, moreover, determines humanity's role or vocation. In Genesis 1, humanity is "blessed" to exercise dominion over creation. In Genesis 2, the *ădām* is tasked to "serve" and "preserve" the soil and its garden: rulership and service. So, which is it? Even the issue of gender is raised as a debatable issue: is humanity fundamentally "male" and "female" (Gen. 1:28) or originally nonbinary (Gen. 2:7)? Other scriptural traditions will have their say as well, providing further dialogical engagement, including the psalms.

PSALM 8: FROM HUMILITY TO MAJESTY

The conversation about human identity and our place in creation expands significantly when certain psalms join in, starting with Psalm 8. This psalm is filled with awe at the starry night sky, a reflection of God's majesty.

> **YHWH, our Lord,**
> **how majestic is your name in all the earth!**
>
> You whose majesty above the heavens is recounted
> by the mouth of nursing infants.
> You have established a stronghold on account of your foes;
> you have utterly vanquished the avenging enemy.
>
> When I gaze upon your heavens, the works of your fingers—
> the moon and the stars that you have established—
> What are human beings that you call them to mind,
> mortals that you care for them?
>
> You have made them just shy of divine;
> with glory and honor you have crowned them.
> You have granted them dominion over the works of your hands;
> you have put everything under their feet:
> All sheep and cattle,
> as well as the beasts of the field,
> birds of the air and fish of the sea,
> those that pass along the paths of the sea.
>
> **YHWH, our Lord,**
> **how majestic is your name in all the earth!**

This beloved psalm is framed by a refrain (in bold) that praises God's majesty throughout creation (Ps. 8:1, 9). Between these bookends, the psalm expresses awe at the vastness of the universe and the majesty of human rule on earth. The pivot from divine majesty to human significance hinges on a poignant question: "What are human beings that you call them to mind?" In other words, why, O God, would you take notice of us in the vastness of the universe you've created? As Carl Sagan famously put it, we live "on a mote of dust suspended in a sunbeam"—why would God care about us, the tiny inhabitants of this "pale blue dot"? The psalmist doesn't need a telescope to feel insignificant before the majesty of God reflected in the starry heavens. The naked eye on a clear, dark night (a rarity for many today) is enough to inspire humility and a sense of our smallness in God's vast universe.

But the psalmist offers a surprising answer to this question: God does care! In fact, God cares a lot, so much so that God has bestowed humanity with its own form of majesty. Not a sovereign majesty over the stars—that's God's domain—but a majesty over the creatures of the earth. Humanity's majesty is drawn according to scale. While God's sovereign majesty spans the cosmos, our majesty covers the earth, encompassing all creatures great and small. On earth, humanity is crowned with "glory and honor" (Ps. 8:5). Here, our identity is royally rooted. Nevertheless, on a cosmic scale, we remain mere dust—but dust that God cares for, dust that shimmers with royal luster.

In Psalm 8, humanity is described as being made "just shy of divine." Such language corresponds well with the idea of humanity being created "in God's image" in Genesis 1. While humanity is not divine, it bears God's "image" (Gen. 1:26). In Psalm 8, we're not quite divine, just slightly "downsized"[8] from divinity (Ps. 8:5). This semi-divine status is evident in humanity's dominion over the creatures of the earth, with everything placed "under their feet" (Ps. 8:6)—language that suggests imperial rule.

8. The literal meaning of the verb *ḥsr* in Ps. 8:5.

When it comes to humanity's place and role in creation, Psalm 8 and Genesis 1 are kindred spirits.

What's distinctive about the psalm's perspective is how this dominion is realized—through humanity's humble posture before God's celestial sovereignty. The journey from humility to majesty implies that human dominion is determined by God alone, grounded entirely in God's gracious mindfulness of humanity. It is only through God's "care" that humanity is "crowned." Furthermore, the psalm's larger structure reinforces that this dominion is a reflection of the divine; human majesty doesn't stand on its own but is derived from and bounded by divine majesty. Human dominion is derived from and ultimately limited by God's sovereign rule.

PSALM 104: CAREFUL COEXISTENCE

If Psalm 8 aligns itself with Genesis 1 regarding humanity's imperial identity and way in the world, another psalm shares greater affinity with the posture given to humanity in Genesis 2: humility. While extending the themes of awe and majesty from Psalm 8, the greatest creation psalm of the Psalter pivots to praise God not for humanity's dominant position over creation but for the countless species of life on earth, including *Homo sapiens.*

> Bless YHWH, O my soul!
> YHWH, my God, you are exceedingly great;
> clothed are you with grandeur and glory
> enwrapping yourself with light as with a garment,
> unfurling the heavens as a curtain.
> You construct the upper chambers upon the waters;
> you make the clouds your chariot,
> riding about on the wings of the wind.
> You make the winds your messengers;
> fire and flame are your ministers. …
>
> You send forth springs into the wadis;

between the mountains they flow,
giving drink to every wild animal,
breaking the onagers of their thirst.
Beside the springs the birds of the heavens make their home,
raising their voices among the foliage.
You water the mountains from your lofty abodes;
from the fruit of your hands the earth is well satisfied.
You make the grass grow for cattle,
and plants for human cultivation
to bring forth food from the earth:
wine, which cheers the human heart,
oil, which makes the face shine,
and bread, which sustains the human heart.
The trees of YHWH are well watered;
the cedars of Lebanon, which YHWH has planted,
where the birds make their nest.
The stork has its home in the junipers.
The high mountains belong to the mountain goats;
the crags are refuge for the coneys.
You made the moon for its seasons,
the sun to know its time for setting.
You bring on the darkness and it is night;
in it creeps every animal of the forest.
The young lions roar for their prey,
seeking their food from God.
When the sun rises, they withdraw,
and to their dens they retire.
Humans go forth to their work,
to their labor until evening.
How manifold are your works, YHWH!
You have made them all in wisdom!
The earth is stock full of your creations!
There is the sea, both vast and wide.

There are the creatures teeming beyond count,
living things small and great.
There go the ships,
And there's Leviathan,
with which you fashioned to play!
May YHWH's glory endure forever;
may YHWH rejoice in creation
who looks on the earth and it trembles,
who touches the mountains and they smoke.
I will sing to YHWH as long as I live;
I will sing praise to my God while I have being.
May my meditation be pleasing to him,
for I rejoice in YHWH.
May sinners cease from the earth,
and the wicked be no more.
Bless YHWH, O my soul.
Hallelujah! (Psalm 104:1-4, 10-35)

This great creation psalm audaciously commands God to enjoy creation, offering numerous reasons for God to do just that, with the main reason being creation's diversity. "How manifold are your works, YHWH! You have made them all in wisdom. The earth is stock full of your creations!" (Ps. 104:24). The psalm paints an unapologetically positive picture of the natural world, including the wilderness, which was often seen as threatening and chaotic in ancient times. Instead of fearing lions and tigers and bears (oh my!), the psalmist essentially proclaims, "Lions and tigers and bears, amen!" (and let's not forget the coneys, onagers, and mountain goats). The psalmist celebrates the richness of the animal kingdom and the God who joyfully sustains it all.

Psalm 104 offers a sweeping view of creation, moving from the theological and cosmological to the ecological and the zoological, all framed—like Psalm 8—by the doxological. But unlike Psalm 8, this expansive creation psalm covers a vast number of creatures without a hint of hierarchy: mountain goats, storks, coneys, lions, and Leviathan all have their rightful place in the world. Each is lovingly detailed in a tone of rapturous praise to the Creator. Even the trees have their place in God's creation:

> The trees of YHWH are well watered;
> the cedars of Lebanon that YHWH planted.
> There the birds build their nests;
> the stork has its home in the fir trees. (Psalm 104:16-17)

The psalmist prizes these trees not for their lumber, but for their majesty and their role in supporting life. The cedars are for the birds! A central theme of the psalm is God's provision for creation. God provides drink to wild animals (Ps. 104:11), "waters the mountains" and "the trees" (Ps. 104:13, 16), causes "grass to grow for the cattle" (Ps. 104:14), and supplies bread, wine, and oil for human beings (Ps. 104:15). God even provides "prey" for the lions (Ps. 104:21) and food for all creatures "in due season" (Ps. 104:27). Provision is the hallmark of God's ongoing work in creation—creation is providential because God is the provider.

But beyond provision, there's another key theme in this psalm, with the cedar trees offering just one example. The clue lies in God's very first act of creation. In the beginning, God created a home—a habitat for divinity—and, in turn, established habitats for every living creature: streams and trees for the birds (v. 12, 17), mountains for the wild goats (v. 18a), and rocks for the coneys (v. 18b). Even the waters have their "appointed" place (v. 8-9). The lions have their dens, just as humans have their homes (v. 26). The earth is not just a habitat for humanity; it's a home for all living beings. As the psalmist declares, "the earth is stock full of your creations" (v. 24). In fact, humans are scarcely mentioned at all until verse 23, and only then alongside lions. According to this psalm, the only real difference between humans and lions within the created order is that lions work the night shift while humans take over during the day. Day and night, the diurnal and the nocturnal, are all part of creation's natural rhythm, where each creature has its own time and place.

Of all the creatures mentioned in the psalm, there's one that seems to bring God the most joy. Like all God's creations featured in Psalm 104, this one also has a home in the created order:

> There is the sea, both vast and wide . . .
> There go the ships, and there's Leviathan,
> with which you fashioned to play. (Psalm 104:25-26)

The vast sea is home to countless living beings, including the greatest of them all—Leviathan, the monster of the deep. In this psalm, ships and Leviathan make quite a pair. Both are remarkable creations: one crafted by human hands and the other by divine power. While the psalm praises the wonders of nature, it also celebrates human ingenuity and technology—the ability to build a craft that can navigate the high seas. But while ships only skim the surface of the waters, God's monstrous creature, Leviathan, dwells in the depths. Both share the sea, but only one truly inhabits it, doing so solely at God's pleasure.

Leviathan's reputation as a monster of the abyss precedes its appearance in Psalm 104. Elsewhere in biblical tradition, Leviathan is depicted as a multi-headed Hydra, God's mortal enemy destined for destruction (Isa 27:1, Job 41). It is not a creature made for play but for combat, and its defeat is considered necessary for the sake of the world and God's sovereignty. But not in this psalm. There is no hint of combat—God's supposed enemy is actually God's playmate. According to the Talmud (*Avodah Zarah* 3b), God's day consists of twelve hours, divided into equal periods. The first three hours are devoted to matters of Torah, the second three are for sitting in judgment on the world, and the third period is focused on exercising mercy, including feeding the world. But the final three hours are reserved for playing with Leviathan—such a delightful way to end the day!

By now, it should be clear that in Psalm 104, humanity is not the only species God cares about. In fact, the psalm doesn't convey any sense of human dominion over other creatures. Instead, it shows them flourishing quite well without human interference. According to Psalm 104, we are not the dominant species on the planet, let alone the culmination of creation—we are simply one of Earth's many inhabitants. Creation is a shared habitation, and if there's an ideal of perfection in the psalmist's view, it's the perfection of biodiversity—the diversity of life and habitat. In God's cosmic mansion, there are many dwelling places, each perfectly suited to the creatures that inhabit it. Humanity's place in this diverse order of creation is as legitimate as that of any other species, right alongside the coney and the onager (or "wild ass"). There's room for everyone, even if the lions get control of the TV remote at night. And God loves them all, making God a true biophile—a lover of all things biological!

For all the psalm's praise of nature's goodness, beauty, and bounty, it ends on a surprisingly sour note. Did you catch it? The psalmist acknowledges that there is something wicked in the land of "lions and tigers and bears...amen!" At its conclusion, the psalm exhorts God to vanquish the wicked (v. 35a). Despite its cosmic scope, which includes even the monstrous Leviathan within the orbit of God's providential care, there's no place for the wicked. For many readers, this grim ending spoils the psalmist's wide-eyed wonder about the world. I used to feel the same at one time. But for the ancient listener, this imprecation against the wicked made sense in a world otherwise seen as harmoniously vibrant, except for one distinctly human flaw. By cursing the wicked, the psalmist takes the evil and chaos traditionally assigned to mythic monsters like Leviathan and places it squarely on human shoulders. The psalm suggests that the most savage, cruel, and wicked conflict occurs among *human* beasts.

We don't know exactly whom the psalmist had in mind when she called on God to consume the wicked. Were they the Babylonians or the Assyrians, empires of domination that ravaged the land and displaced countless people, deporting them to foreign lands through forced migration? Or were they internal threats, like kings who conscripted Israelite farmers for military service or monumental building projects, taking them away from their families and fields for long periods? Whoever the "wicked" were, the psalmist judged them a serious threat to the integrity of creation—a creation built on abundant provision and accommodation.

In the psalmist's view, the wicked deserve to be destroyed "from the earth." Here is an authentic assessment of creation as it stands: a world where the purveyors of chaos are not mythic, animal-like monsters, but monstrously human.

Despite this one glitch in the created order—the threat of the wicked—the psalm concludes with a final burst of blessing (v. 35b), echoing its beginning and forming a framework of praise, much like Psalm 8. The fact that the "wicked" pose a threat to creation, warranting their extermination, suggests that they view themselves as operating hierarchically, above the created order, rather than interdependently with other creatures, both human and otherwise—contrary to how the psalmist sees the world and humanity's place in it. Perhaps the psalmist's concern with the "wicked" is that they are severing the connection between habitat and inhabitant, starting with human beings and their homes, and perpetuating the scourge of forced displacement. In any case, the biocentric perspective of Psalm 104 represents a significant shift from the anthropocentric world of Psalm 8 or Genesis 1. According to Psalm 104, YHWH enjoys creation not for its hierarchy but for its flourishing and diversity. Just as wine "cheers the human heart" (v. 15), so creation's diversity cheers the divine heart. For the poet of Psalm 104, it is humanity's responsibility to ensure that this divine delight in the world is sustained, so that all of creation can be sustained as well.

And so the dialogue continues: while Genesis 1 and Psalm 8 mandate and celebrate humanity's rulership over creation, Psalm 104 offers a counterview—one where humanity is just one species among many, all coexisting, except for the "wicked," who, lamentably, are human. The psalmist not only banishes the "wicked" from the goodness of the created order but also dismisses any notion of human dominion over nonhuman creatures. This raises the question: Does human "dominion" have any place at all in the created order? Or, more broadly, should humans be entirely divested of any distinctive role in creation? Enter Psalm 148.

PSALM 148: ALL CREATION CALLED TO PRAISE

Brimming with the same repeated command, Psalm 148 presents a cosmic roll call of praise, where every realm and creature in creation is called upon to praise God, all in descending order. Interestingly, in this hierarchy from the top down, human beings are listed at the very bottom.

Hallelujah!
Praise YHWH from the heavens!
    Praise him in the heights!
Praise him, all his messengers!
    Praise him, all his host.
Praise him, sun and moon!
    Praise him, all you bright stars!
Praise him, you highest heavens,
    also you waters above the heavens!
Let them praise YHWH's name,
    for he commanded, and they were created;
he established them forever and ever;
    he gave a decree that cannot pass away.

Praise YHWH from the earth,
    you sea monsters and all depths!
Fire and hail, snow and thick smoke,
    storm wind that fulfills his word!
Mountains and all hills,
    fruit trees and all cedars!
Wild animals and all cattle,
    creeping things and winged fowl!

Kings of the earth and all peoples,
    princes and all rulers of the earth!
Young men and women alike,
    old and young together!

Let them praise YHWH's name,
  for his name alone is exalted;
    his majesty is above earth and heaven.
He has raised up a horn for his people,
  the praise for all his faithful,
    for the Israelites, the people close to him.
Hallelujah! (Psalm 148)

In the heavenly realm, the heavenly "messengers" and "host" are commanded to praise YHWH, along with celestial beings and domains. Creatures of the earth—from sea monsters to cattle—along with mountainous landscapes, are next in the roll call. Finally, human beings—kings, youths, men, and women alike—are called upon to offer praise. For Israel, this praise is warranted because YHWH has empowered the leadership ("horn") of the people, who remain "close" to their God. Clearly, being last on the list does not mean being least. However, the psalm does not grant any creature or domain a position of supremacy; the universal call to praise has leveled the playing field—or rather, the praising field. Every creature has its rightful place in the cosmic chorus. Praise has effectively erased all traces of hierarchy as defined by domination.

But what does it mean for "sea monsters" and "cattle" to give praise? For snow and smoke? How do they communicate praise? Psalm 148 credits communicative power to even "nonliving" elements of creation: mountains and hills, smoke and storm winds. In this psalm, nothing in creation is considered inanimate, and therefore nothing lacks the ability to praise God. Everything, both living and nonliving, is waiting and ready to be called upon to give praise.

And what about humanity's place in this cosmic chorus? Humans are certainly one voice among many in creation, a voice further divided into various roles: old and young, women and men, king and commoners, Israel and the nations. But there may be more to humanity's role in the cosmic order when we ask: "Who, pray tell, is giving the command to praise?" None other than humanity itself. Here lies humanity's special role, one that, admittedly, retains a certain distinction, even a "hierarchical" one, between humans and all other creatures. However, this hierarchy is not about domination; it's about enablement. From the psalm's opening "Hallelujah" to its final "Hallelujah," a radically different kind of hierarchy is implied. According to Psalm 148, humanity's prominent (but non-dominant) role in creation is to call all creation to praise. While only God can call creation into being, humanity can call creation into praise, fulfilling God's ultimate purpose for it. Moving from Psalm 8 (and Genesis 1) to Psalm 148, we see a shift from human dominance over creation to humanity enabling and fulfilling creation's praise. The language of subjugation, as found in Psalm 8, transforms into one of liturgical leadership. If humanity's role is to lead nature in praising God, it is also humanity's responsibility to ensure the conditions that make creation's praise possible—to establish a flourishing ecosystem of praise throughout the earth. The psalmist's vision might echo the cosmic temple of Genesis 1, but if so, it enshrines not a humanity of dominion, but a humanity of liturgical leadership—much like a church choir director.

In Psalm 148, humanity is neither merely one species among others, as profiled in Psalm 104, nor is it called to dominate or subjugate creation, as implied in Psalm 8 and Genesis 1. Instead, Psalm 148 presents humanity's unique and powerful role as enabling all creation to offer unhindered praise to God. Rather than placing creation "under the feet" of humanity, this psalm envisions humanity calling forth creation in elevated praise. Humanity is the one species of God's creatures that both summons and is summoned to praise. Throughout the Psalms, humanity's role shifts from being a king over creation to being a priest for creation, ensuring that a creation that can fully praise is a creation that fully flourishes.

PSALM 72: DOMINION FOR THE DOWNTRODDEN

But even with Psalm 148 taken into account, we have not heard the whole story. Yet another voice asserts itself, entering into the dialogue and taking us back to the beginning, back to the beginning of the Bible's first dialogue and that of creation itself. While the creation psalms either amplify human dominion (as in Psalm 8), dismantle it (as in Psalm 104), or transform it into something entirely different (as in Psalm 148), there's yet another option: to refocus and redefine "dominion." This approach is exemplified in Psalm 72, which outlines the king's job description. Beyond praying for the king's longevity, prosperous rule, and international acclaim—all the trappings of imperial power—the psalm emphasizes the king's duty to focus on the most vulnerable in his kingdom, ensuring they receive justice and deliverance. In Psalm 72, we come full circle:

> For Solomon.
>
> Give the king your judgments, O God,
> and your righteousness to the king's son.
> May he judge your people with righteousness,
> and your afflicted with justice.
> May the mountains yield ***shalom*** for the people,
> and the hills (do so) in righteousness.
> May he establish justice for the most afflicted among the people,
> saving children who are destitute
> and crushing the oppressor.
> May he lengthen (his days) as long as the sun (endures),
> and as long as the moon (shines) from generation to generation.
> May he be like rain falling upon a fresh-cut field;
> like showers that drench the land.
> May the righteous flourish throughout his days,
> and ***shalom*** abound until the moon is no more.
> May he rule from sea to sea,
> and from the river (Euphrates) to the ends of the earth.
> Let the desert dwellers bow down before him,
> and his enemies lick the dust.
> Let the kings of Tarshish and of the isles bring tribute;
> let the kings of Sheba and Seba present gifts.

Let all the kings bow down before him,
all the nations serve him.
For he delivers the destitute who cries out for help,
and the afflicted—the one who lacks a helper.
He has compassion on the powerless and the destitute,
and saves the lives of the destitute.
From oppression and violence he redeems their lives;
their blood is precious in his eyes.
Long may he live! May he be given the gold of Sheba!
May he be prayed for always and blessed all day long!
May there be abundant grain in the land!
May it wave on the tops of the mountains!
May its fruit flourish like Lebanon,
and its grain (thrive) like grass upon the land!
May his name endure forever,
and his name propagate as long as the sun (lasts)!
Let them be blessed through him!
Let all the nations consider him most esteemed!

Blessed be YHWH God, the God of Israel,
who alone performs wonders.
Blessed be his glorious name forever,
and may his glory fill all the earth.

Amen and Amen. (Psalm 72)

This is the profile of a supremely powerful king, one to whom all other kings—from Tarshish to Sheba (v. 10-11)—submit, and whose rule extends "from sea to sea" (v. 9), that is, from the Persian Gulf to the Mediterranean Sea. The king's imperial credentials are unquestionable. Moreover, his effective rule is compared to fresh showers and abundant grain—a *prosperous* imperial reign that ushers in an era of unprecedented *shalom*—a time of peace, prosperity, and communal flourishing.

But what stands out most in Psalm 72 is what the king should do with all his imperial might: care for the most vulnerable (v. 4, 12-14). The king's primary responsibility is to care for the impoverished, which includes not only attending to their needs but also "crushing the oppressor" and delivering them from "oppression and violence." This is what "dominion" looks like in Psalm 72: justice for the destitute, deliverance for the disinherited, and liberation for the languishing. It's good news for the poor and bad news for those who keep them impoverished. This is the king's royal vocation—his preferential option for the poor—and it is his royal duty to fulfill it.

And so the dialogue comes full circle. If true dominion, according to the Bible, is demonstrated by the king's care for the least among his people, what does that mean for all humanity created in "God's image"? This prompts an important question: Who or what in all creation should humans care for the most? Just as the king cares for the most vulnerable in his kingdom, who or what are the most vulnerable in all creation? Perhaps Noah offers a clue—the one who best fulfills the mandate to exercise "dominion" over all creatures. Noah's actions in implementing God's version of the Endangered Species Act—saving every species to ensure the survival of creation's diversity in the face of ecological disaster—illustrate a "dominion of deliverance." As a righteous man (Gen 6:9; 7:1), Noah stands as a model of creation-wide dominion in Genesis.

And as for that troublesome word "subdue" (*kābaš*) in Gen 1:28, which reeks of violence, Psalm 72 offers a parallel and redirects it: part of the king's duty is to "crush" (*dākā'*) the "oppressor" (v. 4). More palatably, the coercive aspect of the king's rule includes dismantling agents and structures of oppression so that the vulnerable are no longer vulnerable. Applied to creation, this suggests that humanity's job is to "subdue" systems, agents, and practices that harm the planet, threatening the integrity of creation and its ability to sustain flourishing life—both human and nonhuman. Such destructive forces are irredeemably "wicked."

Conclusion

To retrace our steps, we began with Genesis 1 and its mandate for humanity to exercise dominion over creation, with Psalm 8 serving as its poetic sibling. On the other end of the spectrum, however, Psalm 104 strips humanity of all imperial privilege or royal supremacy. Here, creation is not a kingdom ruled by humanity but a web of interdependence where human beings coexist with all God's creatures. Similarly, Psalm 148 portrays all creation—both animate and inanimate—joining together in praise, but with a liturgical twist: humanity's role is to elicit and ensure creation's praise. Praise levels the field but also underscores humanity's special role in enabling creation's unfettered flourishing. According to Genesis 2, this special role for humanity, the "groundling," is to "serve and preserve" the garden. Indeed, humanity's most fundamental identity—even more so than gender—is found in our connection to the ground, from which all land life emerged, from trees delightful to the sight to sly snakes slithering on the earth. If humanity is to exercise dominion, it must do so by serving the least and wiping away all obstacles that impede or exploit the flourishing of life. All in all, the Bible presents a rich and dialogical picture of humanity in God's creation. It turns out that we are God-endowed, royally invested, take-charge, liberating, nonbinary, binary, problematic, sinful godlings and groundlings. We are both creation's imperial liberator and humble servant—an inimitable *imago*.[9]

---

9. For further detail and more extensive discussion, which includes other biblical creation traditions, see William P. Brown, *Deep Calls to Deep: The Psalms in Dialogue amid Disruption* (Nashville, TN: Abingdon, 2021), 39-76.

DISCUSSION QUESTIONS

1. Recall the dialogue between White and Feenstra, a conversation that is far from finished. After reading this chapter, where do you see yourself in this conversation? If you could join the dialogue, what would you say?
2. Of all the biblical texts discussed, which one do you find most critical today as we live through and respond to climate change? What model of human vocation do you consider most important: dominion, service, stewardship, partnership, liturgical, coexistence, collaboration, reciprocity?
3. In Psalm 104, the "wicked" pose a threat to creation that, in the psalmist's eyes, warrants their extermination. In today's world, who are the wicked? Can anyone be excluded from this classification?
4. The "splitting of the *'ādām*" has resulted in two fully gendered individuals: a man and a woman. "Two out of one; a binary out of unity." How does this understanding support or challenge your understanding of gender?

CHAPTER 3

The Joy of *Torah*

Various images might come to mind when you hear the word "law": a gavel, the "long arm" of the law, a president holding up the Bible after dispersing protesters with tear gas, blindfolded Lady Justice holding the scales, the Constitution, shelves full of legal books, or stone tablets—maybe even two shattered stone tablets. These images reflect different ideas about what "law" is and how it functions. But there's one image notably absent from this list, one that's thoroughly ancient, both biblical and otherwise, and it's the most life-giving of all. In this chapter, we'll explore the different dimensions of biblical law, specifically *tôrâ*, the Hebrew word usually translated as "law," but which carries so much more meaning.

As a body of literature, *tôrâ* in the Bible primarily refers to the diverse prescriptive material collected in the Pentateuch—everything from the Decalogue (often referred to as the "Ten Commandments") found in Exodus 20 to various laws scattered throughout the first ten chapters of Numbers. Laws upon laws, all given to the Israelites at the foot of Mount Sinai, thanks to Moses. But are these laws exhaustive? Are they all really "set in stone," established for all time without change? Or is *tôrâ* adaptable? Is it amendable? Is it subject to revision as contexts shift? What is the primary purpose of *tôrâ*? Is it a burden or a gift? There are no simple answers to any of these questions, as we'll see. But to begin, we need to first understand how *tôrâ* fits in the larger narrative of Israel's origins.

The great Jewish philosopher and holocaust refugee Emil Fackenheim (1916-2003) identified two "root experiences" that define Judaism: 1) God's "saving presence" and 2) God's "commanding presence."[1] The latter refers to the giving of *tôrâ*, both on Mt. Sinai and elsewhere, while God's "saving presence" is exemplified by the Exodus—the defining event of deliverance that shaped ancient Israel's identity. Although these are two distinct themes, they are inseparably linked, as seen in the prologue of the Decalogue:

> I am YHWH your God,
> who brought you out of the land of Egypt,
> out of the house of slavery;
> you shall have no other gods before me.
> (Exodus 20:2-3)

The very first commandment, the first statement of God's "commanding presence" is prefaced by the story of the Exodus, the story of God's "saving presence." This emphatically identifies God, the one who brought the people out of Egypt, as the one who is about to give these commandments to Israel at the foot of a mountain in the wilderness. To view this another way, and more pointedly, consider the following paraphrase of an observation from Brian McLaren: "It took the ten plagues to get Israel out of Egypt, but it took the Ten Commandments to get Egypt out of Israel."[2]

In this context, Egypt is synonymous with slavery. While the Exodus brought the people physical freedom, the Mosaic *tôrâ*, starting with the Decalogue, was meant to rid the people of the mentality of enslavement and help them become a truly free and just community. The "Law" was, first and foremost, an antidote to the lingering legacy of slavery for a newly

1. Emil L. Fackenheim, *God's Presence in History: Jewish Affirmations and Philosophical Reflections* (New York: Harper & Row, 1972), 14-16.
2. Brian McLaren, "I'd Like To Give You the Benefit of the Doubt, But . . ." (May 12, 2011), accessed at http://brianmclaren.net/q-r-id-like-to-give-you-the-benefit-of-the-doubt-but/.

freed people, including the temptation to return to the familiarity of life in Egypt (see Num. 11:4-6, 18-20; 14:2-4).

This link between freedom and law is also addressed in a passage that connects deliverance from Egypt to God's invitation for the people to be bound with God through a covenantal relationship:

> You have seen what I did to the Egyptians and how I lifted you up on eagles' wings to bring you to myself. So now, if you faithfully heed my voice and keep my covenant, you will be my treasured possession out of all the peoples, for the whole earth is mine. You shall be for me a kingdom of priests and a holy nation. (Exodus 19:4-6)

In these three verses, this newly formed community is given a new mission, one that extends beyond the ancestral goal of possessing the land promised to Abraham (Gen. 12:1-2, 7). Their mission is to become a community set apart by God for God's holy purpose. God describes Israel's escape from Egyptian bondage not as fleeing but as flying—on "eagles' wings"—to bring the people to God. Israel now stands at a crossroads: to obey God or not. God invites the Israelites to choose obedience, to "listen to" God's "voice" and "keep covenant," a covenant that is yet to be fully established. This obedience will single out Israel from all the other peoples as God's "treasured possession" (*sĕgullâ*). Israel is to become a special community among the peoples of the earth—a "kingdom of priests and a holy nation"—the collective goal of *tôrâ*.

In this pivotal passage, *tôrâ* serves as the glue that binds Israel and God in a covenantal relationship. It's more than just a collection of laws; it's the sign of a mutually committed relationship: "You shall be my people, and I will be your God" (Exod. 6:7; Jer. 11:4, 30:22). While the Exodus marked God's claim on Israel as God's people, *tôrâ* demonstrates Israel's claim upon God as their God. Exodus and *tôrâ*—freedom *from* Egypt and freedom *for* God—are seamlessly intertwined in the biblical narrative.

These three verses are more than just an introduction; they provide the key to the extensive collection of divine instructions that follows all associated with Mount Sinai. This collection ranges from the Decalogue to Deuteronomy, covering both the sacred and the societal. Together, this sprawling corpus reflects the development of divine instruction, all devoted to the monumental project of community building—forming a viable sociopolitical order that reflects Israel's distinctiveness among the nations. The Decalogue, assuming its primacy of place, opens the *tôrâ* collection at Sinai and is highlighted as God's only public address to the entire community (Exod. 20:2-17; Deut. 5:4, 22-23). Its brevity ("ten words")[3] belies its wide-ranging scope, covering everything from worship to neighborliness, with the Sabbath commandment—the most extensive of the ten—set in the center (Exod. 20:8-11).

The people respond with fear and trembling, beseeching Moses to speak on behalf of God from this point forward (Exod. 20:18-21). From then on, *tôrâ* is mediated by Moses, beginning with the so-called "Covenant Code" (Exod. 20:22–23:19), Israel's earliest law code. This compilation of laws addresses a range of issues, including the possession and release of slaves (Exod. 21:1-11); capital and retributive punishment for violent acts (21:12-26);[4] movable property such as oxen and donkeys (21:28-36); restitution (22:1-14); various social and sacred matters (22:16-31); judicial issues (23:1-9); the sabbatical year and Sabbath (23:10-13); and annual festivals (23:14-19).

But *tôrâ* instruction at Sinai doesn't end there, even after its ratification (Exod. 24:1-11). What follows are detailed instructions for constructing the tabernacle and sacred items (25:1–30:38), Sabbath law (31:12-17; 35:2-3), a renewed covenant that includes another set of "ten words" (34:10-28), and guidelines on offering sacrifices along with various ethical and cultic norms (Lev. 1-27).[5] These instructions cover the duties of the Levites (Num. 3:5-13), including the redemption of the firstborn (3:40-51);

3. See Exod. 34:28; Deut. 4:13; 10:4.
4. Which includes the famous *lex talionis* or "law of retaliation" ("eye for eye . . .") in Exodus 21:23-25.
5. The "Holiness Code" (Lev. 17-26) stands out as a discrete collection regarding matters of moral purity.

special responsibilities of the Kohathites, Gershonites, and Merarites (4:1-33); laws regarding cleanliness, confession, alleged marital infidelity, the Nazirites, a priestly blessing, seven lamps (5:1–6:27; 8:1-4), consecration and duties of the Levites (8:5-26); instructions for participation in the Passover celebration (9:1-14); and instructions on the construction and use of two silver trumpets for war and worship (10:1-10). Whew!

In short, Sinai is the staging ground for the following collections of laws:

1. Decalogue: Exodus 20:2-17
2. Covenant Code: Exodus 20:22–23:19
3. Instructions for the Tabernacle: Exodus 25:1–30:38
4. Covenant Renewed (2nd Decalogue): Exodus 34:10-26
5. Holiness Code: Leviticus 17-26
6. Miscellaneous laws: Numbers 1:1–10:10

The scope of these collections is truly breathtaking, all imparted during Israel's encampment at Sinai. You can imagine this mountain as a magnet, pulling in a vast array of legal material that was historically developed over centuries of Israel's communal life. Narratively, however, it is combined and presented as a singular, mountainous experience. And what happens at Sinai is not meant to stay at Sinai.

The giving of *tôrâ* at Sinai serves a significant purpose within the broader narrative of Israel's journey to becoming a people. Between Egypt and Sinai, the Israelites wander in the wilderness. They frequently complain about the lack of water and food. In response, God provides abundantly: "bread (manna) from heaven" in the morning, meat (quail) in the evening (Exod. 16:1-21), and water from the rock (Exod. 17:1-7). Despite their complaints being directed "against YHWH" (Exod. 16:8), God graciously responds.

However, after spending almost a year at Sinai receiving *tôrâ*, the Israelites resume their wanderings, but things are different. While they continue to complain—déjà vu—God responds differently. This time, God gets angry and even consumes some with fire (Num. 11:1-3). Later, God provides quail, but it's accompanied by a "very great plague" (Num. 11:31-34). When the people complain again, this time considering a return to Egypt, God is ready to destroy them all (Num. 14:1-12). But Moses intervenes, pleading for forgiveness and appealing to God's "slow-to-anger" nature (vv. 17-18). Though God does begrudgingly forgive, there's a caveat: the first generation that witnessed God's glory in Egypt must pass away before reaching the Promised Land (vv. 20-23). Even Moses is barred from entering the land for rashly performing the water-from-the-rock miracle (Num. 20:2-13).

In short, the post-Sinai wanderings mirror the pre-Sinai wanderings: the Israelites remain a complaining, stubborn people. But God's treatment of them has changed. Before Sinai, God relents from punishing the people despite their complaints; after Sinai, God does punish them. The difference lies in *tôrâ*—the law received at Sinai.

To understand this, we need to take a step back and look at how Israel's story has evolved since the Exodus, highlighting the milestones in Israel's formation as a people. If we think of Israel's story as a narrative of the people's growth, then this is what we observe:

Exodus	Israel's Birth
Wilderness Wanderings	Israel's Adolescence
Tôrâ at Sinai	Israel's Bar Mitzvah
More Wilderness Wanderings	Israel's Age of Accountability

If the Exodus marks Israel's birth through the waters, then their constant complaining in the wilderness symbolizes something like the rebellious phase of adolescence—a time of testing and pushing boundaries. In fact, "Test" becomes a place name in the narrative (*Massah*), along with its counterpart, "Quarrel" (*Meribah*), in Exodus 17:7. These could be seen as Israel's teenage years. During this period, God's patience is certainly tested, but instead of punishment, God provides for the people's immediate needs with miraculous abundance. God simply accepts their complaints as a natural part of their development—those teenage years!

After Sinai, however, although God continues to provide for the people despite their complaints, there's a shift. God also begins to inflict punishment, especially when the people start contemplating a return to Egypt after all that God has done for them. While Israel's behavior hasn't changed much (call it "arrested development"), God's response certainly has, and it's tied to the giving of *tôrâ* at Sinai. Within the broader story of Israel's formation, *tôrâ* marks the passage from adolescence to adulthood, when one becomes accountable for one's actions. Call it a corporate bar mitzvah.

This analogy between Israel's journey after Egypt with an individual's maturation according to Jewish custom is telling. Now that the people have received God's instructions, they're expected to have grown up, ready to obey and enter the Promised Land as a fully formed community with its own social order. But they don't—they still act like rebellious juveniles, longing to return to Egypt. Has *tôrâ* failed?

On the surface, it seems so. The desire to return to the "womb" of enslavement in Egypt remains strong, while the courage to move forward into the Promised Land is lacking (Num. 13:25–14:4). In the wilderness, nostalgia and cowardice converge—a fatal combination. As a result, God resolves to consign the people to forty years of wandering, allowing a new generation to rise in the wilderness and take their place.

So, did *tôrâ* actually fail? In the short term, yes. But now a new generation must be taught and prepared, just as the old generation was, to live in the land across the Jordan. What happened at Sinai extends to a new generation. This is where Deuteronomy comes in, recounting Moses' teaching to this subsequent generation after forty years.

> Moses summoned all Israel and said to them: "Hear, O Israel, the statutes and ordinances that I am recounting to you today. You must learn them and observe them diligently. YHWH our God made a covenant with us at Horeb. Not with our ancestors did YHWH make this covenant, but with all of us, we who are here and alive today. (Deuteronomy 5:1-3)

And so begins Moses' (re-)education program, with *tôrâ* repurposed for a new generation. In the long run, *tôrâ* succeeds, spanning across generations. It had to find the right generation to fulfill its role in building God's community. In the process, *tôrâ* also had to adapt, demonstrating that it's a living, evolving body of instruction, not a set of unchanging laws carved in stone once and for all.

On the plains of Moab, in Deuteronomy, Moses extends *tôrâ* by revisiting and revising the events at Sinai (now referred to as Mt. Horeb) for a new generation. Take, for example, a comparison of some prescriptions from the "Covenant Code" (Exod. 20:23–23:19) with those in Deuteronomy:[6]

Topic	**Covenant Code Stipulations in Exodus**	**Revised Stipulations in Deuteronomy**
Altars	Multiple altars authorized (20:24)	Single altar prescribed (12:1-28)
Slavery	Enslaved men are to be released after six years; female slaves are not released except under mitigating circumstances (21:1-11)	Both enslaved men and women are to be released after six years; masters must provide reparations on release (15:12-18)
Marriage/ Adultery	A man who seduces a virgin either marries her or pays a fine equal to the bride-price (22:16-17)	A man who seduces a virgin either marries her (without ever divorcing her) or pays a fixed fine (22:28-29)
Carcass disposal	Animals that died naturally are to be thrown to the dogs (22:31)	Animals that died naturally may be sold to foreigners (14:21)

6. Adapted and expanded from Michael LeFebvre, *Collections, Codes, and Torah: The Re-Characterization of Israel's Written Law* (LHB/OTS 451; London/New York: T&T Clark, 2016), 69-70.

Topic	**Covenant Code Stipulations in Exodus**	**Revised Stipulations in Deuteronomy**
Festivals	Three feasts: Unleavened Bread, Harvest, and Ingathering (Passover is conducted at home), to be celebrated by the males (23:14-17)	Three feasts: Passover/ Unleavened Bread (combined), Weeks, and Booths to be celebrated at the central shrine by men, women, children, slaves, immigrants, orphans, Levites, and widows (16:1-17)
Sabbatical Year	Land left fallow (23:10-11)	Debts released (15:1-11)
Returning another's property	Ox and donkey (23:4-5)	Ox, sheep, donkey, cloak, or anything else lost by the neighbor; provision for keeping neighbor's property until claimed (22:1-4)

Notice how Deuteronomy's stipulations for festival observance are more inclusive, involving family members and the most vulnerable in society, whereas the earlier Covenant Code limits participation to males. On the other hand, while the Covenant Code assumes local observance, Deuteronomy requires a pilgrimage to Jerusalem, placing a heavier burden on families. Additionally, Deuteronomy introduces what could be called reparations for the formerly enslaved, including the release of both men and women. In contrast, the earlier code allows only for the release of enslaved men, without any recompense, though it does allow for them to be freed "without debt" (Exod. 21:2).

It is telling that the Deuteronomic version of the enslavement prescription includes the following commendation:

> Remember that you were enslaved in the land of Egypt, and YHWH your God redeemed you; for this reason, I lay this command upon you today. (Deuteronomy 15:15-16)

Or consider this from the Covenant Code:

> You shall not wrong or oppress an immigrant, for you were immigrants in the land of Egypt. (Exodus 22:21)
>
> You shall not oppress an immigrant; you know the heart of an immigrant, for you were immigrants in the land of Egypt. (Exodus 23:9)

As part of *tôrâ*, Deuteronomy repeatedly emphasizes "remembering" the time of slavery in Egypt as a motivation for various prescribed practices. These include observing the Sabbath (5:15), celebrating the Festival of Weeks by joyfully sharing produce with slaves, strangers, orphans, and widows (16:11-12), acting justly toward immigrants, orphans, and widows (24:17-18), and allowing them to glean your fields (24:21-22). All of this is done because "you"—meaning the people's ancestors—were once enslaved in Egypt.

Nevertheless, nowhere in Deuteronomy or elsewhere do we find a commandment that says, "Remember that you were enslaved in the land of Egypt; therefore, I command you not to enslave others." Or, with a slight modification of the Covenant Code: "You shall not enslave a fellow Hebrew or foreigner, for you were once enslaved in the land of Egypt." The Bible does not make this necessary leap of faithful logic—a striking failure of moral imagination. The closest it comes to prohibiting slavery is in Leviticus 25, which prescribes the Year of Jubilee, the fiftieth year, when "liberty" or "release" (*dĕrôr*) is proclaimed "throughout the land" (Lev. 25:10), including the return of previously-sold property to its original owners. As for Israelites who have become so impoverished that they had to sell themselves, Leviticus makes it clear that they are to be treated not as slaves but as "hired laborers," to be released in the Year of Jubilee (Lev. 25:39).

In Leviticus, enslaving fellow Israelites is forbidden: "For they are my servants, whom I brought out of the land of Egypt; they shall not be sold as slaves" (Lev. 25:42). However, enslaving foreigners and immigrants (those "from the nations around you") is allowed: "They may be your property" (Lev. 25:45). Again, this reveals a significant failure of moral and theological imagination—a lamentable shortcoming of Mosaic *tôrâ*. It seems that the enslaving mentality of Egypt could not be fully erased from the minds of the ancient Israelites. Yet, the dialogue continues, into the Decalogue itself (see Chapter 4).

In summary, *tôrâ* is a complex and multifaceted concept: sprawling, evolving, dynamic, and inherently dialogical. While the prescriptions in Deuteronomy were meant to replace the older Covenant Code historically, they did not do so canonically. Both are preserved in the Bible, coexisting side by side, albeit in separate books, without one canceling out the other. Consequently, they are held in dialogue with each other. There is no more dramatic example than the case of Zelophehad's daughters in Numbers 27, which occurs while the Israelites are still journeying in the wilderness. After the death of their father, the four daughters of Zelophehad bring their case before Moses, questioning the inheritance of property in a family without sons. "Why should the name of our father be taken away from his clan because he had no son? Give us a possession among our father's brothers," they plead (Num. 27:4).

According to biblical custom, when the household patriarch died, family property would be passed down to the sons, with the firstborn receiving a double portion (Deut. 21:15-17). If there were no sons, the property would go to the nearest male relative. When the case of Zelophehad's daughters was brought to Moses, he consulted with YHWH, who declared, "The daughters of Zelophehad are right" (Num. 27:7), and Moses granted them their father's inheritance. This statute is given further refinement in Numbers 36:1-12, demonstrating that law in ancient Israel was dynamic and open to amendment, judged on a case-by-case basis. The journey through the wilderness, it turns out, was also a journey of evolving jurisprudence.

So far, we've delved into the dialogical tensions within the various legal traditions in the Pentateuch, all contributing to the complexity of *tôrâ*. And we haven't even done much with Leviticus yet, which brings its own diverse prescriptions (see Chapter 5 on holiness). For now, though, let's shift to a very different view of *tôrâ* found outside the Pentateuch. In the Psalms, *tôrâ* takes on a life of its own, both in connection to and distinct from *tôrâ* in the Torah.

TÔRÂ OF THE PSALMS

Three psalms are devoted to showing off *tôrâ* in a very different light—Psalms 1, 19, and 119. Unlike in the Pentateuch, *tôrâ* in the Psalms doesn't serve as a charter for Israel's political order. In fact, it offers little in the way of legal content—there are no codes or stone tablets to speak of. Moses isn't even closely associated with *tôrâ* in the Psalms, with only a brief reference in Psalm 103:7, which may not even be related to *tôrâ*. Moses has other roles to play in the Psalter (see Psalm 77:20; 106:23). In the Psalms, *tôrâ* takes on a more poetic and evocative quality. We start with Psalm 1, which opens the entire Psalter:

> How happy is the one who neither walks in the counsel of
> the wicked,
> nor stands in the pathway of sinners,
> nor sits in the seat of the insolent!
> Rather, in YHWH's *tôrâ* is their[7] delight;
> they ponder [YHWH's] *tôrâ* day and night.
> They are like trees transplanted beside channels of water,
> yielding its fruit in due season,
> whose leaves do not wither.
> Everything that they do proves efficacious.
>
> Not so the wicked:
> they are like chaff,
> which the wind drives away.

7. In Hebrew, the subject is singular ("he") throughout the first half of the psalm, which is pluralized in translation for inclusive readability.

No wonder the wicked have no standing (in the court of)
justice,[8]
neither sinners in the assembly of the righteous.
Surely, YHWH knows the pathway of the righteous,
but the pathway of the wicked will perish. (Psalm 1)

In this poetic reflection on what distinguishes the wicked from the righteous, Psalm 1 commends the way of the *tôrâ*-lover. Instead of mingling with the wicked, this "happy" person meditates on YHWH's *tôrâ* continuously, finding in it the ultimate source of guidance and an irresistible source of delight. Those who dwell on *tôrâ* are compared to well-rooted, fully nourished trees, standing in stark contrast to the "wicked," who are blown about like "chaff." Like fruit-bearing evergreen trees, the righteous thrive, endure, and are impactful in all they do.

Notably, the psalm doesn't specify what *tôrâ* actually is. The only thing we know is that it's an object of devotion and delight. This kind of language is never used to describe *tôrâ* in the Pentateuch, where it's all about obedience and strict adherence to its many rules and legal codes. In those books, *tôrâ* is more about legislation than it is about flourishing. But in Psalm 1, *tôrâ* takes on a spiritual dimension; it becomes a source of nourishment, like the channels of water that sustain a tree. If the person grounded in *tôrâ* is like a tree, then *tôrâ* itself is like the soil and flowing water that keep the tree alive. In this sense, *tôrâ* in Psalm 1 feels fluid, emphasizing its life-sustaining and nourishing role.

But what exactly is *tôrâ* in Psalm 1? Clearly, for the psalmist, *tôrâ* is more than just legal codes. To explore this further, let's turn to the psalm that C. S. Lewis called "the greatest poem in the Psalter and one of the greatest lyrics in the world."[9] A single reading is enough to know that Lewis was right. In Psalm 19, *tôrâ* takes on a cosmic dimension:

8. The poetic parallel in the verse ("assembly") suggests a judicial context.

9. C. S. Lewis, *Reflections on the Psalms* (New York: Harcourt, Brace, Jovanovich, 1958), 63.

The heavens declare the glory of God;
    and the firmament proclaims [God's] handiwork.
Day to day gushes forth speech;
    and night to night dispenses knowledge.
There is no speech or words
    —their sound cannot be heard—
Yet their voice extends throughout the world,
    so also their words to the ends of the earth.

For the sun God has set a tent in the heavens.
Like a bridegroom it bursts forth from his wedding canopy,
    rejoicing like a warrior running the path.
From one end of the heavens is its rising,
    and its circuit is complete at the other.
    There is nothing hidden from its heat.

The *tôrâ* of YHWH is impeccable,
    restoring the self.
The testimony of YHWH is sure,
    making wise the simple.
The precepts of YHWH are upright,
    gladdening the heart.
The commandment of YHWH is clear,
    giving light to the eyes.
The fear of YHWH is radiant,
    enduring forever.
The ordinances of YHWH are reliably true,
    altogether righteous.
They are more desirable than gold,
    more than abundant fine gold,
sweeter also than honey, the drippings of the honeycomb.

Indeed, your servant is enlightened by them;
    in observing them there is great reward.

Who can discern [my] errors?
  From hidden iniquities clear me!
Deliver your servant from insolent thoughts;
  let them not gain mastery over me.
Then I will become entirely whole,
  and innocent of great transgression.

May the words of my mouth and the meditation of my heart
  be acceptable to you, YHWH, my rock and redeemer.
    (Psalm 19)

Scholars have long debated whether Psalm 19 was originally composed from two separate psalms—one celebrating God's glory in creation (vv. 1-6) and the other praising the qualities and benefits of *tôrâ* (vv. 7-14)—or whether it was always intended as a single, unified piece. Regardless, in its present form, Psalm 19 invites the reader to merge these two perspectives: creation and *tôrâ*, God's world and YHWH's word. What do they have in common? Is one more important than the other? And what exactly is *tôrâ* in such a cosmic context? Psalm 19 sets the stage for this kind of deep, dialogical reflection.

However one answers these questions, it's clear that *tôrâ* is connected to creation, and creation is connected to *tôrâ*—a mutual association that isn't found in the Pentateuch, where *tôrâ* is focused solely on its prescriptive content. The first half of Psalm 19 presents creation as the arena for God's glory: the heavens proclaim it, day and night communicate it, and the sun embodies it with vigor and joy as it journeys across the sky.

The psalm suggests that *tôrâ* is like the sun—it radiates and gleams, "giving light to the eyes." Just as the sun "runs" its path with joy, so *tôrâ* "gladdens the heart." *Tôrâ* is restorative, like the sun warming the earth with its heat. It's as if *tôrâ* reflects the sun's energy, running on solar power! At the same time, the sun mirrors *tôrâ*'s prescriptive nature while "running" its set path across the heavens (see Ps. 119:32). Both *tôrâ* and sun communicate God's glory and guidance.

This association isn't entirely innovative, even if the psalmist develops it in a uniquely poetic way. The connection between the sun and law goes back to ancient Mesopotamia, where the sun god Shamash was also the deity of justice. For example, the Code of Hammurabi features a relief at the top that likely depicts the enthroned Shamash giving laws to the king. In Mesopotamian religion, sun and law are closely linked, a connection paralleled in Psalm 19.

However, in the psalm, the sun is no enthroned deity. Instead, it's described as a bridegroom bursting forth from his wedding canopy, running with joy—a figure of vitality, joy, and warmth, just like *tôrâ*. Both are lifegiving, joy-giving, enlightening, guiding, and restorative. The efficacy of *tôrâ* is like the breaking of dawn, when the earth, having survived the chaos of the night, is reordered and restored. The rising of the sun and the giving of *tôrâ* are equally lifegiving for creation and community.

In Psalm 19, *tôrâ* is defined more by what it does than by what it is, and its effects are manifold. The psalm doesn't refer to specific rules or legal content, as found in Exodus through Numbers. Instead, it celebrates *tôrâ*'s attributes and benefits, leaving the question of what *tôrâ* actually consists of completely open. The psalm doesn't presuppose any particular legal material—whether from Deuteronomy, the Covenant Code, or Leviticus. *Tôrâ* in Psalm 19 is all-encompassing and left undefined, suggesting that any commandment, precept, ordinance, and testimony of God that restores the self, gladdens the heart, and imparts wisdom qualifies as *tôrâ*. In fact, *tôrâ* in Psalm 19 isn't confined to what happened at Sinai or what is inscribed on two tablets. It's open-ended, defined by its impact rather than by its specific content.

Equally remarkable is the absence of both Moses and a mountain in the psalmist's portrayal of *tôrâ*. Instead, the focus is on what *tôrâ* does for the well-being of the individual, whose voice takes center stage at the end of the psalm (Ps. 19:11-14). YHWH's "servant" is "enlightened" by *tôrâ* which reveals the speaker's "errors" and "hidden iniquities" (Ps. 19:11-12). The speaker seeks from God freedom and wholeness ("entirely whole"), the kind of perfected wholeness inherent in *tôrâ* itself: "The *tôrâ* of YHWH is impeccable" (Ps. 19:7a). The qualities attributed to *tôrâ*—"righteous," "upright," "reliably true," and "sure"—mirror the moral character one strives for. What *tôrâ* provides is life-giving radiance and enlightenment for the soul. In the end, *tôrâ* is not a book or tablets of stone, but something like a sunrise. That's the life-giving image of "law" offered by the psalmist.

In summary, *tôrâ* in the Bible represents an ever-evolving, dynamic process of discerning divine instruction. It starts as something set in stone (the Decalogue), only to be shattered, revised, and expanded by other law codes that address the shifting challenges of building community—all of which are preserved together. Although Moses urged the people to "diligently observe everything that I command you; never add to it or take anything from it" (Deut. 12:32), he might have also been heard quietly muttering, "Never say never." While the Bible's law traditions haven't "taken" anything away, they have certainly "added" to an ever-growing collection of divine instruction. The "law of Moses," it turns out, is a mosaic in more ways than one.

DISCUSSION QUESTIONS

1. How do biblical notions of *tôrâ* differ from your understanding of "law" or "law and order" in American society?
2. In what ways is the American Constitution, with its Bill of Rights, similar to and different from biblical *tôrâ*?
3. If "law" feels too narrow when defining biblical *tôrâ*, what would be a better word?
4. Do you see Old Testament "law" as a burden, as it's often viewed among Christians, or a source of joy, as held in Jewish tradition (*Simchat Torah*)? Or do you see it as something else entirely?
5. Jesus said, "Do not think that I have come to abolish the law or the prophets; I have come not to abolish but to fulfill" (Matt. 5:17, NRSVUE). How do you interpret this statement in light of Psalms 1 and 19?
6. How should we approach discussing certain biblical laws that allowed for slavery and excluded certain groups from worship?
7. If God's *tôrâ*, as described in Psalm 19, is meant to restore the self, gladden the heart, and impart wisdom—and is therefore amendable—what does that say about God, both then and now, and about our responsibilities today?

CHAPTER 4

Decalogical Dialogues

On a towering mountain in the middle of the wilderness, God makes a dramatic appearance before Moses and the Israelites. The scene is set with all the required props of a theophany: storm clouds, lightning bolts, fire, smoke, and an earthquake, all building up to God's public address. But what does God look like in such terrifying glory? The text does not say; instead, the pyrotechnics seem to obscure rather than reveal God's presence. According to Deuteronomy, the people perceive only the voice of God, speaking "out of the fire" (Deut. 4:12, 15). One ancient testimony in Exodus suggests that the Israelites not only heard God's thunderous voice but also *saw* it! An ancient Greek version of Exodus 20:18a reads, "And all the people saw the voice," while the Hebrew text refers to "voices" or "sounds," usually interpreted as thunder and lightning.[1] But in the Greek version, God's voice itself becomes visible. When God speaks, the verbal turns visual. One can only imagine what God's thunderous voice might have sounded like—let alone *looked* like—to the trembling Israelites. One stream of Jewish thought even imagined God's voice as flames of fire striking the tablets.[2]

1. The Septuagint or Old Greek version likely preserves the older reading. See Azzan Yadin, "*Qôl* as Hypostasis in the Hebrew Bible," *JBL* 122, 4 (2003), 617-23.
2. Attributed to Rabbi Akiba in Lauterbach, ed., *Mekhilta de-Rabbi Ishmael*, 338. The midrash goes on to imagine the Israelites able to interpret the visible words ushering from God's mouth.

This pyrotechnical display of divine power underscores the significance of what God is about to do and say (Exod. 20:1-17; Deut. 4:13). Amid all the sound and fury, God's aim is clear: to make Israel "my treasured possession out of all the peoples" by establishing a covenantal bond sealed by *tôrâ* (Exod 19:5). This covenant establishes God's formal bond with a group of formerly enslaved people. God's public appearance is meant to leave a permanent mark on the collective memory of the people, demonstrating God's power to initiate a relationship and inspire obedience—to "instill the fear of [God] so that you do not sin" (Exod. 20:20). As Deuteronomy explains, this moment is a profound teaching experience: "So that they may learn to fear me as long as they live on earth and may teach their children so" (Deut. 4:10). This "fear of YHWH" is a *learned* fear, a fear passed down from generation to generation through the retelling of the mountain experience and the reciting of *tôrâ*, both of which are inseparably linked at Sinai. This "fear" marks the beginning of obedience, and the "how" of obedience is revealed in what follows, starting with the Decalogue—literally the "ten words" (Exod. 34:28; Deut. 4:13, 10:4)—"ten words" that speak volumes.

And so begin the dialogues of the Decalogue. One version of the Decalogue unfolds in "real time" before the Israelites' very eyes and ears at the foot of Mt. Sinai (Exod. 20:2-17). Another version comes from Moses' memory on the plains of Moab (Deut. 5:6-21). Although similar in content, there's a major difference in the lengthiest commandment—the one about the Sabbath. Below, you will find the distinctive language used in these two accounts highlighted in bold (NRSVUE with author's alterations).

Exodus 20:8-11	Deuteronomy 5:12-15
Remember the sabbath day and keep it holy. Six days you shall labor and do all your work.	**Observe** the Sabbath day and keep it holy, as YHWH your God commanded you. Six days you shall labor and do all your work.

Exodus 20:8-11	Deuteronomy 5:12-15
But the seventh day is a Sabbath to YHWH your God; you shall not do any work—you, your son or your daughter, your male or female slave, your livestock, or the immigrant in your towns.	But the seventh day is a Sabbath to YHWH your God; you shall not do any work—you, your son or your daughter, or your male or female slave, **or your ox or your donkey**, or any of your livestock, or the immigrant in your towns, **so that your male and female slave may rest as well as you**.
For in six days YHWH made heaven and earth, the sea, and all that is in them, but rested the seventh day.	**Remember that you were enslaved in the land of Egypt, and YHWH your God brought you out from there with a mighty hand and an outstretched arm.**
Therefore, YHWH blessed the Sabbath day and consecrated it.	Therefore, YHWH your God commanded you to keep the Sabbath day.

The key difference between the two versions of the Decalogue lies in their respective reasons for observing the Sabbath. What is the primary reason for keeping the sabbath? The Exodus account and the Deuteronomic version offer two quite different explanations. The version in Exodus ties the Sabbath to the seventh day of creation (Gen. 2:1-3), while Deuteronomy connects it to the story of Israel's release from Egypt (Exod. 1-15). Deuteronomy commands rest for people who are enslaved (which isn't mentioned in Exodus), based on the historical memory of Israel's own enslavement in Egypt, where there was no relief from the grueling labor of building Pharaoh's massive storage facilities (Exod. 1:11) and performing field labor (Exod. 1:13). In Deuteronomy, Sabbath rest is portrayed as an experience of liberation. In Exodus, it's a way of emulating God's rest on the seventh day after finishing creation. Both reasons point to divine initiative—whether in creating the heavens and the earth or in liberating the enslaved from Egypt. However, they diverge in what they identify as the Sabbath's purpose: emulating God in creation or remembering enslavement in Egypt. This difference highlights their dialogue. Not even the Decalogue is "set in stone"!

What are we to do with two very different reasons for observing such a fundamental practice in the life of faith? We could choose one over the other after carefully considering which resonates more with us. Or, we could weave them together, as the Qumran community did—those who preserved what we now call the "Dead Sea Scrolls." In Cave 4, a fragmentary version of Deuteronomy was discovered that rewrote the Sabbath commandment of the Decalogue, combining both reasons in **4QDeut^{n}, col. iii 12- col. iv 7** (the Deuteronomic version is italicized and the Exodus version is bolded for clarity):

> Observe the Sabbath day to sanctify it, as YHWH your God has commanded you. Six days you shall labor and do all your work, but on the seventh day is a sabbath to YHWH your God; you shall not do in it any work, you, your son, your daughter, your male servant or your female servant, your ox or your ass or your beast, your sojourner who is in your gates; in order that your male servant and your female servant might rest like you. *And remember that you were a slave in the land of Egypt, and YHWH your God brought you forth from there with a mighty hand and an outstretched arm; therefore, YHWH your God commanded you to observe the Sabbath day to sanctify it.* **For six days YHWH made the heavens and the earth, the sea and all which is in them, and he rested on the seventh day; therefore, YHWH blessed the Sabbath day to sanctify it.**[3]

---

3. Based on the translation by Sidnie White Crawford, "41. 4QDeut^{n}," in Eugene Ulrich et al., *Qumran Cave* 4.IX: *Deuteronomy, Joshua, Judges, Kings* (DJD 14; Oxford: Clarendon, 1995), 124-125.

Now we have a third version of the Decalogue—an expanded Deuteronomic version that combines the two Decalogues as preserved in the canonical tradition. In other words, this version of Deuteronomy discovered at Qumran adds the Exodus rationale for the Sabbath commandment in the Decalogue. Instead of choosing one reason over the other, this scribe included both, and why not?

MORE DECALOGICAL DIALOGUES

This point of dialogical contact in the Decalogue is just the tip of the iceberg, one of many concerning the most succinct body of law in the Old Testament. Allegedly written by the finger of God on two tablets (Exod. 31:18; Deut. 9:10), the Decalogue holds a special place within the Bible's various legal traditions. But why two tablets? This is a matter of debate. It's often assumed that two tablets were needed to separate the commandments into two halves: the first five dealing with God and the people, and the second five focusing on community building. However, this assumption presents a problem—the first "half" contains almost five times as many words (146) as the second half (26). The commandments in the second half are simply much shorter. Moreover, the fifth commandment deals with parental relations, which isn't directly about God.

A more plausible explanation is that the two tablets were actually two copies of the same commandments: one for God and one for Israel. This idea is supported by the practice in ancient international treaties, where multiple copies were made—one for each party involved—to be preserved and stored in a prominent place.[4]

Before the Decalogue was written down by "the finger of God"—and possibly in duplicate form (Exod. 31:18; Deut. 9:10)—it was communicated directly to the people by God, without any human intermediary.

4. See the discussion of Exodus 24:12 in William H.C. Propp, *Exodus 19-40: A New Translation with Introduction and Commentary*. Volume 2A (The Anchor Yale Commentary; New Haven & London: Yale University Press, 2006).

This direct communication continued until the people could no longer endure the sound of God's thunderous voice (Exod. 20:1, 18-20). Only then did Moses step in as the intermediary between God and the people: God spoke to Moses, and Moses relayed the message to the people. Of all the prescriptive codes in the Old Testament (and there are several), the Decalogue is the only one delivered directly by God to the entire community (Exod. 20:2-17). But after the last commandment, the people had heard enough of God's voice, and Moses was chosen to speak for God and on their behalf (Exod. 20:19).

Decalogue and Covenant Code in Dialogue

The Decalogue, literally the "ten words" (Exod. 34:28), is a powerful condensation of *tôrâ* that spans everything from theological principles to societal guidelines. It begins with the prohibition against worshiping other gods (Exod. 20:2b) and concludes with the prohibition against "coveting your neighbor's house" (Exod. 20:17). Much of the Decalogue focuses on being a good neighbor. It's far more than just a list of commandments, despite modern depictions on monuments, plaques, and yard signs that often reduce it to a set of abbreviated commands. The Decalogue includes narrative context and motivations behind each commandment. To illustrate how the commandments form only part of the Decalogue, I've bolded the commandments themselves, highlighting how much more there is to the Decalogue than just the commands. The Decalogue is also dialogically related to the Covenant Code (Exod. 20:22–23:19), which follows it. (Most scholars consider the Covenant Code to be the earliest law code in the Bible.) In the right-hand column you'll find specific stipulations from the Covenant Code that closely relate to the commandments in the Decalogue (NRSVUE with author's alterations).

Decalogue	Covenant Code
20:2 I am YHWH your God, who brought you out of the land of Egypt, out of the house of slavery; 20:3 **you shall have no other gods before me**. 20:4 **You shall not make for yourself an idol, whether in the form of anything that is in heaven above, or that is on the earth beneath, or that is in the water under the earth**.	22:20 Whoever sacrifices to any god, other than YHWH alone, shall be devoted to destruction.
20:5 **You shall not bow down to them or worship them**; for I YHWH your God am a jealous God, punishing children for the iniquity of parents, to the third and the fourth generation of those who reject me, 20:6 but showing steadfast love to the thousandth generation of those who love me and keep my commandments. 20:7 **You shall not make wrongful use of the name of YHWH your God**, for YHWH will not acquit anyone who misuses his name.	23:13b Do not invoke the names of other gods; do not let them be heard on your lips. (See Deut. 6:13, 10:20)

20:8 **Remember the Sabbath day and keep it holy.** 20:9 **Six days you shall labor and do all your work.** 20:10 **But the seventh day is a Sabbath to YHWH your God; you shall not do any work—you, your son or your daughter, your male or female slave, your livestock, or the immigrant in your towns.** 20:11 For in six days YHWH made heaven and earth, the sea, and all that is in them, but rested the seventh day; therefore, YHWH blessed the Sabbath day and consecrated it.	23:12 Six days you shall do your work, but on the seventh day you shall rest, so that your ox and your donkey may find relief, and your homeborn slave and the immigrant may be refreshed.
20:12 **Honor your father and your mother**, so that your days may be long in the land that YHWH your God is giving you.	21:15 Whoever strikes father or mother shall be put to death. 21:17 Whoever curses father or mother shall be put to death.
20:13 **You shall not kill.**	21:12 Whoever strikes a person mortally shall be put to death. 21:13 If it was not premeditated, but came about by an act of God, then I will appoint for you a place to which the killer may flee. 21:14 But if someone willfully attacks and kills another by treachery, you shall take the killer from my altar for execution. (See also Gen. 9:6; Num. 35:6, 9-31.)
20:14 **You shall not commit adultery.**	(See Deut. 22:22-29.)

20:15 **You shall not steal.**	21:16 Whoever kidnaps a person, whether that person has been sold or is still held in possession, shall be put to death. 22:1 When someone steals an ox or a sheep, and slaughters it or sells it, the thief shall pay five oxen for an ox, and four sheep for a sheep. The thief shall make restitution, but if unable to do so, shall be sold for the theft. 22:2 If a thief is found breaking in, and is beaten to death, no bloodguilt is incurred; 22:3 but if it happens after sunrise, bloodguilt is incurred. 23:4 When you come upon your enemy's ox or donkey going astray, you shall return it.
20:16 **You shall not bear false witness against your neighbor.** 20:17 **You shall not covet your neighbor's house; you shall not covet your neighbor's wife, or male or female slave, or ox, or donkey, or anything that belongs to your neighbor.**	23:1 You shall not spread a false report. You shall not join hands with the wicked to act as a malicious witness. 22:9 In any case of disputed ownership involving ox, donkey, sheep, clothing, or any other loss, of which one party says, "This is mine," the case of both parties shall come before God; the one whom God condemns shall pay double to the other.

Notice the major difference in form: the commandments in the Decalogue are presented as straightforward commands, both positive and negative (i.e., prohibitions). In contrast, the rules in the Covenant Code are cast in a casuistic form, meaning they are framed as "case law" with conditional statements that begin with words like "when" or "whoever." The lone exception is Exodus 23:1, which is a prohibition similar to the one in Exodus 20:16 ("You shall not . . ."). The Decalogue is known for its brevity and directness, as it is God's direct address to the community ("you"), treated as a single entity—much like a parent addressing a child. The Covenant Code, however, communicates its legal content more indirectly, often in the third person, and dives into the weeds of legislating behavior, including penalties like capital punishment for various violations. The Decalogue, with its straightforward commands, avoids these details. It's also worth noting that the Decalogue doesn't cover everything found in the Covenant Code, such as building altars, emancipating the enslaved, caring for the most vulnerable, lending money, and observing the annual festivals. On the other hand, the Covenant Code doesn't address the issue of misusing God's name, as in the case of oath-swearing, which figures prominently in the Decalogue (Exod. 20:7).

A few key differences stand out when comparing the Decalogue and the Covenant Code. For example, the Sabbath command in the Covenant Code lacks any reference to God resting on the seventh day. The only rationale given for observing the Sabbath is to provide "relief" for domestic animals, enslaved persons, and immigrant laborers (Exod. 23:12; Deut. 5:12-15). There's nothing about emulating the Creator God. Additionally, the Decalogue's prohibition, "You shall not kill," broadly covers both murder and accidental killing, such as manslaughter or causing death without premeditation. The Covenant Code, however, makes allowances for killing in the context of executing the perpetrator—a murderer deserves death. Furthermore, the distinction between murder and manslaughter is carefully detailed in Numbers 35:6, 9-31. In Numbers 35, God designates "cities of refuge" to protect those who kill without premeditation from the "blood avenger." These legal provisions in the Covenant Code qualify the Decalogue's blanket prohibition against killing, which seems to prohibit any kind of killing, whether justified or not. This creates an inescapable tension between the two, captured well by the following dictum in Genesis 9:6:

> Whoever sheds the blood of a human,
> by a human shall that person's blood be shed;
> for God made humankind in [God's] own image.

The tension arises from the fact that, on one hand, the "image of God" is considered so inviolable that killing another person constitutes the gravest of offenses, warranting the death penalty. Yet, on the other hand, the execution of the perpetrator—who is also made in God's image—is deemed a necessity. In other words, the very reason given for capital punishment could also be used to argue against it, since it involves killing someone made in God's image, which applies to everyone. This makes the general prohibition against killing a topic ripe with dialogical opportunity.

When it comes to capital punishment, the Decalogue's command to "honor" one's parents contrasts sharply with the Covenant Code's approach. In the Covenant Code, a child who "strikes" or "curses" either parent is given a death sentence. The Decalogue, however, carefully avoids such language, instead framing the rule positively: "honor" your parents. It also adds a motivational purpose—honoring your parents will lead to a long and prosperous life in the land given to you by God. The implication is that parents deserve the same honor from their children as the land, as both are gifts from God that merit gratitude and care. In this commandment, gratitude and honor go hand in hand. Parents and land alike are to be revered for their roles in sustaining life. This middle commandment of the Decalogue transforms what was once a prohibition against abusing one's parents into a call for deep respect, positivity, and motivation to care for one's parents.

The prohibition against stealing likely had its roots in the practice of kidnapping, as indicated in the Covenant Code, which directly addresses the stealing of people for forced labor through enslavement or indentured servitude. The fact that the Decalogue's commandment is phrased without specifying any particular object suggests that "stealing" can also be understood broadly, encompassing everything from individuals to farm animals. Relatedly, the prohibition against "coveting" a neighbor's belongings also addresses stealing, but in a very different way. This language applies not only to property but also to a person's spouse ("wife").

Coveting Spouse, Adultery, and Rape

It's worth noting that the "wife" is listed among possessions like the ox and donkey in Exodus, something that one certainly can—and should—object to. It cannot be denied that patriarchy was alive and well in ancient Israel. However, in the Deuteronomic version, the spouse is placed at the top of the list, rather than buried within it, suggesting a subtle shift in how the "neighbor's wife" was regarded—perhaps as more than a possession. This difference hints at an ongoing conversation within ancient Israel's patriarchal culture regarding the status of women.

Exodus 20:17 (NRSVUE)	Deuteronomy 5:21 (NRSVUE)
You shall not covet your neighbor's house; you shall not covet your **neighbor's wife**, male or female slave, or ox, donkey, or anything that belongs to your neighbor.	Neither shall you covet your **neighbor's wife**. Neither shall you desire your neighbor's house, or field, or male or female slave, or ox, or donkey, or anything that belongs to your neighbor.

The command not to "covet," which applies to both spouse and property, also introduces a psychological component—the deep emotion of desire, specifically illicit desire, the urge to claim something as "mine" when it is not, in fact, yours. In this case, a fitting translation might be "lust." The Decalogue's inclusion of this language of lust adds a new dimension to the discussion about stealing, foreshadowing Jesus' own admonition in Matthew 5:27-28:

> You have heard that it was said, "You shall not commit adultery." But I say to you that everyone who looks at a woman with lust has already committed adultery with her in his heart.

As for adultery, the Decalogue's prohibition against this is not explicitly addressed in the Covenant Code (notwithstanding Exodus 20:16-17). However, it is covered elsewhere, as in Leviticus: "If a man commits adultery with his neighbor's wife, both the adulterer and the adulteress shall be put to death" (Lev. 20:10). This rule, however, does not consider the crime of rape. Deuteronomy is more specific; it lays out the conditions of adultery in greater detail, including cases of rape. Having sexual relations—whether consensual or nonconsensual—with a woman who was unmarried or not engaged did not actually constitute adultery for the married man (Exod. 22:16-17; Deut. 22:28-29). In such cases, the woman was required to marry the perpetrator, and the perpetrator had to pay restitution: "The man who lay with her must pay fifty shekels of silver to the young woman's father, and she will become his wife. Because he humiliated her, he will not be allowed to divorce her as long as he lives" (Deut. 22:29).

Such "punishment" for the rapist focuses solely on the man, with little regard for the woman. However, in a patriarchal society where women's survival often depended on marriage, this could have been a lifeline. The act was only considered adulterous—and a capital offense for both the man and the woman—if the woman was married or betrothed (Deut. 22:22-26). An exception is made if the rape occurs in the "open country," where the woman is presumed to have resisted without anyone present to hear her (Deut. 22:25-27). In such a case, only the man is put to death.

Back to the Basics and the Positive

Such details, however, are not the concern of the Decalogue. Given its brevity, the Decalogue addresses the more fundamental issue of agency rather than consequences, as it also does in the case of coveting. One might say that in the Decalogue God addresses the heart of the matter—human will—while the Covenant Code and much of Deuteronomy deal with the practical challenges of law and order. In this way, the Bible recognizes the need for both direct commandments and detailed legal consequences.

The Decalogue's shift from a negative command to a positive one, as seen in the case of honoring parents, invites us to consider how its other prohibitions, or negative commands, could also be construed positively. This opens up room for more dialogue, as shown below.

Decalogue Prohibitions	Possible Positive Constructions
20:3 *You shall have no other gods before me.* 20:5 *You shall not bow down to them or worship them.*	You shall worship YHWH alone, the God who freed you from enslavement in Egypt.
20:4 *You shall not make for yourself an idol.*	You shall make only what glorifies God.
20:13 *You shall not kill.*	You shall preserve the life of others.
20:14 *You shall not commit adultery.*	You shall honor and support the relational commitments of others.
20:15 *You shall not steal.*	You shall respect what others possess and return anything your neighbor has lost.
20:16 *You shall not bear false witness against your neighbor.*	You shall speak truthfully of your neighbor in all situations.
20:17 *You shall not covet your neighbor's house; you shall not covet your neighbor's wife, or male or female slave, or ox, or donkey, or anything that belongs to your neighbor*	You shall respect everything that belongs to your neighbor.

This exercise encourages a deeper exploration of each prohibition's significance and allows us to consider their broader implications. For instance, the prohibition against killing takes on a wider meaning when viewed positively: preserving life involves more than simply preventing death. The same goes for the prohibitions against adultery and stealing. The commandment against worshiping other gods can be positively reframed as an edict to exclusively worship the God (YHWH) who freed the enslaved. In other words, only the God who liberated you is worthy of your worship; idols, no matter how artistically impressive (like golden calves), ultimately enslave and diminish the worshiper (see the satirical account in Isa. 44:9-20). A positive formulation of the prohibition against making idols doesn't imply that all human creativity is bad; rather, this creativity should be directed toward glorifying God alone. Constructing the tabernacle and, later, the Temple are two biblical examples of this.

The Decalogue has its own story. Spoken by God and written on two tablets, the first version of the Decalogue (both copies) is shattered when Moses, in a fit of anger, destroys them after discovering his people worshiping a golden calf. This act of idolatry stemmed from the people's impatience and lack of trust in Moses during his extended time on the mountain, with Aaron's complicity adding to the betrayal (Exod. 32:1-20). Though initially considering whether to destroy the people, God ultimately relents and instructs Moses to cut two new stone tablets saying, "I will write on the tablets the words that were on the former tablets" (Exod. 34:1). However, the actual words dictated by God in this new version are strikingly different. While it prohibits the worship of other gods (v. 14), forbids the casting of idols (v. 17), and emphasizes observing the Sabbath (v. 21), this new Decalogue also addresses issues not covered in the original, including the observance of particular festivals (v. 22-23), proper sacrifices and offerings (v. 25-26), and the dedication of the firstborn (v. 19-20). Compared to the original Decalogue this Decalogue focuses much more on matters of ritual.

Additionally, the narrative elements of this Decalogue differ: instead of emphasizing God's liberation of the Israelites from slavery (see Exod.

20:2), it focuses on God driving out the inhabitants of the Promised Land to make way for its occupation by the Israelites. It includes the command, "You shall not make a covenant with the inhabitants of the land" (Exod. 34:15). While the original Decalogue looks back at Israel's exodus from Egypt, this Decalogue looks forward to the "eisodus," that is, Israel's entrance into a new land. However, the earlier Decalogue is not lost; Moses revives it in Deuteronomy for a new generation, as previously discussed (Deut. 5:6-21). In the broader biblical narrative, we encounter not one, not two, but three Decalogues each reflecting the growth of a people from enslavement to community. Their differences provide a rich source for dialogue and deeper understanding.

DISCUSSION QUESTIONS

1. What additional differences do you notice between the three Decalogues: Exodus 20:2-17, Deuteronomy 5:6-21, and Exodus 34:11-26?
2. How would you reframe the negative commands of the Decalogue in a positive way?
3. How might you use these texts to argue for or against the death penalty in America?
4. How important is the Sabbath commandment to you? Does comparing the two versions make the commandment more compelling?

CHAPTER 5

Wisdom Controversies

Wisdom is an elusive concept in the Bible, partly because it's so hard to define. Wisdom is always evolving, and because of that, it thrives on dialogue. Picture the ancient sages or scribes engaged in lively discussions about fundamental questions: What is the purpose of life? How can we understand God? What shapes good character? What is the value of experience? Where does wisdom come from, and how can it be shared? Is wisdom something pursued and possessed by those who seek it, or is it a gift from God, available to everyone? The answer to this last question is "simple": Yes.

But first, a word from the prophet Jeremiah. This sixth-century BCE prophet was not at all impressed with the wisdom of the scribes or sages:

> How can you say, "We are wise, and YHWH's *tôrâ* is with us," when in fact the false pen of the scribes has made it into a lie? The wise shall be put to shame; they shall be dismayed and taken, for they have rejected YHWH's word. What wisdom is in them? (Jeremiah 8:8-9)

Jeremiah accuses the "wise" scribes of distorting YHWH's *tôrâ*, turning it "into a lie." He doesn't specify how this distortion occurred—perhaps they "watered down" God's word in some way. Jeremiah was a radical prophet, steeped in the Deuteronomic tradition, trying to convince his people that Babylon's imperial control was God's just punishment and could not be resisted. He argued that surrender and acceptance of exile were the only viable options. Resistance, he warned, would be a suicide mission. History proved him right.

One issue that particularly angered the prophet was the status of the enslaved. According to Deuteronomy 15:12-17, the sabbatical or seventh year was meant to be a time of release for those held in slavery, both male and female. Jeremiah applauded King Zedekiah's "proclamation of liberty" to free all who were enslaved (Jer. 34:8-9). However, for reasons unknown, this proclamation was later rescinded, and the formerly freed individuals were enslaved once again. Jeremiah saw this as a covenantal betrayal and a gross injustice. In response, he invoked God's poetic justice against the slaveholders: "I am going to grant a release to you . . . a release to the sword, to pestilence, and to famine!" (Jer. 34:17). Could the sages have played a role in justifying the reversal of this Deuteronomic command, thereby "rejecting YHWH's word"? For Jeremiah, true wisdom was found exclusively in adhering to YHWH's *tôrâ* or "word," not in any other source, even so-called wisdom.

Another critique of the wise by the prophet cuts to the heart of what wisdom truly is:

> Thus says YHWH: "Do not let the wise boast in their wisdom; do not let the powerful boast in their might; do not let the wealthy boast in their wealth. But let those who boast boast in this, that they understand and know me, that I am YHWH; I act with faithful love, justice, and righteousness in the earth, for in these things I delight," says YHWH. (Jeremiah 9:23-24)

Jeremiah identifies the cardinal sin of the wise: boasting in their own wisdom. Or, as it says in Proverbs, they see themselves "wise in their own eyes" (Prov. 26:5, 12). The wise should no more boast in their wisdom than the powerful and wealthy should boast in their power and privilege—in other words, never! For Jeremiah, pride is a clear and present danger to true wisdom.

DEFINING WISDOM

So much for a critical view from the outside looking in. But what do the sages themselves have to say about wisdom? How might they respond to these scathing criticisms from a prophet? Welcome to the Wisdom Literature! Scholars typically classify the books of Proverbs, Job, and Ecclesiastes as the wisdom corpus because of their focus on, well, wisdom—though Job is a bit of an outlier (more on that later). Despite their shared theme, these three books are strikingly diverse. Proverbs discerns a clear connection between human actions and their consequences, while Job questions and ultimately severs that link, and Ecclesiastes seems to leave everything to chance. Where Proverbs sees cosmic order, the character of Job sees only disorder and chaos, and Ecclesiastes perceives an inscrutable mystery. Across these books, biblical wisdom spans the spectrum from confident certainty to unsettling uncertainty. One reason for this diversity is that much of biblical wisdom is grounded in human inquiry and experience, which is naturally never fully settled. If anything, wisdom is fluid by necessity.

While it's impossible to define biblical wisdom by a common outlook, we can identify some general features, starting with what wisdom is *not*. The Wisdom Literature in the Hebrew Bible says nothing about history or prophecy and very little about worship. Instead of focusing on national history, it explores creation and human experience. Rather than Zion's temple, the landscape of Wisdom Literature is shaped by the home, the city gates, and the royal court. In the broadest sense, wisdom focuses on human understanding and conduct outside the context of worship.

The wisdom corpus also has other defining features, ranging from practical guidance for success and moral instruction to reflection on the ups and downs of daily life and the mysterious wonders of God and creation. But beneath all these aspects lies a fundamental dynamic: wisdom imparts wisdom. Though this may sound circular, it highlights two key aspects of wisdom: 1) the active nature of wisdom and 2) wisdom's purpose.

First, wisdom, by its very nature, must be shared and received. Wisdom kept to oneself is not truly wisdom; it's merely a secret that dies along with its keeper. Wisdom becomes wisdom when it is imparted. From the simplest maxim to the stiffest rebuke, wisdom is always in motion, passed on to those who have ears to hear and hearts to receive. Moreover, wisdom is not just meant to be received but also tested (Job 12:11-12). Second, wisdom is wisdom when it is deemed *worthy* of sharing—when it provides some benefit, including the fundamental benefit of understanding.

When it comes to understanding, it's important to distinguish between knowledge and wisdom. It's often said that while knowledge is knowing that a tomato is a fruit, wisdom is knowing it doesn't belong in a fruit salad. Wisdom is all about the right application of knowledge. It's as much about doing as it is about knowing. But here's the thing: I recently had a fruit salad with mango, strawberries, kiwis, and grape tomatoes—and it was surprisingly good! It just goes to show that, sometimes, wisdom can break its own rules.

WHERE IS WISDOM TO BE FOUND?

Another striking feature of wisdom is the diversity of its sources. "Where shall wisdom be found? And where is the place of understanding?" (Job 28:12). In Job, the answer is that mortals don't have a clue (Job 28:13-22). Only God knows the way to wisdom (Job 28:23-27). So much for *Homo sapiens* ("the wise human"). Maybe our species' self-designated title was a bit too self-congratulatory anyway—just look at the state of the world.

However, not all the voices of biblical wisdom agree with such a pessimistic outlook. In Proverbs, wisdom is seen as something that begins in the family. The father addresses his son with, "Listen, my son, to your father's instruction, and do not dismiss your mother's teaching" (Proverbs 1:8). Later, he continues, "My son, be attentive to my wisdom; incline your ear to my understanding" (Proverbs 5:1). The direct parental address "my son" (or "my child" in more inclusive translations) appears twenty-four times in Proverbs, and "my children" is used twice (Proverbs 7:24; 8:32).

This form of direct address emphasizes that wisdom is deeply rooted in parental instruction and guidance, essential for children not only to survive, but to thrive.

But there's more to consider. The biblical sages didn't just find wisdom within their own culture, often attributing it to Solomon; they also recognized wisdom in other cultures, among non-Israelites. Take, for example, the final two sections of Proverbs: "The words of Agur son of Jakeh" (Proverbs 30:1) and "The words of King Lemuel, king of Massa, which his mother taught him" (Proverbs 31:1). Beyond this reference, there is no biblical record of an "Agur," and "the king of Massa" likely hailed from a region in northern Arabia. Additionally, Job and his friends, who dominate nearly twenty-five chapters of dialogue, are all non-Israelites. Perhaps most surprising, the collection of proverbs known as the "words of the wise" in Proverbs 22:17–24:22 is drawn mostly from an even more ancient Egyptian work, the *Instruction of Amenemope.*

The biblical sages saw wisdom as something that cut across and transcended cultures, free to be borrowed and adapted. In the ancient world, there were no copyright laws, and plagiarism wasn't a concept. In this world, wisdom is universal, even if its expressions are culturally specific.

The ancient sages also drew wisdom from creation itself, seeing it as a reflection of God's wisdom:

> By wisdom YHWH founded the earth;
>   by understanding he established the heavens;
> By his knowledge the deeps broke open,
>   and the clouds drop dew. (Proverbs 3:19-20)

Divine wisdom is woven into the very fabric of creation. Creation itself reveals God's wisdom, and studying it is a means for discerning that wisdom. It's no coincidence that God's response to Job focuses entirely on God's wisdom in creation (Job 38-41). Similarly, Proverbs frequently draws on examples from nature, especially its creatures, to offer wisdom of some sort (Prov. 6:6-8; 30:15-19, 24-31). For the sages, creation was their classroom.

Finally, wisdom can also be found wherever wisdom has *her* say. In Proverbs, wisdom is uniquely personified as a woman, who stations herself "in the street," in the city's "squares," at the "busiest corner," and at the "city gates" (Prov. 1:20-21), as well as at the "crossroads" (Prov. 8:2). Amid the hustle and bustle of life, in the heart of social interaction, wisdom can be found, fully accessible and direct. According to Proverbs, Woman Wisdom never hides; she is always beckoning, challenging, and inviting. She even invites her guests to a meal:

> She has slaughtered her animals;
>   she has mixed her wine;
>   she has also set her table.
> She has sent out her servant girls;
>   she calls from the highest places in the town,
> "You who are immature, turn in here!"
>   To those without sense she says,
> "Come, eat of my bread and drink of the wine I have mixed.
>   Lay aside immaturity, and live, and walk in the way of
>   insight." (Proverbs 9:2-6)

Wisdom invites her guests to a banquet of rich fare—a feast of wisdom. What follows her invitation, beginning in chapter 10, is a veritable smorgasbord of proverbial sayings that extend nearly to the end of the book. These proverbs range from bite-size nuggets to more substantial insights, getting richer and more complex as one proceeds. It's a full multi-course meal, meant to be savored and digested slowly, each bite to be tasted and tested. But be warned—some may be harder to swallow than others! There's tension within these proverbs; some even seem to duel with each other, as we saw earlier in Proverbs 26:4-5 (see Chapter 1). There's a time to "answer fools" and there's a time to walk away from them. It's up to you to decide which is which, after carefully weighing the consequences.

Another point of dialogue and controversy within the proverbs is the topic of poverty. Some proverbs denigrate the poor:

> How long will you lie down, you sluggard? When will you get up from your sleep? A little sleep, a little slumber, a little folding of the hands to rest, and poverty will come upon you like a robber, and destitution, like an armed warrior. (Proverbs 6:9-11)

> The wealth of the rich is their stronghold; the poverty of the poor is their ruin. (Proverbs 10:15)

The first passage attributes poverty to laziness and neglect, serving as a dire warning. The second laments poverty as a state of ruin, contrasting it with the wealth of the rich. On the opposite end of the spectrum, there's an acknowledgment that poverty is caused by injustice:

> The poor person's land may yield much food, but it is swept away from injustice. (Proverbs 13:23)

One can easily imagine foreclosed properties and predatory loans driving farmers into poverty—for instance, a once-thriving family farm lost to insurmountable debt and seized by the wealthy. This was the dire reality in eighth-century Israel, as prophets like Amos and Isaiah attested.

Other proverbs, however, esteem the poor, highlighting their integrity in contrast to the wealthy:

> Some pretend to be rich, yet have nothing; others pretend to be poor, yet have great riches. (Proverbs 13:7)

> Better to be poor and walk in integrity than to be crooked in one's ways and wealthy. (Proverbs 28:6)

> It is better to be humble among the destitute than to divide the plunder with the proud. (Proverbs 16:19)

> A rich man is wise in his own eyes, but an insightful poor person sees through him. (Proverbs 28:11)

Poverty and wealth are not always what they seem. Proverbs like these add nuance to the extremes, even suggesting that wealth is problematic and poverty less of a bane than it is feared to be. Laziness isn't part of the equation here.

Finally, there are proverbs that focus on protecting the poor from oppression and abuse.

> Those who exploit the poor insult their maker, but those who are kind to the needy honor [God]. (Proverbs 14:31)

> Whoever is gracious to the poor lends to YHWH and will be repaid in full. (Proverbs 19:17)

Taken together, these proverbs facilitate a dialogue about the causes of poverty, ranging from laziness to systemic injustice, and what can be done about it. Not all proverbs think alike! Wisdom offers up a diverse menu to satisfy all palates and compel her guests to converse.

FOR WHOM AND FOR WHAT IS WISDOM?

Another question for discussion: For whom is wisdom and what is its purpose? Let's start with the beginning of Proverbs, where the book's purpose is outlined. If Proverbs were an educational course, then Proverbs 1:2-7 would be its statement of objectives:

> To learn about wisdom and instruction,
> **to understand words of insight,**
> *to gain instruction in wise dealing,*
> *righteousness, justice, and equity;*
> *to teach shrewdness to the naive,*
> *knowledge and prudence to the young—*
> *May the wise also hear and gain in learning,*
> *and the discerning acquire skill,*
> **to understand a proverb and a figure,**
> **the words of the wise and their riddles.**
> The fear of YHWH is the beginning of knowledge,
> but fools despise wisdom and instruction. (Proverbs 1:2-7)

This formal introduction highlights all the reasons for pursuing wisdom, presenting a motley list of virtues and values. What might initially appear to be a haphazard collection is, on closer inspection, carefully structured. The first and last lines of the passage refer to the general terminology of wisdom: "wisdom," "instruction," and "knowledge." Moving toward the center, these portions (bolded in the text) focus on the literary forms of wisdom: "words of insight," "proverb," "figure," "words," and "riddles." Closer still to the center (italicized in the text) are various skills and practices that help one succeed in life: "wise dealing," "shrewdness," "prudence," "learning," and "skill." These are what ethicists might call "instrumental virtues"—qualities that help get you where you want to go in life.

Finally, at the very heart of the text (underlined in the text), are the inherently moral virtues: "justice, righteousness, and equity." It's no accident that these are positioned at the thematic core of the passage. If this passage were a mountain, these particular virtues would rest at the summit. They also respond to Jeremiah's critique, which identified similar moral values that YHWH delighted in but the wise had allegedly forgotten (Jer. 9:24). In Proverbs, these values take center stage. Altogether, this preface to Proverbs demonstrates how wide-ranging wisdom is, encompassing everything from justice to commerce, from equity and righteousness to success in navigating life.

And whom is wisdom for? A cursory glance at this passage would suggest that wisdom is primarily aimed at the "young" and the "naive," as they are clearly in the greatest need of wisdom. However, Proverbs 1:5 makes it clear that the "wise" and the "discerning" are also among wisdom's intended recipients. Just like the young, the wise are in constant need of more wisdom. There is no endgame to wisdom; there is no finish line. The wise can never assume they have learned it all, so there's no room for boasting—echoing Jeremiah's critique. The path of wisdom is never-ending; both the novice and the most advanced remain wisdom's humble disciples. There's no graduation ceremony in the study of wisdom because there's no final day of class. There is always more to learn.

Speaking of more, the last verse in this prologue lays the theological foundation for the entire wisdom project (Prov. 1:7). Often called the book's motto, this verse grounds wisdom in the context of reverence: "The fear of YHWH is the beginning of knowledge" (or wisdom; see also Prov. 9:10; Ps. 111:10). Elsewhere in the Bible, the fear of God can elicit terror (2 Chron. 14:14; Exod. 20:20). In fact, the first mention of fear in the Bible is when Adam, filled with shame, hides from God in the Garden after eating from the forbidden tree of the knowledge of good and evil (Gen. 3:10).

Fear is typically defined as an avoidance response, an emotion that triggers fight or flight. In Proverbs, however, godly fear is not meant to terrorize someone into submission or make them flee from God. Instead, this fear is intended to evoke a sense of reverence and humility that draws one closer to wisdom by acknowledging its divine source. Call it an "affiliative fear" (which sounds like an oxymoron), a fear that brings a person nearer to God through the pursuit of wisdom. "The fear of YHWH" is the beginning of one's growth in wisdom. Elsewhere in Proverbs, this kind of fear "prolongs life" (Prov. 10:27), promotes "strong confidence" (Prov. 14:26), and is the "fountain of life" (Prov. 14:27; see also 19:23). It is far from terror.

This language opens up a dialogue about the role of fear in relation to God. In Deuteronomy, the fear of God is a motivator for serving God (Deut. 6:13; 13:4), and "walking in all [God's] ways" (Deut. 10:12; see also 8:6). There, fear is tied to obedience, driven by the fear of punishment in light of the horrific curses mentioned in Deuteronomy 28:1-68. So, what is the appropriate way to understand fear in relation to God? In Proverbs, it's not about obedience or punishment; it's about the pursuit of wisdom. Without such fear—without proper reverence for God as the "beginning" of wisdom—wisdom becomes a lost opportunity and a temptation toward self-pride. In Proverbs, the "fear of the YHWH" is an awe-filled, humbling reverence of the source of wisdom.

WISDOM AS POSSESSION OR PROCESS OR . . . ?

Another point of dialogue within Proverbs is the nature of wisdom in relation to the human subject. Is wisdom something that can be possessed? This idea is implied in the following advice from a father to his children:

> Listen up, children, to a father's instruction. . . . When I was a son to my father, tender, and my mother's favorite, he taught me and said to me, "Let your heart hold on to my words; keep my commandments and live. *Get wisdom*; *get understanding*: don't forget, and don't turn away from the words of my mouth. Do not forsake her, and she will keep you; love her, and she will protect you. The beginning of wisdom is this: *Get wisdom*, and whatever else you get, *get understanding*. Prize her, and she will exalt you; she will honor you if you embrace her." (Proverbs 4:1-8)

A father reminisces about the advice his own father gave him as a child, which can be summed up in just two words: "Get wisdom!" But more than a possession, wisdom is also personified as a woman, heightening her appeal to the son on the brink of adulthood. In other words, wisdom is to be possessed and prized. But wisdom is no mere trophy; she reciprocates by "exalting" and "honoring" the one who embraces her. She offers the gifts of longevity and prosperity:

> How happy are those who find wisdom,
>   and those who get understanding,
> for her profit is better than silver,
>   and her gain better than gold.
> She is more precious than jewels;
>   nothing you desire can compare with her.
> Long life is in her right hand;
>   in her left hand are wealth and honor. (Proverbs 3:13-16)

Although Wisdom is priceless and far surpasses material abundance, she does offer "wealth and honor," as well as a "long life" to those who embrace her.

Possession, however, isn't the only metaphor for attaining wisdom in Proverbs; another is the idea of a "path" or "way."

> I have taught you the way of wisdom;
> I have led you in straight paths.
> When you walk, your step will not be hindered;
> and if you run, you will not trip. (Proverbs 4:11-12)

> But the path of the righteous is like the light of dawn,
> which gets brighter and brighter until full day.
> (But) the path of the wicked is like deep darkness;
> they do not know what they will trip over.
> (Proverbs 4:18-19)

The metaphor of the "way" or "path" is foundational in Proverbs. The book presents two distinct paths that wind their way through the book: the path of wisdom and righteousness and the path of wickedness. The difference is stark. The path of wisdom is illuminated, shining "brighter and brighter," while the path of wickedness is shrouded "like deep darkness." On the path of wisdom, one walks steadily and does not trip, even when running. In contrast, stumbling is inevitable on the dark path of wickedness. This metaphor of a path emphasizes that wisdom is a way of life, requiring constant diligence and practice. Moreover, it's not an individual journey. A path is formed through the passage of many feet; one does not walk this path alone.

So, which is it? Is wisdom a possession or a path? Both perspectives are prominently featured and, in fact, are intertwined in Proverbs. Immediately following Proverbs 3:16, which we discussed earlier ("Long life is in her right hand . . ."), we find the following verse: "Her ways are pleasant, and all her paths are peace" (Prov. 3:17). Elsewhere, personified Wisdom boasts:

My fruit is better than gold, even fine gold,
and my yield is better than choice silver.
I walk on the way of righteousness,
on the paths of justice,
to enrich those who love me,
and fill their treasuries. (Proverbs 8:19-21)

Wisdom can both walk and provide, so gifted is she. But to "possess" her, one must walk with her and be guided by her. In Proverbs, she is portrayed as both an object to be possessed and a companion along the path. The reasons for Wisdom's dual nature becomes clear through comparison. As an object of possession and source of provision, Wisdom awakens a deep desire within the self. Her alluring qualities, verging on the erotic, make Wisdom an object of deep and profound longing:

How happy is the one who listens to me,
watching daily at my doors,
waiting beside my doorposts,
for whoever finds me finds life
and gains favor from YHWH.
But the one who misses me injures themselves;
all who hate me love death. (Proverbs 8:34-36)

Watching, waiting, lurking, and ultimately finding—such is the process of possessing wisdom. It may sound a little creepy, but remember, wisdom is a metaphor, portrayed as an alluring object of desire. Like a hidden treasure waiting to be discovered (Matt 13:44), Wisdom invites us to seek her out.

On the other hand, wisdom isn't just a possession or an object of desire for young men. Wisdom is the path of life itself—challenging and joyful in equal measure. It's a continuous process, never-ending, and always evolving. To pursue wisdom, you must keep moving forward, never settling for less. The desire for wisdom is never fully quenched because if it were, the journey would end. As possession and process, wisdom is both something to be acquired and a guide along the way, never fully attained but always leading us onward.

Another important aspect of wisdom extends beyond the book of Proverbs and is illustrated in the story of Solomon, to whom much of Proverbs is attributed (Prov. 1:1; 10:1; 25:1). In 1 Kings 3, early in his reign, Solomon receives a vision from God at Gibeon, where God says, "Ask what I should give you" (1 Kings 3:5). Solomon responds:

> YHWH, my God, you have made your servant king in my father David's place, although I am only a young child; I do not know how to go out or to come in. Your servant lives amid the people you have chosen, a great people, too numerous to be numbered or counted. So give your servant a discerning mind to govern your people, able to distinguish between good and evil; for who can govern this great people of yours? (1 Kings 3:7-9)

In short, Solomon asks for wisdom to govern, speaking from a place of deep humility, even likening himself to a "young child" who knows nothing. God is pleased:

> Because you have asked this rather than asking for yourself long life or wealth, or for the life of your enemies, but instead have asked for yourself understanding to discern what is right, I will now do according to your word. I hereby grant you a wise and discerning mind; no one like you has been before you and no one like you shall rise up after you. I give you also what you have not asked, both wealth and honor all your life. No other king shall compare with you. (1 Kings 3:11-13)

"A wise and discerning mind" and "understanding to discern what is right"—this is the wisdom of a king, which Solomon soon demonstrates in the well-known story of the two prostitutes and their children, one living and one dead (1 Kings 3:16-27). This "wisdom of God" earns Solomon international acclaim (1 Kings 3:28; 4:29-34). "People came from all the nations to hear Solomon's wisdom," including the Queen of Sheba, who came to “test him with hard questions” and left awestruck (1 Kings 10:1-10)—and, according to Ethiopian legend, with a child. But that’s another story.

The point is that Solomon’s unparalleled wisdom began with a prayer. Resisting the urge to ask for riches, power, or military might, the great king asked for the wisdom to govern God’s “great people,” approaching the request with the humility of a “child.” Here, wisdom is God’s gift, not something to be pursued but rather received through prayer and a humble, listening heart.

WISDOM AND FAILURE

Wisdom promises so much, including the protection of the wise:

> When you walk, your step will not be hindered;
> and if you run, you will not trip. (Proverbs 4:12)

Stumbling is reserved for the wicked, whose path plunges into utter darkness (Prov. 4:19). But what about the wise or righteous—can they ever fall? According to this verse, it seems not; even running doesn’t pose a danger (even with scissors). Yet, in other parts of scripture, the answer is different.

> The righteous may fall seven times,
> but they will rise back up.
> As for the wicked,
> they will trip in evil. (Proverbs 24:16)

What sets the righteous apart from the wicked is not that the wicked trip and fall—both do. The key difference is that the righteous have the capacity to pick themselves back up and continue on their path. What might such a fall look like? It could be a lapse in judgment, a moral misstep, complicity in wrongdoing, indifference to a pressing moral issue, or even a crime—anything that could tarnish their character or cast them as wicked or ignorant. However, the righteous who fall will correct themselves and continue walking the path of wisdom. They may fall seven times, no less—a number signifying completeness or perfection in biblical tradition. The righteous, thus, fall "perfectly" by acknowledging that falling and failing are an expected part of the journey, as perfection is never fully attainable in the pursuit of wisdom.

But getting back up after a fall isn't just a matter of "pulling yourself up by your bootstraps," as the cliché goes. It involves the support of others. Enter the power of rebuke:

> Whoever corrects a scoffer gets insulted;
> whoever rebukes the wicked gets hurt.
> Do not rebuke a scoffer, or he will hate you,
> but rebuke the wise, and they will love you.
> Teach the wise,
> and they will become wiser still.
> Instruct the righteous
> and they will gain in learning. (Proverbs 9:7-9)

In this passage, what distinguishes the wise and the righteous from the wicked or the scoffer is that the wise will not only accept "rebuke" or correction; they will love you for it! Those who embrace critique and correction prove themselves to be truly wise, showing a willingness to learn from their mistakes, even when those mistakes are pointed out by others. Sometimes this process involves considerable unlearning. Past assumptions and preconceptions may need to be questioned and either overturned or revised. Although it may sound harsh, the art of rebuke is meant to be constructive, offering an opportunity for growth within the community of the wise. Those who offer critique are just as willing to receive it. A room full of rebukes might sound like a graduate school seminar, but in Proverbs, it's the school of life.[1]

---

1. For more on the connection between wisdom and failure, see William P. Brown, "When Wisdom Fails" in *"When The Morning Stars Sang": Essays in Honor of Choon Leong Seow on the Occasion of His Sixty-Fifth Birthday*, ed. Scott C. Jones and Christine Roy Yoder (BZAW 500; Berlin: Walter de Gruyter, 2018), 209-223.

WISDOM AS TREE OF LIFE

Speaking of life, wisdom is often presented as the very source of life, emphasized most pointedly in the following passage:

> She is a tree of life to those who embrace her;
> those who hold her fast are happy. (Proverbs 3:18)

Wisdom's ultimate metaphor in the book of Proverbs is the "tree of life," an image that appears elsewhere only in Genesis and Revelation, both referring to the tree of life in the Garden of Eden. In Genesis 2-3, two trees are mentioned: "the tree of the knowledge of good and evil" and "the tree of life." The first is forbidden, while the latter remains hidden in the narrative, only reappearing at the end when Adam is barred from the garden to prevent him from partaking from it and becoming immortal as a result (Gen. 3:23). It's a tragic story.

But Proverbs tells a different story: wisdom is a "tree of life" freely available to all who seek it, inviting them to partake. She offers the knowledge of good and evil—that is, the ability to make moral judgments—along with a long and prosperous life. It's as if wisdom in Proverbs combines the qualities of both trees in the Garden, grafting them into one. She is the one tree, the tree of wisdom *and* life, leading to an enlightened, moral, and flourishing existence.

Comparing Genesis 2 and Proverbs 3, one wonders if the notion of wisdom as a tree of life predates the two trees of the Garden. Together, these two trees represent wisdom's full scope, from complete knowledge and moral understanding to the pursuit of a long life, if not immortality itself. In the Garden, the tree of wisdom is divided into two, representing the two defining aspects of wisdom but now separated. The story's purpose in splitting the trees is to demonstrate that while humans have the capacity to attain wisdom, they cannot achieve immortality. Their lives remain inherently fragile and finite: "You are dust and to dust you shall return" (Gen. 3:19). One tree is forbidden, the other inaccessible. Only through disobedience is the fruit of moral discernment tasted. This divinely prescribed restriction underscores that obedience is valued more highly than wisdom gained through human effort. From the Garden's perspective, the wisest course is to obey God's command, even if it means forsaking wisdom. In Proverbs, however, the wisest choice is to embrace Wisdom and enjoy her benefits—to partake in the "tree of life" without a fiery sword to guard it. Wisdom is open access, accompanied by God's blessing. And with this, the dialogue continues—as it began—all in response to Jeremiah's critique. But there is more.

WISDOM'S PLAY

As a counterpart, if not counterpoint, to "fear" as the beginning of wisdom (Prov. 1:7, 9:10), personified Wisdom talks about her own beginning in a passage that establishes her preeminent place in creation and her close relationship with God. The poem is her soliloquy of self-praise, infused with a distinctly rhetorical purpose: to assert her inestimable worth and authority in relation to humanity.

> YHWH had me at the beginning of creation,
>   the first of [God's] acts of long ago.
> Of old I was woven at the very beginning,
>   even before the earth itself.
> When there were no depths, I was given birth;
>   when there were no springs abounding with water,
> When the mountains were not yet anchored,
>   before the hills themselves, I was birthed.
> When YHWH had not yet made earth and fields,
>   or the world's first bits of soil,
> When God established the heavens,
>   I was there; when God drew a circle on the face of the deep,
> When God secured the skies above,
>   when God established the fountains of the deep,
> When God assigned the sea its limit,
>   so that the waters might not transgress God's command,

When God marked out the foundations of the earth,
    I was beside God growing up.[2]
I was sheer delight day by day,
    playing before God every moment,
playing in God's inhabited world
    and delighting in the offspring of Adam. (Proverbs 8:22-31)

In this evocative passage, Wisdom asserts her existence before all things, witnessing God's work in creation. She also talks of playing with both God and the world (Prov. 8:30-31), highlighting her intimate and lively connection with both Creator and creation through the bond of play. While God is depicted as the architect of the cosmos, establishing the heights and depths of the universe and ensuring its stability amid the onslaught of chaos, Wisdom describes herself as having been birthed by God, begotten before all things. This imagery suggests that God has a womb, and that Wisdom, once a child, was raised by God, "growing up" beside the Creator.

Why does Wisdom describe herself this way? Perhaps to show that even she was once a child, specifically God's only begotten daughter. This creates a paradox: Wisdom, as God's child, grows in wisdom by witnessing with wide-eyed wonder the creation of the universe. Unique to this passage is the emphasis on her playfulness. Play is the means by which she grows in wisdom from childhood to adulthood. By the next chapter, Wisdom has indeed matured—she builds her house with seven pillars and invites the world to partake of her banquet (Prov. 9:1-5). While modeling hospitality, Wisdom also retains the wonder of a child seeing the world for the very first time. Instead of fear, she claims wonder as the true beginning of Wisdom, her genesis.

---

2. See the footnote reference in the NRSV: "little child." The translation of the enigmatic term *'āmôn* remains hotly debated by scholars. Alternatives include "master worker" and "confidant." I agree with Michael V. Fox's argument in *Proverbs 1-9: A New Translation with Introduction and Commentary* (The Anchor Bible 18A; New York: Doubleday, 2000), 285-87.

Jesus would concur. Once a child himself, he grew in wisdom (Luke 2:40), and as an adult, he told his followers, "Unless you change and become like children, you will never enter the kingdom of heaven" (Matt. 18:3; see also 19:14). Or, for that matter, walk the path of wisdom. Young and old, wise and immature—all walk the path, taking baby steps along the way.

JOB

Finally, we encounter wisdom in a stand-alone poem found in the book of Job. After Job and his friends have spent nearly twenty-five chapters in their heated debates, seemingly getting nowhere, another voice intrudes with these words on wisdom:

> But as for wisdom, where can it be found?
> Where is the place of understanding?
> No mortal knows the way to it;
> it is not found in the land of the living.
> The deep says, "It is not in me";
> the sea says, "It is not with me."
> Gold cannot be given for it;
> Silver cannot be weighed out as its price. . . .
> Gold and glass cannot compare with it,
> nor can it be exchanged for gold jewelry.
> No mention shall be made of coral or crystal;
> the price of wisdom is above pearls. . . .
> Where then does wisdom come from?
> Where is the place of understanding?
> It is hidden from the eyes of all the living,
> concealed from the birds of the air.
> Abaddon and Death say,
> "We have heard a report of it with our ears." (Job 28:12-15, 17-18, 21-22)

Earlier in the chapter, the poet waxes eloquently on the effort and expertise of miners as they dig deep into the earth to extract precious metals like gold, silver, iron, copper, and sapphires (Job 28:1-2, 6). But wisdom, according to the poet, is not something that can be extracted like minerals can be through mining. Wisdom's worth far exceeds the finest gold, yet it remains hidden from all—except one:

> God understands the way to it;
> he knows its place.
> For he looks to the ends of the earth,
> and sees everything beneath the heavens.
> When he gave the wind its weight,
> and measured out the waters;
> when he issued a decree for the rain
> and a way for the thunderbolt,
> he saw it and declared it;
> he established it and searched it out.
> And he said to humankind,
> "See, the fear of the Lord, that is wisdom;
> to depart from evil is understanding." (Job 28:23-28)

Only God knows the way to wisdom; only God can search wisdom out. This wisdom is beyond human reach, echoing Qoheleth's lament in Ecclesiastes: "I said, 'I will be wise,' but it was far from me. That which is, is far off, and deep, very deep; who can find it?" (Eccl. 7:23-24). This "deep" wisdom is reserved only for God, much like the "tree of knowledge" and the "tree of life" in the Garden, both forbidden to human beings. Job 28 deems wisdom to be beyond all human pursuits; thus, seeking it out is a futile endeavor and a monumental waste of time and effort, akin to miners digging in vain for something that can be found only in heaven. In today's terms, Job 28 asserts that we cannot innovate and technologically advance our way to wisdom. Despite our rapid technological progress, wisdom remains elusive. Our rapid advancement does not make us wiser, just more dangerous.

In light of the open accessibility of wisdom in Proverbs, Job 28 offers a contrast, a testimony to wisdom's *inaccessibility*. Taken together, it becomes clear that some wisdom is within our reach, while other wisdom remains beyond our grasp. Job 28 emphasizes the limits of human understanding, asserting that only God is truly wise. However, at the end of the poem there is a reminder that a portion of wisdom is reserved for human beings. This brings us almost full circle: "The fear of the Lord, that is wisdom" (Job 28:28). We are back to the idea of reverential fear, which is where Proverbs begins (Prov. 1:7; see also 9:10), but with a subtle difference. Let's compare the two mottos:

The fear of YHWH is the beginning of wisdom. (Proverbs 9:10)

The fear of the Lord, that is wisdom. (Job 28:28)

What's missing in the Joban version is the key word "beginning." In Proverbs, reverence for God is just the start of a journey toward greater wisdom. But in Job, this same reverence constitutes the entirety of wisdom—there's nothing beyond it. This wisdom isn't about acquiring knowledge, searching for truths, or possessing anything, for that matter. Instead, wisdom is about practicing humility before God. Period. Full stop. Now *that's* a perspective Jeremiah would appreciate.

DISCUSSION QUESTIONS

1. Of all the different perspectives on wisdom in the Bible, which one resonates with you the most?
2. Describe someone you consider wise. What qualities or actions make them wise?
3. Share an example of wisdom you've received that you truly appreciated.
4. How would you define wisdom?
5. Does age always bring greater wisdom? What is the relationship between experience and wisdom?
6. In what ways could wisdom be considered more a gift than an object of pursuit?

CHAPTER 6

Holy Contentions

In everyday conversation, the word "holy" easily conjures negative images of exclusion or self-righteousness, like a "holier-than-thou" attitude. Even worse, it's often linked with violent conflict, like the seemingly intractable conflict in the "Holy Land." But in the Bible, holiness takes on a different meaning. It touches on issues such as power and divine election, but it also weaves in themes of gratitude, mercy, and grace. Holiness, in this way, holds its own sacred tensions, making it both complex and, at times, paradoxical.

FIGHTING OVER HOLINESS

We begin our dialogue on holiness with a heated argument, one that quickly escalates into violence. The scene is set in the wilderness, a place where unmet expectations have boiled over into talk of revolt. After years of wandering, the Israelites are once again growing restless with their divinely appointed leaders, Moses and Aaron. Ever since escaping the bonds of Egyptian slavery, they've been stuck in the desert for what would eventually become forty long years. A rebellion is brewing. Many have grown tired of Moses' heavy-handed leadership, feeling like he is leading them deeper into the wilderness, depriving them of basic necessities like food and water—both of which, they point out, had been available in

Egypt. This complaint against Moses is voiced by Dathan and Abiram, conveying the people's growing frustration:

> Is it not enough that you have brought us up out of a land flowing with milk and honey to kill us in the wilderness, that you must also lord it over us? Clearly, you have not brought us into a land flowing with milk and honey or given us an inheritance of fields and vineyards. (Numbers 16:13-14)

As if that wasn't enough, another group, led by Korah and his followers, accuses Moses and Aaron of hoarding holiness for themselves:

> Now Korah son of Izhar son of Kohath son of Levi . . . rose up against Moses, along with two hundred fifty Israelite men, leaders of the congregation, chosen from the assembly, well-known men. They gathered against Moses and Aaron, and said to them, "You have gone too far, for the entire assembly is holy, every one of them, and YHWH is in their midst. So why then do you exalt yourselves above YHWH's congregation?" (Numbers 16:1-4)

This was no trivial dispute; it represented a significant disagreement about the nature of holiness. On one side, Moses and Aaron claimed God's holiness as the basis for their leadership over the entire community. On the other, certain leaders were crying foul, arguing that holiness could not be monopolized by just two people. They believed that holiness was inherent to the whole community because YHWH was "in their midst." You could even call it the "priesthood of all believers." At the heart of confrontation was the exclusivity of holiness and how it intersects with power and authority.

What follows in this dispute is not a civil discussion about the relative merits of each position, but rather an escalation. Moses' reaction doesn't bode well: "When Moses heard it, he fell on his face" (Num. 16:4). While in other passages, the narrator immodestly declares Moses the humblest person "on the face of the earth" (Num. 12:3), that humility does not lead to a cordial resolution in this case. Moses doesn't give an inch; compromise is apparently not an option when it comes to holiness. Instead, the decision is left up to God: "In the morning YHWH will make known who is his, and who is holy, and who will be permitted to approach him; the one whom he will choose he will permit to approach. . . . You Levites have gone too far!" (Num. 16:5-7). Moses then accuses Korah and his followers, the Levites, of a power grab:

> Hear now, you Levites! Is it not enough for you that the God of Israel has separated you from the congregation of Israel, to allow you to approach him in order to perform the service of YHWH's tabernacle, and to stand before the congregation and serve them? He has allowed you to approach him, and all your brother Levites with you; yet you also seek the priesthood? (Numbers 16:9-10)

There's a backstory here. Moses identifies Korah and his followers with the Levites, a special class of priestly officials. The Levites had the privilege of carrying the ark of the covenant (Deut. 31:26), setting up and dismantling the tabernacle while in the wilderness (Num. 2:17), performing "service at the tabernacle" (Num. 3:7), and assisting Aaron, the High Priest, and his son Eleazar (Num. 3:32). Numbers makes it clear that the Levites are subordinate to Aaron and his priestly house; they are described as a "gift to Aaron and his sons" (Num. 8:19). Additionally, the Levites held the special status of "substitutes for all the firstborn that open the womb among the Israelites" (Num. 3:12), with YHWH declaring "The Levites shall be mine, for all the firstborn are mine" (Num. 3:12b-13a; see also Num. 8:16-18).

In short, the dispute over holiness has a lot to do with hierarchy and exclusion. In Moses' eyes, Korah's claim of collective holiness represents a push toward claiming equality with the holy priests of Aaron's family. The story doesn't resolve with a truce or compromise—it ends violently. Korah and his followers are swallowed up by the earth (Num. 16:32-33). What a way to win an argument! However, not all of Korah's descendants perished. Later, it's noted that "the sons of Korah did not die" when the earth swallowed (most of) them (Num. 26:11). In fact, no less than eleven psalms in the Psalter are attributed to the "sons of Korah" (Pss. 42, 44–49, 84, 85, 87 and 88). And what do these psalms say about holiness? Only that God and God's dwelling places—throne, hill, mount, and mountain—are holy (Pss. 43:3, 46:4, 47:8, 48:1, 87:1). Human holiness, however, is notably absent.

This story is just one dispute about holiness. To dive deeper into the different perspectives in this story and elsewhere, we must ask some fundamental questions: What is holiness? What does it mean for God to be holy? And what does it mean for humans to be holy? These questions don't have a single, uniform answer in the biblical tradition.

FROM HOLY HORROR TO SANCTIFYING SEPARATION

At its core, holiness refers to a state of separation. Theologically, it refers to God's own separation from the ordinary or profane. Indeed, it is God's very nature to be entirely distinct from the world, wholly other. For something to be considered sacred, it must be set apart; holiness requires separation first and foremost. But what exactly sets God apart from everything else? The Old Testament lists several aspects exclusive to God: glory, power, and divinity, to name a few. Many scholars reference Rudolph Otto's famous description of God's holiness as *mysterium tremendum et fascinans* (literally, "awe-filled and fascinating mystery").[1] This captures God's transcendent power and majesty along with the rapturous fascination and attraction that draws people in. The most personal account of God's holiness in its *tremendum* form comes from the prophet Isaiah in the context of his own calling:

> In the year that King Uzziah died, I saw the Lord sitting on a throne, high and exalted, the hems of his robe filling the temple. Seraphim were stationed above him; each had six wings: with two

---

1. John Webster, *Holiness* (Grand Rapids, MI: Eerdmans, 2003), 19; John G. Gammie, *Holiness in Israel* (Overtures to Biblical Theology; Minneapolis: Fortress, 1989), 49.

> they covered their faces, and with two they covered their feet, and with two they flew about. One called to another, saying:
>
> "Holy, holy, holy is YHWH of hosts;
> all the earth is full of his glory."
>
> The doorposts shook at the voices of those who called, as the house filled up with smoke. I said, "Woe is me, for I am lost! I am a man of unclean lips, and I live among a people of unclean lips; yet my eyes have seen the king, YHWH of hosts!" (Isaiah 6:1-5)

God's holiness is on horrifying display in the Temple, as proclaimed by the monstrous-looking seraphim (the Hebrew plural for *seraph*), fiery-winged serpents (see Isa. 14:29; 30:6). They cry out the *Trisagion*, the threefold proclamation of "holy," followed by testimony of God's glory. As God's holy presence fills the Temple, symbolized by the hems of YHWH's robe and the rising smoke, so God's glory extends across the earth. Even the celestial seraphim must cover their faces before God's holiness, while the Temple itself trembles violently. No wonder Isaiah cries out with lament—God's holy presence sharply contrasts his own unclean status. Impurity and holiness cannot coexist, and Isaiah is ready to die now that he has seen the Holy One. But God has other plans for him.

> Then one of the seraphim flew over to me, and in his hand was a live coal that he had taken from the altar with tongs. He touched my mouth with it and said: "Now that this has touched your lips, your guilt has departed and your sin is purged." Then I heard the Lord's voice saying, "Whom shall I send, and who will go for us?" And I said, "Here I am; send me!" (Isaiah 6:6-8)

Through this intense and painful ritual, Isaiah is cleansed from "guilt" and "sin," making him ready to be sent out as God's prophet.

In similarly dramatic—and arguably traumatic—fashion, Exodus 19 vividly portrays God's holy theophany on Mt. Sinai: God descends upon the mountain in dark clouds and thunder; the earth quakes, striking fear into the hearts of the Israelites encamped below. Yet, despite their terror, the Israelites desire to get closer, filled with a sense of awe and fascination—*fascinans*—even as they are warned not to touch the mountain or approach God, lest they perish (Exod. 19:12-13, 21-22). The dynamic reflects a vital tension: God's unapproachability is matched by the human desire to approach. At the same time, there's something profound about God choosing to come down and appear on the mountain in the first place. While God's holiness emphasizes separation, this unapproachability is matched by God's act of approach, seeking relationship with the community. As God declares, "I am God and not a human being, the Holy One in your midst" (Hos. 11:9). God's transcendence isn't holy if it is not in relationship. This reveals the central paradox at the core of God's holiness: relationship amid separation.

Put simply: God's holiness is sanctifying, as seen in the cases of Isaiah, Moses, and even the people. While God remains wholly other and utterly transcendent, the biblical witness testifies that God chooses to extend holiness ("sanctify") to certain things in the world. These things are set apart as belonging to God—marked as holy. This includes people, places, objects, and even specific moments in time. For example, God sanctifies—or sets apart—the Sabbath day (Gen. 2:3; Exod. 20:11), priests (Exod. 29:44; 31:13; Lev, 21:8), the firstborn (Num. 3:13; 8:17), and sanctuaries like the tabernacle and the Temple (Exod. 29:44; 1 Kings 9:3; 2 Chron. 7:16, 20). Holiness is a marker of God's ownership, separating the holy from the ordinary, the common, and the mundane. Israel, as God's covenant people, is also called holy, though this holiness stipulates obedience to the covenant on the part of the people (Exod. 6:7; Jer. 7:3). Before God's grand appearance on Sinai, God instructs Moses to tell the people:

> You saw what I did to the Egyptians and how I lifted you up on eagles' wings to bring you to myself. So now, if you faithfully heed my voice and keep my covenant, you will become my treasured possession out of all the peoples, for the whole earth is mine. You shall be for me a kingdom of priests and a holy nation. (Exodus 19:4-6)

Israel's identity as a "holy nation" comes from two key elements: God's loving choice and Israel's covenantal obedience. On one hand, God chose Israel as God's "treasured possession," setting them apart from "all the peoples." On the other hand, this special status is sustained by the people's commitment to keeping the covenant.

Echoing Exodus 19, 1 Peter 2:9-10 offers a different twist on this special status, emphasizing that it rests entirely on God's action:

> But you [new Christians] are a chosen people, a royal priesthood, a holy nation, God's own possession, so that you may proclaim the stupendous acts of the one who called you out of darkness into his marvelous light. Once you were no people, but now you are God's people. Once you had not received mercy, but now you have received mercy. (1 Peter 2:9-10)

As in Deuteronomy, which we will explore next, holiness is rooted in God's choice—a choice that transforms "no people" into "God's people," shifting their status from "no mercy" to "receiving mercy" (Hos. 1:9-10; 2:23). While holiness is a matter of divine selection, it also has a purpose. Holiness enables a people to proclaim God's "stupendous acts" and bear witness to God's presence in the world. Holiness is not an end in itself; it serves an evangelical purpose.

PRIESTLY CONTOURS OF HOLINESS

The contested issue of holiness in the Bible revolves around how far holiness can be extended in the world, particularly among human beings. This tension is dramatically illustrated in the story of Korah's rebellion, a narrative fraught with historical context. The dispute between Korah and Moses (along with Aaron) highlights two diverging views of holiness, particularly regarding its scope, as seen in the books of Leviticus and Deuteronomy.

In Leviticus, holiness is something that priests receive through ritual but must maintain through their behavior:

> [The priests] shall be holy to their God . . . for they offer YHWH's offerings by fire, the food of their God; thus, they shall be holy. They shall not marry a prostitute or a woman who has been defiled . . . they are holy to their God, and you shall treat them as holy, since they offer the food of your God. They shall be holy to you, for I YHWH, I who sanctify you, am holy. (Leviticus 21:6-8)

The priests—including Aaron and his sons—embody a special and exclusive kind of holiness, conferred upon them through their ordination. This process, outlined in Leviticus 8, includes several steps: wearing special vestments (vv. 6-9), being anointed by oil (vv. 10-13), and offering animal sacrifices, namely a bull and two rams, the last one designated as an "ordination offering" (vv. 14-21). Their sanctification involves the application of anointing oil and the blood of the sacrifice to their vestments and body, repeated consistently for seven days in the entrance of the tabernacle (vv. 33-35). It is a solemn and elaborate affair.

No comparable ordination ritual is prescribed for the Levites. Instead, they undergo an installation or dedication rite that involves purification by water and the laying on of hands (Num. 8:5-22). And that's it. The Levites are cleansed but not consecrated—they are not made holy like their priestly "brothers," who alone perform the sacred services of God (Num. 8:26). The Levites can only assist. This categorical distinction, which seemed elitist and hierarchical to Korah and his followers, was at the heart of their grievance. Elsewhere, the Levites are simply given to Aaron to assist him:

> Bring near the tribe of Levi, and set them before Aaron the priest, so that they may assist him. . . . You shall give the Levites to Aaron and his descendants; they are assigned to him from the Israelites. But you shall appoint Aaron and his descendants to be responsible for the priesthood, and any outsider who comes near shall be put to death. (Numbers 3:6, 9-10)

The passage makes clear who has holiness, and with it, the power and privilege of ministering before YHWH. The Levites, on the other hand, were tasked with doing the heavy lifting of the tabernacle, responsible for setting it up and dismantling during their travels through the wilderness (Num. 1:50). In other words, the Levites did the grunt work at the priests' bidding.

So what recourse would the Levites have had to assert their own claim to holiness before Moses and Aaron? Were they just making up their case? To the contrary, the Levites had a strong argument, an ace in the hole if you will, and it was grounded in their vocational identity. By God's command, the Levites served as substitutes for the firstborn of Israel:

> I hereby take the Levites from the Israelites as substitutes for all the firstborn that open the womb among the Israelites. The Levites are mine, for all the firstborn are mine. When I killed all the firstborn in the land of Egypt, I consecrated for my own all the firstborn in Israel, both human and animal; they are mine; I am YHWH. (Numbers 3:12-13)

Given the significance of the exodus and the death of the firstborn during the plagues, along with the ritual practice of sacrificing the firstborn of the flock to God, Korah and his followers had a strong case for claiming their own holiness. After all, they served as substitutes for the Israelite firstborn, who were deemed holy or "consecrated" by God (see Exod. 13:2). In a later tradition, the Levites are considered just as holy as the priests (2 Chron. 23:6; 35:3). But in Numbers and Leviticus, this isn't the case. Despite their service to the tabernacle—God's mobile dwelling—and their role as substitutes for the firstborn, they are still barred from holiness. You could call it a substitutionary demotion.

HOLINESS FOR THE PEOPLE

The question of the Levites and their disputed holiness raises a larger issue about holiness in relation to the entire community. While the priests in Leviticus are deemed holy through their sanctifying ordination, the book also extends the opportunity for holiness to the whole community of Israel, as seen in the following passages addressed to the people:

> Because I am YHWH your God, sanctify yourselves and be holy, for I am holy. You must not defile yourselves with any swarming creature that moves on the earth. For I am YHWH who brought you up from the land of Egypt, to be your God. You must be holy, for I am holy. (Leviticus 11:44-45)

> Say to the whole congregation of the Israelites: You must be holy, for I, YHWH your God, am holy. You must each revere your mother and father, and you must keep my Sabbaths: I am YHWH your God. (Leviticus 19:2-3)

> But I have told you: You will possess their land, and I will give it to you to possess, a land flowing with milk and honey. I am YHWH your God; I have separated you from the peoples. . . . You must be holy to me; for I YHWH am holy, and I have separated you from the other peoples to be mine. (Leviticus 20:24, 26)

In these three passages and elsewhere in Leviticus, a recurring refrain rings out with only slight variations: "You must be holy, for I, YHWH, am holy." Unlike God's inherent holiness, the Israelites are not holy by nature—they must strive to become holy. In Leviticus, holiness is not something automatically granted through God's separation of Israel from other nations. Instead, that separation provides the opportunity for holiness, but it must be pursued. And how does a people become holy once they are set apart by God? Through obedience:

> Speak to the Israelites and tell them to make fringes on the edges of their garments throughout their generations and to place blue cords on the fringe on the edges. This will be your fringe. When you see it, you will remember all the commandments of YHWH and do them. . . . So you shall remember and do all my commandments, and you must be holy to your God. (Numbers 15:38-39)

Holiness is a matter of consequence, the outcome of the people's behavior. Like the priests with their vestments, the people are instructed to don special attire, specifically blue-colored fringes. This color is also used for the cloth in the tabernacle (Num. 4:6-12). However, these fringes are not holy in themselves; they simply serve as reminders of YHWH's commandments. In Leviticus, these commandments cover a wide range of topics, from ritual practices to ethical issues. They're often mixed together, seemingly at random. For example, look at these commandments found in Leviticus 19:

> You must each revere your mother and father, and you must keep my Sabbaths: I am YHWH your God. (Leviticus 19:3)
>
> Do not turn to idols or make cast images for yourselves: I am YHWH your God. (Leviticus 19:4)
>
> You must not strip your vineyard bare or gather the fallen grapes of your vineyard; you must leave them for the poor and the immigrant: I am YHWH your God. (Leviticus 19:10)
>
> And you must not swear falsely by my name, profaning the name of your God: I am YHWH. (Leviticus 19:12)
>
> You must not take vengeance or bear a grudge against any of your people, but you must love your neighbor as yourself: I am YHWH. (Leviticus 19:18)
>
> You must not round off the hair on your temples or mar the edges of your beard. You must not make any gashes in your flesh for the dead or tattoo any marks upon you: I am YHWH. (Leviticus 19:27-28)
>
> The immigrant who resides with you shall be to you as the citizen among you; you must love the immigrant as yourself, for you were immigrants in the land of Egypt: I am YHWH. (Leviticus 19:34)

> You must have accurate balances, accurate weights, an accurate ephah, and an accurate hin: I am YHWH your God, who brought you out of the land of Egypt. (Leviticus 19:36)

From facial hair and idolatry to accurate weights and gleaning fields, Leviticus 19 is a hodgepodge of ritual, customary, and moral prescriptions (and that's not even mentioning the sexual prohibitions). Amid such an eclectic list, you may have noticed a command that Jesus himself identifies as the second greatest: "You shall love your neighbor as yourself" (Lev. 19:18b; Matt. 22:39; Mark 12:31; see Rom. 13:9). Jesus didn't invent this principle. But what is often overlooked is the follow-up command found in Leviticus: "You must love the immigrant as yourself," because Israel once lived as immigrants in Egypt (Lev. 19:34). In Leviticus, all these commands are aimed to foster communal holiness, and the rationale is simple: "I am YHWH," the one who freed Israel from Egyptian enslavement, the one who is preeminently holy. If you want to *be* holy, then *act* holy—that's the mantra of Leviticus. Holiness here is essential and a call to action.

HOLINESS IN THE NEW TESTAMENT

The refrain in Leviticus, "You must be holy, for I am holy," appears again in 1 Peter, but this time it's not tied to a list of specific rules like those found in Leviticus 19. Instead, it's part of a broader call to live a holy life:

> Therefore, gird up your minds for action, exercising self-control; set all your hope on the grace that Jesus Christ will bring you when he is revealed. Like obedient children, do not be conformed to your former desires, (rooted) in ignorance. Instead, be holy yourselves in all your conduct, just as the one who called you is holy; for it is written, "You must be holy, for I am holy." (1 Peter 1:13-16)

Here, holiness is reflected in conduct, but it is conduct that stands in stark contrast to the past, which was driven by "desires" born of "ignorance." This new way of living looks forward, rooted in hope for Christ's grace to be revealed. Just as in Leviticus, holiness in 1 Peter is demonstrated through actions that reflect the holiness of the one "who called you." Holiness, in this sense, is a calling—a vocation from the one who is holy.

The statement echoes what Paul writes in his letter to the church in Rome, where he similarly urges nonconformity as essential to embodying holiness:

> I encourage you therefore, brothers and sisters, by the mercies of God, to present your bodies as a living sacrifice, holy and acceptable to God, your appropriate service. Do not be conformed to this age (*aiōn*), but be transformed by the renewing of your minds, so that you may ascertain what is the will of God—what is good and acceptable and morally complete. (Romans 12:1-2)

In 1 Peter, holiness is separation from the personal past, but in Paul's letter to the Romans, it's about standing apart from the present age. Transformation (literally "metamorphosis") and renewal are key to a life of holiness. Paul goes so far as to liken our very lives to a "living sacrifice." No longer are animal sacrifices needed, nor is death required. Instead, holy humans become "living sacrifices" presented to God. Just as Christ is portrayed as the high priest who becomes the ultimate holy sacrifice, the author of Hebrews suggests that all believers can embody holiness through their actions (Heb. 2:17; 4:14; 7:26). The only distinction is that Christ died (Heb. 2:14; 9:11-12). But for Paul, everyone can be a "living sacrifice" through holy conduct. Korah would likely agree: anyone, Levites included, can be holy.

So, where is God in all of this? In both 1 Peter and Romans, the weight of agency falls on human conduct. (In Hebrews, the focus is entirely on Christ.) For Paul, holiness leads to the fulfillment and fullness of moral "completeness" (*teleios*; Rom. 12:2). In 1 Peter, holiness is seen as a quality of God that humans are called to emulate. Paul also acknowledges God's "mercies" or compassion as a necessary foundation that makes holy living possible. In Deuteronomy, however, it's all God's work from start to finish. Human holiness is entirely rooted in divine action.

HOLINESS GROUNDED IN GOD'S CHOICE

Holiness in Deuteronomy differs remarkably from what we find in Leviticus. Consider these examples:

> You are a people holy to YHWH your God; YHWH your God has chosen you out of all the peoples on earth to be his people, his treasured possession. (Deuteronomy 7:6; see also 14:2)

> You must not eat anything that dies naturally; you may give it to immigrants residing in your towns for them to eat, or you may sell it to a foreigner. For you are a people holy to YHWH your God. You shall not boil a kid in its mother's milk. (Deuteronomy 14:21)

> Today YHWH has obtained your agreement: to be his treasured people, as he promised you, and to keep his commandments; to set you high above all nations that he has made, in praise and in fame and in honor, so that you are a people holy to YHWH your God, as he promised. (Deuteronomy 26:18-19)

In Deuteronomy, holiness is extended by God to the people from the very beginning, based in God's decision to choose them (Deut. 7:6; 14:2). Such language is not used in Leviticus. In Deuteronomy, Israel is referred to as YHWH's "treasured possession," echoing the language from Exodus 19:5. The concept of "choice" in Deuteronomy is, not coincidentally, also applied to the Levites, implying their own unique holiness.

> For YHWH your God chose Levi out of all your tribes to stand and minister in YHWH's name, him and his sons for all time. (Deuteronomy 18:5)

Throughout Deuteronomy, the Levites are consistently called "priests" (Deut. 18:1; 21:5), a title that Leviticus studiously avoids when speaking about the Levites. As for Aaron, he is mentioned only briefly in Deuteronomy (Deut. 10:6; 32:50), with just one reference to his son, Eleazar, as a priest (Deut. 10:6). Apart from reporting Aaron's death, Deuteronomy critiques him for provoking God's anger, with Moses stepping in to save him (Deut. 9:20). In doing so, Deuteronomy diminishes Aaron's role and, in turn, elevates both Moses and the Levites, who take on a much greater role than in Leviticus:

> If a Levite leaves one of your towns, from wherever he has been residing in Israel, and comes to the place of YHWH's choosing (and he may come whenever he pleases), then he may minister in the name of YHWH his God, like all his fellow-Levites who stand to minister there before YHWH. They shall have equal portions to eat, even though they have income from the sale of family possessions. (Deuteronomy 18:6-8)

In Deuteronomy, the Levites are considered bona fide priests, enjoying the privilege of eating the sacrifices offered by the people (Deut. 18:1-4). Additionally, they play a role in judicial proceedings (Deut. 17:8-9) and are involved in matters pertaining to teaching and interpretation of *tôrâ* (Deut. 17:18). They are entrusted with placing incense before YHWH and "whole burnt offerings" on YHWH's altar (Deut. 33:10)—tasks that, in the book of Numbers, the Levites are explicitly forbidden to perform!

All in all, the people's holiness according to Deuteronomy is entirely dependent on YHWH's choice. Their holiness is established by God prior to any act of obedience on their part. The people are holy from the start. While Deuteronomy contains many prescriptions, obedience is not a condition for holiness as it is in Leviticus. Instead, it is an outgrowth of holiness. "You are a holy people" is a declaration of fact in Deuteronomy, an affirmation of communal identity grounded in divine action. In contrast, sanctification in Leviticus ("You *must be* holy") stems from a divine command. Obedience in Deuteronomy is driven by gratitude, a response to being chosen by God, while obedience in Leviticus is aspirational, a striving for holiness that makes one holy.[2] Deuteronomy emphasizes divine agency, while Leviticus focuses on human agency. This reflects the distinction between the indicative (Deuteronomy) and the imperative (Leviticus) of holiness.

One might think that the tension between these two perspectives is just a matter of divine action versus human conduct, with Deuteronomy and Leviticus taking opposing sides. But the issue is far more nuanced. Both books acknowledge that holiness involves both divine action and human responsibility. Leviticus, for example, does affirm that God has set apart God's people from the nations:

> You must be holy to me; for I YHWH am holy; I have separated you from the other peoples to be mine. (Leviticus 20:26)

But, again, Leviticus does not use the language of "choice" as Deuteronomy does. However, Leviticus does acknowledge that holiness isn't entirely dependent on human conduct. God's action plays a critical role:

> You must sanctify yourselves and be holy; for I am YHWH your God. Uphold my statutes and observe them; I am YHWH, who makes you holy. (Leviticus 20:7-8)

> You must not profane my holy name, so that I may be sanctified among the people of Israel: I am YHWH, who makes you holy. (Leviticus 22:32)

While declaring the importance of obedience, Leviticus recognizes that holiness ultimately comes from God. When the people live a life of holiness, they are, in turn, sanctified by God. Self-consecration ("sanctify yourselves") and God sanctifying the people ("who makes you holy") are bound together—divine agency manifest through human agency, and human agency reflecting divine action.

On the other side, Deuteronomy, for all its emphasis on divine action, recognizes the crucial role of obedience in maintaining holiness:

2. Gammie, *Holiness in Israel*, 109.

> YHWH will establish you as his holy people, just as he swore to you, if you keep the commandments of YHWH your God and walk in his ways. (Deuteronomy 28:9)

In Deuteronomy, while holiness is established by God, it is sustained by the people's obedience. The interesting question then is whether holiness can be lost through disobedience. For Leviticus, the answer is a definitive yes, as the people's holiness was never a given in the first place. In Deuteronomy, however, the question remains open. When the people sin, Deuteronomy doesn't declare their holiness irretrievably lost; instead, it reminds them that they are failing to live up to their true identity as a holy people. Holiness is part of their DNA. Punishment is certainly warranted—Deuteronomy contains the longest list of curses in the Bible (Deut. 28:15-68)—but do the people of God remain holy regardless? The authors of Deuteronomy may not explicitly say it, but their theological reasoning suggests that they do.

TO SACRIFICE OR NOT TO SACRIFICE?

A related issue to this discussion about holiness is the matter of sacrifice. To sacrifice or not to sacrifice—that is the question! In the Pentateuch, particularly Leviticus, Numbers, and Deuteronomy, offering sacrifices is indispensable for maintaining holiness. But for the prophets, the necessity of sacrifice is called into question. Take Isaiah, for example, who avoids referring to anyone as holy other than Israel's God, the magisterial "Holy One" (Isa 1:4; 6:3; 8:13):

> What to me is the multitude of your sacrifices? says YHWH; I am fed up with whole burnt offerings of rams and the fat of well-fed beasts; I do not delight in the blood of bulls, or of lambs, or of goats. When you come to appear before me, who asked this from your hand? Trample my courts no more; bringing offerings is futile; incense is an abomination to me. New moon and sabbath and calling of convocation—I cannot stand solemn assemblies

> with iniquity. Your new moons and your appointed festivals I hate; they have become a burden to me, I am tired of bearing them. When you stretch out your hands, I will hide my eyes from you; even when you make many prayers, I will not listen. Your hands are filled with blood. (Isaiah 1:11-15)

Isaiah's blistering critique of animal sacrifice is clear: God can no longer tolerate the people's sacrifices. "Who asked this from your hand?" the prophet asks. The obvious answer is the priests. But, as Isaiah implies, these requirements didn't actually come from God, contrary to the way Leviticus presents them as divine instruction. The problem lies in the "hands" making the sacrifices; they are "full of blood" (Isa. 1:15)—the blood of injustice, as Isaiah clarifies in the next two verses:

> Wash yourselves! Be clean! Remove the evil of your doings from before my eyes! Cease to do evil, learn to do good; seek justice, deliver the oppressed, defend the orphan, plead for the widow! (Isa. 1:16-17)

Injustice not only renders sacrifices to God ineffective but also turns them into an affront to God. The prophet clearly favors acts of justice over acts of sacrifice. The same sentiment can be found in the writings of Amos:

> I hate, I reject your festivals. I take no delight in your solemn assemblies. Even when you offer me your burnt offerings and grain offerings, I will not accept them. The offerings of well-being of your fatted animals I will not even look upon. Remove from me the cacophony of your songs; I will not listen to the melody of your harps. But let justice roll down like waters, and righteousness like an ever-flowing torrent. Did you bring to me sacrifices and offerings during the forty years in the wilderness, O house of Israel? (Amos 5:21-25)

Amos's words are just as harsh—if not harsher—than Isaiah's. He finds everything from various offerings to singing praises with musical accompaniment completely unacceptable, creating a scene of total disgust for God. How so? Is it because God hates worship as a matter of principle, or is it the *kind* of worship that irks God? That remains an open question. Still, the elements of worship that Amos abhors seem quite comprehensive. The last two verses are particularly revealing. The text asks, what is worship without the music and the singing, without the sacrificial offerings and festive liturgies? Strip it all away, and what do you have left? Perhaps nothing at all.

Is there something essential to worship that God finds lacking—a critical, missing element that undergirds it all? If you take away the music and the singing, what does God really hope to hear? Does God prefer silence? As the last verse makes clear, God does want to hear something: the "sound" of justice, likened to the roar of gushing, cascading waters—the constant rumble of a torrent that never subsides, a wadi that never runs dry. So how is justice related to rushing water? Is it destructive or sustaining, overwhelming or satisfying? The prophet leaves us to ponder the ambiguity of this powerful imagery. Perhaps it all depends on where you stand in the water. Some people float, while others drown.

Amos leaves open the question of whether worship and justice are themselves reconcilable. *If* they are (and that's a big "if"), what does worship look, sound, and smell like when it's shaped by justice? Do the songs change? Are the sacrificial offerings presented differently? Do the prayers matter, or are they all just wiped away? One wonders. One thing is clear, though: in God's ears, worship that lacks justice is just noise. Without justice, worship stinks. With justice, worship works.

Isaiah and Amos, two eighth-century prophets, are united by their passion for justice and their disdain for the way worship is practiced, including animal sacrifice, as a means of maintaining holiness. Interestingly, neither prophet refers to the people being holy; that title is reserved solely for God. While humans can strive to be just and righteous before God, holiness belongs to the divine. However, Isaiah adds an intriguing twist on this idea of divine exclusivity:

> On that day YHWH's branch will be beautiful and glorious, and the fruit of the land will be the pride and splendor of Israel's survivors. Whoever remains in Zion and is left in Jerusalem will be called holy, everyone who is inscribed for life in Jerusalem, when the Lord has washed away the filth of Zion's daughters and cleansed Jerusalem's bloodstains from its midst by a wind of judgment and a wind of purging. (Isaiah 4:2-4)

Isaiah speaks of a time of judgment and cleansing, describing a "wind of purging" that ultimately leads to a remnant that survives to enjoy the fruits of the land. These survivors will "be called holy," but not because of any sacrifices they make, or their ministry to YHWH, or even their righteous conduct. Instead, they are deemed holy simply by surviving. Their survival itself signifies their status as chosen by God.

AN ESCHATOLOGICAL RESOLUTION

Isaiah and Amos are not priests; they're prophets. Both focus more on justice than maintaining holiness. So, what would a priest who is also a prophet have to add to this conversation? Enter Ezekiel, the prophetic priest of the exile. He laments the sins of his people, who have "profaned" YHWH's name through illicit worship, including idol worship and disregarding the Sabbath (Ezek. 20:39; 22:8), among other things (see Amos 2:7). Ezekiel also condemns his fellow priests for blurring the lines between what is holy and what isn't:

> Its priests have done violence to my *tôrâ* and have profaned my holy things. They have made no distinction between the holy and the ordinary, neither have they taught the difference between the unclean and the clean, and they have disregarded my Sabbaths, so that I am profaned in their midst. (Ezekiel 22:26)

This is the cardinal sin of the priests: breaking down the essential distinction between "the holy and the ordinary." At its core, holiness means setting something apart from everything else. In other words, you can't have holiness without the existence of something that is not holy, something that is "ordinary." Things get so bad among the priests, according to Ezekiel, that God has no choice but to abandon the Temple. A holy God cannot simply dwell among an impure people as if it were an ordinary thing; therefore, the Temple must be kept holy. And the priests have failed in this task. As a result, Israel is also forced to abandon the land, or to borrow Leviticus's evocative phrase, they are "vomited out" (Lev. 18:28). Ezekial points out that the people's exile and dispersion among the nations is a direct consequence of their actions in profaning God's name.

Is all lost? Is holiness gone for good? The prophet offers his own solution, one that brings us full circle back to divine action:

> I dispersed them among the nations . . . in accordance with their conduct and their deeds I judged them. . . . But I had compassion on my holy name, which the house of Israel had profaned among the nations to which they came. Therefore, say to the house of Israel, Thus says the Lord YHWH: It is not for your sake, O house of Israel, that I am about to act, but for the sake of my holy name, which you have profaned among the nations to which you came. I will make my great name holy, which has been profaned among the nations, and which you have profaned among them; and the nations shall know that I am YHWH, says the Lord YHWH, when through you I display my holiness before their eyes. I will take you from the nations . . . and bring you into your own land. I will sprinkle clean water upon you, and you shall be clean from all your uncleannesses, and from all your idols I will cleanse you. A new heart I will give you, and a new spirit I will put within you; and I will remove from your body the heart of stone and give you a heart of flesh. I will put my spirit within you, and make you follow my statutes and be careful to observe my ordinances. Then you shall live in the land that I gave to your ancestors; and you will be my people, and I will be your God. (Ezekiel 36:19-28)

The prophet envisions a future in which YHWH's holiness is the sole motivating force to restore the exiled people. For the moment, Israel is no longer separated from other nations but rather dispersed among them. The need to maintain the holiness of God's name—which has been tainted by Israel's actions—motivates YHWH to take the lead and do the heavy lifting in sustaining Israel's collective holiness, which Ezekiel describes as a "cleansing." He paints this transformation as an act of new creation, whereby a "new heart" and a "new spirit" will replace a "heart of stone" (similar to Pharaoh's "hardened heart") with a "heart of flesh." By putting God's holy spirit within them, the people will naturally abide by God's statutes and ordinances. This renewal rests entirely on God, God will sanctify Israel (Ezek. 20:12; 37:28). Israel's role is simply to receive this gift and follow along. Ezekiel concludes this vision of holiness by repeating the heart of God's covenant: "You will be my people, and I will be your God." God and Israel are mutually bound together because of God's initiative and commitment. Holiness, then, isn't just about God setting a people apart from the nations; it's also about their restoration and covenantal fulfillment with God.

Ezekiel isn't the only prophet who envisions holiness being fulfilled in the future. Isaiah shares this same vision with regard to the remnant, as we saw earlier. Zechariah also prophecies about a time when YHWH's sovereignty over the nations is fully realized (Zech. 14:9). In Zechariah, this is demonstrated through the elevation and vindication of Jerusalem, which will be "never again doomed to destruction" (Zech. 14:11). When that day comes, the circle of holiness widens beyond just the furnishings of the Temple:

> On that day "Holy to YHWH" will be inscribed on the bells of the horses. And the cooking pots in YHWH's house will be as holy as the bowls in front of the altar; and every cooking pot in Jerusalem and Judah will be sacred to YHWH of hosts, so that all who sacrifice may come and use them to boil the flesh of

> the sacrifice. And there will no longer be traders in the house of YHWH of hosts on that day. (Zechariah 14:20-21)

Horse bells and cooking pots—these everyday items, these common things, are themselves invested with divine holiness. The specific inscription on the bells indicates that holiness is fundamentally about belonging. For something to be considered "holy," it must belong to God. In priestly tradition, this would have included only the Temple furnishings and the priests serving inside. The inner curtain of the Temple (the "second temple" in Hebrews 9:3) created a strict boundary that protected God's most holy presence, enthroned upon the cherubim, from the larger nave or (less) holy place inside. This inner sanctuary was further protected from the outside world of the ordinary by the Temple walls. Traditionally, holiness required clear boundaries to separate the holy from the profane. However, in Zechariah's vision, even horse bells and cooking pots share in holiness. God's holiness is unleashed, and as a consequence, merchants "in YHWH's house" are "no longer" there. It's no wonder that Jesus drove the money changers out of the Temple area (Matt. 21:12-13; Mark 11:15; John 2:14-16). His actions were all about preserving and extending God's holiness in Zion.

EXCLUSION AND INCLUSION

If holiness is all about creating boundaries—specifically delineating what belongs to God and what does not, as well as who is included in the worship of God and who is not—then where exactly are those lines drawn? We've seen how the boundary for holy objects has shifted from what's inside the Temple to what's outside. But what about people?

Despite its expansive approach to holiness, Deuteronomy draws strong boundaries between who can be admitted to YHWH's assembly and who cannot:

> No man whose testicles are crushed or whose penis is cut off will be admitted to the assembly of YHWH. No one born of

> an illegitimate union will be admitted into YHWH's assembly. Even to the tenth generation, none of their descendants shall be admitted to YHWH's assembly. No Ammonite or Moabite will be admitted to YHWH's assembly. Even to the tenth generation, none of their descendants will be admitted to YHWH's assembly. (Deuteronomy 23:1-3)

Deuteronomy is quite clear: those with certain bodily impairments as well as certain foreigners are excluded from the worshiping community. Their admittance would compromise God's holiness. Among those prohibited are eunuchs, who figure prominently elsewhere in scripture—think of all eunuchs in the book of Esther, not to mention the Ethiopian eunuch in Acts 8:27-39. However, according to Deuteronomic law, they are not allowed to participate in worship.

This is not so in later traditions. Isaiah pronounces a divine declaration that breaks down such divisions:

> Thus says YHWH: Do justice, and do what is right, for my salvation will come soon, and my deliverance be revealed. . . . Do not let the foreigner joined to YHWH say, "YHWH will no doubt exclude me from his people"; and do not let the eunuch say, "I am just a dry tree." For thus says YHWH: To the eunuchs who keep my Sabbaths, who choose what I desire and hold fast to my covenant, I will give, in my house and within my walls, a monument and a name better than sons and daughters; I will give them an everlasting name that will not be cut off. And the foreigners who join themselves to YHWH, to minister to him, to love YHWH's name, and to be his servants, all who keep the Sabbath, do not profane it, and hold fast to my covenant—these I will bring to my holy mountain and make them joyful in my house of prayer; their burnt offerings and their sacrifices will be accepted on my altar; for my house shall be called a house of prayer for all peoples. (Isaiah 56:1, 3-7)

What Deuteronomy forbids, Isaiah embraces: eunuchs and foreigners are welcomed to be "joined to YHWH," fully included in worship. Isaiah describes the Temple as a "house of prayer for all peoples" (Isa. 56:7), a sentiment echoed by Jesus in Mark 11:17. Even foreigners can "minister" to God like the priests do. So, where is holiness now? It seems to have grown ever wider.

Perhaps the most significant shift occurs much later, at the crucifixion, as described in the Gospel of Matthew:

> Then Jesus cried out again with a loud voice, and he breathed his last. At that moment the curtain of the temple was torn in two, from top to bottom. The earth shook, and the rocks split. (Matthew 27:50-51)

The Temple curtain represented an inviolable boundary between God's holy presence—the most sacred part of the Temple complex—and the rest of the Temple. When the curtain is "torn," holiness is unleashed into the world, rendering the Temple itself extraneous. In Christ, holiness is accessible to everyone, as Paul himself affirmed. The community of Christ is now considered the Temple:

> Do you not realize that you are God's temple and that God's Spirit dwells in you? If anyone destroys God's temple, God will destroy that person. For God's temple is holy, which is what you are. (1 Corinthians 3:16-17)

Paul later elaborates on this idea:

> Or do you not realize that your body is a temple of the Holy Spirit within you, which you have from God, and that you are not your own? For you were bought with a price. So, glorify God in your body. (1 Corinthians 6:19-20)

In both passages, Paul is talking not about our individual bodies but about the corporate body, the "body of Christ"—the church—in all its diversity (Rom. 12:4-5; 1 Cor. 12:12-27). This a is a holy community that embraces its differences.

This is where our discussion on holiness must end, having only scratched the surface by reviewing just a few examples of the various contours of holiness featured in the Bible. Holiness is contested, restricted, expanded, and (re)defined—it truly has many faces. Who can be holy; what can be considered holy? One thing stands clear across all the traditions we've explored: God is holy. The essence of holiness lies with God. But what God chooses to do with holiness is the presenting issue. God cannot keep holiness to God's self because, as we've seen, holiness is fundamentally relational. It's also paradoxical, balancing God's incomparable transcendence with God's resolute desire to be in community. After all, "The Holy One" is only holy "in your midst" (see Hos. 11:9). That's the essence of holiness.

What about the other side of the relationship? How do we reflect or embody holiness? How effective is sacrifice in this process? What role does human agency play in manifesting holiness? Do we become holy through our actions, or are we already holy because of God? And ultimately, what's the point of being holy? All these questions are addressed throughout the Old Testament, albeit in different ways, given the sheer complexity of holiness. Amid these various perspectives, the New Testament aims to provide clarity. If you're looking for *the* example of holiness, look no further than Christ Jesus, who is recognized as "the Holy One of God," even by unclean spirits and demons (Mark 1:24; Luke 4:34). In Christ, empowered by God's Spirit to baptize with the "Holy Spirit and fire" (Matt. 3:11; Mark 1:8), human and divine agency come together in the pursuit of holiness. This is a mystery worth exploring further. In the meantime, Paul (or someone writing in his name) offers these words of advice, blending together the indicative and the imperative: "As God's chosen ones, holy and loved, put on compassion, kindness, humility, gentleness, and patience" (Col. 3:12). Such qualities are the telltale signs of holiness for a people chosen and made holy by God.

DISCUSSION QUESTIONS

1. What's the first thing that comes to mind when you hear the word "holy" or "holiness"? Is it a positive or negative thought?
2. What biblical tradition do you think is most relevant when it comes to holiness?
3. Describe a place that you regard as holy. What makes it holy?
4. Do you think of yourself as holy? What about your community of faith? Why or why not?
5. What's something you've learned about holiness in this study that you didn't know before?

CHAPTER 7

The Chosen: Problems and Promises

"Chosenness"—or as my fellow Presbyterians would say, "election"—is a controversial topic often linked to exclusivism and even violence. Just mentioning it brings up a flood of questions: What does it mean to be "chosen" by God? Does God play favorites? For what purpose is someone chosen? Who gets to be chosen by God, and why? And what does it mean for those who aren't chosen? The Old Testament, from Genesis to the Prophets, offers a wide and complex spectrum of views.

Let's go back to the beginning, when God created human beings on the sixth day, making them "in the image of God . . . male and female" (Gen. 1:27). The first account of creation in the Bible categorically states that all human beings are created equally in God's eyes; there are no preferences for one over another. God's "image" is shared by everyone, regardless of gender or status. As discussed in chapter 2, the language of royalty—terms like "image of God" and "dominion"—is thoroughly democratized. From the very start, there's no room for a hierarchy where some humans hold special status over others.

But things turn out quite differently later in Genesis, especially in the story of Cain and Abel found in Genesis 4. This tale becomes a tragic one, in part, due to a divine choice. Born to Eve, these two brothers are Cain, a farmer, and Abel, a shepherd. The very first family in the Bible also showcases the diversity of work. No preference is given to either profession; both are essential for surviving in the harsh world outside of Eden.

Each brothers gives an offering to God: Cain offers the "fruit of the ground," while Abel presents the "firstlings of his flock." Everything seems fine until God chooses one over the other, and we're left wondering why. The text doesn't offer any clues. It's certainly not that God prefers meat over grain or vegetables—both offerings are fully acceptable (see Leviticus 2). Cain's offering isn't inherently inferior, but for whatever reason, God looks favorably on Abel's offering (Gen. 4:4-5).

Cain's reacts with anger and resentment—literally his "face falls"—but we aren't told whether this anger is directed at God, his brother, or both. In any case, God challenges Cain to "master" his sin, which is poised to strike (Gen. 4:7). Strike is exactly what Cain does, committing fratricide—the murder of his brother—marking the first act of violence in the Bible. It is also the first mention of the word "sin" (Gen. 4:7).

God famously questions Cain regarding his brother's whereabouts. Cain feigns ignorance and expresses disdain for the idea that he is his "brother's keeper." But God hears Abel's blood crying out from the ground (Gen. 4:10-11) and curses Cain "from the ground": the soil will no longer yield anything for him, the farmer, condemning him to a life of nomadic wandering. Despite this curse, God marks Cain to protect him, warning that anyone who kills him will face sevenfold retribution (Gen. 4:13-15). So, while Cain is cursed to a life of foraging, he does so under God's protective deterrence.

In this first story of sibling rivalry, with its tragic outcome, we encounter a God who favors one brother over the other by accepting one sacrifice and rejecting the other. In Cain's case, we witness the destructive power of human jealousy that arises from divine favor. Why couldn't God have simply accepted both sacrifices to maintain peace between the brothers? As the judge of sacrifices, God chose to be partial. Favor for one brother becomes a test for the other, ultimately leading to murder.

We don't know what motivated God's choice of Abel's offering. Trying to explain it, as countless interpreters have done, misses the point of the story, which focuses on Cain's response rather than the reasons behind God's decision. The rationale for God's choice remains a mystery, but the outcome we know all too well, and it is shockingly tragic.

ELECTION WITH A FOCUS ON THE FAMILY

One might think that God would have learned a lesson from this—perhaps regretting such an arbitrary choice. But no. As we dive into the narratives of the patriarchs and matriarchs in Genesis, beginning with chapter 12, we encounter even more examples of sibling rivalry, each triggered by God choosing one brother over another: Isaac over Ishmael, Jacob over Esau, Joseph over his brothers. These divine choices lead to feelings of enmity and, in two cases, inspire murderous wrath. Behind these choices lies the call given to their forefather, Abraham (who is called Abram until Genesis 17):

> Now YHWH said to Abram, "Go forth from your country, from your kindred, and from your father's house to the land that I will show you. I will make of you a great nation, and I will bless you, and make your name great, so that you will be a blessing. I will bless those who bless you, but the one who belittles you I will curse; and in you all the families of the earth will gain a blessing." (Genesis 12:1-3)

Abram's call from YHWH begins with a command to separate himself from his extended family and journey to a land that will be shown to him (and Sarai). He, along with Sarai, is singled out because God has chosen him to become a "great nation" with a "great name." But the most expansive blessing is saved for last: through Abram, "all the families of the earth will gain a blessing," a blessing of international significance that's repeated twice in Genesis (Gen. 18:18, 28:14). With Abraham, the drama of blessing begins, driven by God's choices about who will bear this blessing from one generation to the next, eventually carrying it all the way to Israel's formation as a nation.

Along the way, certain members of Abraham's growing family are chosen over others, often with scandalous results. It would have been much easier if each generation had only one child, but things always get a lot more complicated with two siblings, let alone twelve! Abraham has two sons, Isaac (from Sarah) and Ishmael (from Hagar). Then Isaac and Rebekah have two sons, Esau and Jacob. Jacob himself has twelve sons and a daughter from four women (two wives and two concubines): Leah, Rachel, Bilhah, and Zilpah. Each generation has its own story to tell about God's chosen blessing, and each story is filled with its share of heartache, intensifying with every generation.

Take Isaac and Ishmael. Ishmael is born to Hagar, Sarah's Egyptian maidservant, who was given to Abraham because Sarah was thought to be infertile at the time. However, Hagar's pregnancy inspires contempt (Gen. 16:4-6), and so Hagar must flee due to Sarah's harsh treatment (Gen. 16:6). But then, YHWH's angel reassures Hagar that her son, named Ishmael ("God listens"), will father a multitude of offspring (Gen. 16:10), echoing the blessing given to Abraham in Genesis (Gen. 12:2; 15:5; 17:4, 16). As for Ishmael, he will be a "wild ass of a man," prone to conflict with everyone around him (Gen. 16:12), but he will thrive in the wilderness.

While Abraham hopes for Ishmael to be his heir, God firmly says no, instead promising that Sarah will give birth to her own child, to be named Isaac (Gen. 17:18-19). This news prompts incredulous laughter from both Sarah and Abraham (Gen. 17:17, 18:12, 21:6). Indeed, Isaac's name means "laugh." However laughable the circumstances surrounding his birth (and even the circumstances of his life since he is often a comical character in the narrative),[1] Isaac is clearly the chosen one over Ishmael. It is through Isaac that "offspring shall be named for" Abraham (Gen. 21:12). While Isaac is chosen to carry the Abrahamic blessing, Ishmael receives his own: God promises that Ishmael will become a great "nation" as well because of his heritage as Abraham's son (Gen. 21:13, 18).

1. Joel S. Kaminsky, "Humor and the Theology of Hope: Isaac as a Humorous Figure," *Interpretation* 54, 4 (2000): 363-75.

The relative equity of these blessings is also illustrated in the covenant of circumcision that God establishes with Abraham. God instructs Abraham to circumcise every male in his household, which includes not just his offspring but also every enslaved person, even those bought from a foreigner (Gen. 17:9-14). This means Ishmael is included, and he receives the blessing of becoming "the father of twelve princes" (Gen. 17:20). But when it comes to the covenant, it is specifically restricted to Isaac (Gen. 17:21). For Isaac, who carries on Abraham's chosen lineage, God promises to be the God of Abraham's offspring ("I will be their God") and to give them the land of Canaan (Gen. 17:7-8). While Ishmael is circumcised, he remains outside this covenant, despite the covenant being signified by circumcision. His position regarding the covenant is ambiguous: Ishmael is essentially an inside outsider.

Regarding the next generation, the issue of covenantal election becomes much less ambiguous—and, frankly, downright cruel. Isaac and Rebekah have twins: Jacob and Esau as rivals. From the start, they are sibling rivals as indicated by a prenatal announcement: "Two nations are in your womb, and two peoples born of you will be divided; the one shall be stronger than the other, the older one shall serve the younger one" (Gen. 25:23). God's choice is clear: Jacob, the younger twin whose name means "heel," proves to be a trickster. With his mother's help, he dupes his blind father Isaac into giving him the blessing meant for the firstborn.

When Esau discovers the ruse, he cries out, "Bless me, me also, father!" (Gen. 27:34) and laments that his younger brother had taken away his blessing. His grief quickly turns into a deep-seated grievance:

> "Isn't this why he's named Jacob? He has supplanted me twice now. He took away my birthright; and now he has taken away my blessing." Then he said, "Have you not reserved a blessing for me?" Isaac answered Esau, "I have already made him your lord, and I have given him all his brothers as servants, and with grain and wine I have sustained him. What then can I do for you, my son?" Esau said to his father, "Have you only one blessing, father?

> Bless me, me too, father!" And Esau lifted up his voice and wept. (Genesis 27:36-38)

Once recovered, Esau plots to kill Jacob. So, Jacob goes on the run, claiming that he's off to find a wife from his mother's family in Syria, but really he's trying to escape his brother's murderous wrath. On his journey, while stopping at Bethel, God confirms Jacob as God's chosen. In the famous dream, often referred to as "Jacob's ladder" (better translated as "staircase"), God speaks to Jacob, saying:

> I am YHWH, the God of Abraham, your father, and the God of Isaac; the land on which you are lying I will give to you and to your offspring; and your offspring will be like the dust of the earth, and you shall spread abroad to the west and to the east and to the north and to the south; and all the families of the earth will gain a blessing in you and in your offspring. Know that I am with you and will keep you wherever you go, and I will bring you back to this land; for I will not leave you until I have fulfilled what I have promised you. (Genesis 28:13-15)

God has chosen Jacob to continue the lineage that will receive the land, promising to be "with" him and never to leave his side. Later, under mysterious circumstances, Jacob is given the name "Israel" (Gen. 32:27-28), thereby becoming the father of a nation of twelve tribes. However, being God's chosen isn't easy. Jacob is pursued by his brother, tricked by his uncle Laban, and has to work for fourteen long years to marry his favorite wife, Rachel. Her life isn't easy either, as she constantly rivals her sister, who is also married to Jacob. Jacob shows marital favoritism, much like God shows favoritism among brothers, leading to endless rivalry and resentment. This story suggests that one of the strongest arguments against polygamy is that it just doesn't work well. But that's a discussion for another time.

In Genesis, God seems to favor the younger brother over the older one. There is, admittedly, something like a reconciliation between Jacob and Esau; at least Esau no longer wants to kill his brother. It's clear that both brothers have matured enough to peacefully coexist, but they're not exactly close. There's even a hint that Jacob gives back to Esau his rightful blessing (Gen. 33:11). The trickster brother has grown up and is trying to repair the damage he caused in his youth. He even tells Esau, "To see your face is like seeing the face of God—since you have so graciously welcomed me" (Gen. 33:10). Yet, despite this progress, Jacob remains the one chosen, not Esau. Paul points out this painful truth when he writes, "As it is written, 'I loved Jacob, but I hated Esau'" (Rom. 9:13, taken from Mal. 1:2b-3a).

The challenges of familial favoritism really come to a head in the story of Joseph, whose very name stems from the rivalry between Jacob's two wives (Gen. 30:24). We first meet Joseph as a teenager who is quick to tell on his brothers, bringing "bad reports" about them to his father (Gen. 37:2). The very next verse reveals that Joseph is Jacob's favorite: "Now Israel loved Joseph more than any of his other sons" (Gen. 37:3). Jacob has chosen Joseph, the son of his preferred wife. To show his favoritism, Jacob makes Joseph a "long tunic," which the Greek translates as a "variegated tunic," that is, a multicolored robe. Whether it's made distinctive by its length or its vibrant colors, Joseph's robe is a clear symbol of favoritism, and it only fuels his brothers' hatred.

To make matters worse, Joseph has two dreams that suggest his royal supremacy—dreams involving bowing sheaves and celestial bodies—which he eagerly shares with his family. This not only sparks jealousy among his brothers but also earns him a rebuke from his father. The result? His brothers "hated him even *more*" (Gen. 37:5, 8). This repeated mention of their hatred is telling, especially since Joseph's name means "more" or "add." Joseph has inspired only more animosity, truly living up to his name by provoking an *excess* of emotion against him. And it is all because he flaunts his status as Jacob's chosen son and, as we'll see, as God's chosen one. It seems that God has chosen a jerk.

With some dissent from Reuben and Judah, Joseph's brothers plot to kill this "dreamer" before deciding to throw him into a pit instead. Although his life is spared, he is sold into slavery in Egypt. There, he rises to prominence in Potiphar's household, only to be falsely accused of sexual assault and sent to prison. The chosen one has gone from one pit to another. But through it all, "YHWH was with him" (Gen. 39:2-3, 23), extending "loyal love" (*ḥesed*) to him (Gen. 39:21). It's in prison that Joseph discovers his gift for dream interpretation. The dreamer becomes the dream interpreter, and his success in this role becomes his ticket out of prison after two years of languishing behind bars. Remarkably, Joseph remains humble about his gift, attributing it solely to God (Gen. 40:8) : "It is not I; God will give Pharaoh a favorable response" (Gen. 41:16).

However, the interpretation isn't entirely good news: Joseph announces seven years of plenty for Egypt, followed by seven years of famine (Gen. 41:25-27). He also offers some wise advice: "Let Pharaoh select a man who is intelligent and wise and set him over the land of Egypt" (Gen. 41:33). Pharaoh does just that and chooses Joseph, the chosen one. Thus begins Joseph's ascent to high rank and authority in Egypt, where he becomes Pharaoh's second-in-command. The Egyptians now bow down to him (Gen. 41:37-45). Joseph successfully navigates the years of plenty and famine with the wisdom of a seasoned administrator. "All the world came to Joseph in Egypt to buy grain, because the famine had become severe throughout the world" (Gen. 41:57). This fulfills Joseph's part within the Abrahamic blessing, positioning him as a means of blessing to "all the families of the earth" (Gen. 12:3). Indeed, when Jacob eventually arrives in Egypt, he "blesses Pharaoh" (Gen. 47:10).

Joseph also becomes a blessing to his family, helping them survive the famine and even prosper by settling them into the fertile land of Goshen in Egypt. But for any of that to happen, his brothers must acknowledge his authority and follow his commands: "Joseph's brothers came and bowed before him with their faces to the ground" (Gen. 42:6; see also Gen. 43:26). Joseph's dreams about his family are now fulfilled. They don't recognize him, but he knows who they are. When Joseph finally reveals his identity, the bowing turns into a heartfelt reconciliation, filled with tears and much conversation (Gen. 45:14-15).

To reach that, however, Joseph tests—some might say tortures—his brothers. One could argue they had it coming, given how they treated Joseph. But retribution doesn't seem to be the goal. Nevertheless, Joseph toys with them by planting incriminating evidence of theft on them and demanding that Benjamin, the youngest son and Jacob's other favorite child, be brought to Egypt against their father's wishes. Joseph also plays favorites himself by lavishing more attention on Benjamin (Gen. 43:34). These tactics not only cause distress among his brothers but also elicit moments of heroism from Judah and Reuben (Gen. 42:37-38, 43:8-10). In this way, the theme of divine election inspires both good and bad behavior among those who are not chosen.

Joseph's election ultimately leads to reconciliation, blessing, survival, and prosperity. But it was a difficult journey for both him and his family. Reflecting on everything that happened, Joseph addresses his brothers, who are now worried that he might want to kill them for what they did to him:

> Now do not be upset or angry with yourselves that you sold me here; for God sent me before you to save life. Now the famine has been in the land these two years; and there are five more years in which there will be neither plowing nor harvest. God sent me before you to ensure your survival on earth, and to keep you alive by this great deliverance. So it was not you who sent me here but God; he has made me a father to Pharaoh, and lord of all his house and ruler over all the land of Egypt. (Genesis 45:5-8)

Joseph credits it all to God, who sent him and was with him to "save life." This sentiment is famously echoed at the end of Genesis:

> But Joseph said to them, "Do not be afraid! Am I in the place of God? Although you intended to do me harm, God intended it for good, in order to save a numerous people, as he is doing today. So have no fear; I myself will provide for you and your little ones." In this way he reassured them, speaking kindly to them. (Genesis 50:19-21)

Malicious intentions from Joseph's brothers are providentially used for good, specifically to "save a numerous people." Throughout all of Joseph's (mis)adventures and rise to power, God was at work. Joseph's position of supremacy, a direct result of his chosenness, paves the way for saving lives—from his family to all of Egypt. He represents the pinnacle of the ancestral blessing that began with Abraham's call in Genesis 12. It's no coincidence that Genesis concludes with blessings for each of the twelve tribes of Israel, represented by Jacob's sons (Gen. 49:2-27).

ISRAEL'S ELECTION AMONG THE NATIONS

So, we conclude the stories of chosenness with a focus on family, filled with moments of blessing and anguish, promise and tragedy. These narratives are a mix of scandalous trickery and hopeful tales of growing up, blessing, reconciliation, and salvation. With God's choice of Abraham, Isaac, Jacob, and Joseph, there are those who are, by definition, excluded: Ishmael, Esau, and Joseph's brothers. Yet the rejected ones still find ways to benefit despite their exclusion; they aren't doomed to damnation. These themes also play out on the national level as we shift from family to nation, exploring what it means for Israel to be God's chosen people among all the nations.

If there's a manifesto about Israel's election, it might just be God's declaration to Moses while Israelites are encamped at Mt. Sinai, waiting for further instructions:

> You saw what I did to the Egyptians, and how I lifted you up on eagles' wings and brought you to myself. So now, if you faithfully obey me and stay true to my covenant, you will be my treasured possession out of all the peoples, for the whole earth belongs to me. You will be a kingdom of priests for me and a holy nation. (Exodus 19:4-6a)

The liberation of enslaved Israelites in Egypt was a clear sign of God's choice for Israel to be God's "treasured possession" (*sĕgullâ*). The language suggests a deep intimacy: the Israelites are "brought" from Egyptian bondage to be embraced by God. Additionally, there's a purpose behind God's loving choice of Israel: to become a priestly and holy people, both internally and externally. Israel is the priest for "all the peoples," serving as an intermediary for God's blessings to the world (see Gen. 12:3). However, this privilege hinges on Israel's faithful obedience as a community. It's no surprise that this divine declaration serves as a preface to the Sinai covenant, which begins with the Decalogue (Exod. 20:2-17). Israel's special status with God must be sustained through their obedience.

A different but related perspective on Israel's election is found in Isaiah, who uses the language of love and servanthood:

> But you, Israel, my servant, Jacob, whom I have chosen, offspring of Abraham, whom I love, you whom I took from the ends of the earth, and called from its farthest corners, saying to you, "You are my servant; I chose you and did not reject you." Do not fear, for I am with you; do not be afraid, for I am your God; I will empower you, I will help you, I will uphold you with my right hand of righteousness. (Isa. 41:8-10)

Israel is chosen as the object of God's love, lifted from the margins of the world. And as God's chosen people, Israel need not fear because God promises to support and protect them. This promise is echoed in God's name, Immanuel, which means "God with us" (Isa. 7:14). God's choice of Israel is not just about protection; it's also about establishing a covenantal relationship. Finally, Israel is designated as God's "servant." While Israel is chosen for servanthood, the nature of that servanthood can take many forms:

> [YHWH] says, "It is not enough that you are my servant to raise up the tribes of Jacob and to bring back the survivors of Israel. Hence, I will appoint you as a light to the nations, so that my salvation may reach to the end of the earth." (Isaiah 49:6)

Here, the servant represents exiled Israel—or at least a portion of it—living on foreign soil as "survivors" who hope for restoration. God promises that this servant will be empowered for deliverance. But beyond that, servant Israel will shine as a beacon of salvation for the world, much like Abraham, who was a source of blessing to "all the families of the earth" (Gen. 12:3). So, what does this "salvation" look like? The very next verse offers an imperial perspective:

> Thus says YHWH, Israel's Redeemer and Holy One, to one despised, abhorred by the nations, to the slave of rulers, "Kings shall see and stand up, princes, and they shall prostrate themselves, because of YHWH, who is faithful, the Holy One of Israel, who has chosen you." (Isaiah 49:7)

In this context, the first step toward salvation for the nations is to submit to Israel and Israel's God. This idea of submission as a consequence of Israel being "chosen" is also stressed in Isaiah 14:1-2.

> But YHWH will have compassion on Jacob and again choose Israel and give them rest in their own land. Immigrants will join them and attach themselves to the house of Jacob. And the peoples will take them and bring them to their own place. The house of Israel will possess the nations as male and female slaves in YHWH's land. They will take captive those who were their captors, and rule over those who oppressed them. (Isaiah 14:1-2)

Israel's chosenness leads to a great reversal: those who once took Israel captive will now find themselves as Israel's captives. The nations that enslaved Israel will become enslaved themselves. Here, Israel's election by God requires the nations to serve Israel.

A "softer" version of this, however, is found in Zechariah:

> Many peoples and mighty nations shall come to seek YHWH of hosts in Jerusalem and to seek YHWH's favor. Thus says YHWH of hosts: In those days ten men from nations of every tongue will take hold of a Judean, grasping his garment and saying, "Let us

> go with you, for we have heard that God is with you." (Zechariah 8:22-23)

It's not enslavement but envy that drives the nations to seek YHWH's favor and to ask Israel's permission to do so. Another reason for the nations to come to Jerusalem is found in Isaiah:

> In days to come, the mountain of YHWH's house will be established as the highest of the mountains. It will be raised above the hills; all the nations shall stream to it. Many peoples shall come and say, "Come, let us head up to YHWH's mountain, to the house of the God of Jacob, so that he may teach us his ways and that we may walk in his paths." For out of Zion shall go forth instruction, and YHWH's word from Jerusalem. (Isaiah 2:2-3)

The nations come not only to seek YHWH's favor but also to receive YHWH's "instruction" (the Hebrew word is *tôrâ*). This instruction teaches the way of peace as opposed to war: "They will beat their swords into plowshares, and their spears into pruning tools; nation will not take up sword against nation; they will never again learn to wage war" (Isa. 2:4). The nations have been raging long enough, according to Isaiah.

In all these passages, Israel's election as God's beloved people comes at the expense of the nations, at least in terms of their national autonomy, even if it is seen as "good" for them. However, there is an outlier—a passage with a very different vision of Israel and the nations:

> On that day there will be a highway from Egypt to Assyria, and the Assyrian will come to Egypt, and the Egyptian to Assyria, and the Egyptians will worship with the Assyrians. On that day Israel will be the third with Egypt and Assyria, a blessing at the center of the world, for YHWH of hosts will bless them, saying, "Blessed be Egypt my people, and Assyria the work of my hands, and Israel my heritage." (Isa. 19:23-25)

In this vision of the future, Assyria and Egypt—historically considered enemy superpowers—will worship YHWH together with Israel, becoming "a blessing at the center of the world." The result is a profound blessing from God for everyone, described in the most intimate of terms: God declares Egypt "my people" and Assyria "the work of my hands." These titles are otherwise reserved for Israel alone (see Exod. 3:7, 8:23, Ps 50:7, Isa. 29:23, 45:11, 60:21). God's covenant with Israel has now been extended to the nations, suggesting that Israel was only the first to be chosen by God.

However inclusive this international vision may sound, it's significantly tempered by earlier statements that set the stage for it: Judah will be a "terror" to the Egyptians (Isa. 19:17), and God will "strike" the Egyptians in order to bring about "healing" (Isa. 19:22). For better or worse, these words of punishment lay the groundwork for the radical vision that unfolds in Isaiah 19:23-25.

Together, these passages express conflicting views on how the nations fit into Israel's election. Are they meant to be subservient to Israel, possibly even enslaved, as a form of retribution (see Gen. 12:3b)? Or do they ultimately have equal standing with Israel as recipients of God's electing love, beginning with Egypt and Assyria—both known for their imperial abuse of Israel? When it comes to Assyria, we can't overlook Jonah's anguish over God sparing Nineveh (the capital of Assyria) from judgment. Jonah laments God's acknowledgment that there are people in Nineveh "who do not know their right hand from their left, and also many animals" (Jonah 4:11). They deserve compassion, despite their brutality toward Israel. In stark contrast, the prophet Nahum revels in Nineveh's downfall with an almost sadistic glee.

What is the fate of the nations in relation to Israel's special status? Are they destined for punishment or consigned to servitude? Or can they be reconciled with Israel as equals on the global stage? The ancient scriptures grapple with these questions, rightly so, given the inherent tension between Israel's chosen status and the other peoples of the world. This tension exists in relation to a God who is both creator of all and covenant partner with one, a God who is both universal in scope and particular in action. This is the God who created all humankind in God's image (Gen. 1:27) and "formed Israel in the womb" (Isa. 44:2).

ENTITLEMENT VS. SERVICE

In addition to considering the status of the nations in relation to Israel, we should also ask: What does Israel receive and do as God's uniquely elected people? Does Israel enjoy the privileges and benefits that come with being chosen by God? Does Israel's election come with certain responsibilities?

As God's elect, Israel has a uniquely intimate relationship with God. Through the covenant established first with Abraham, God promises to be with Israel and always be their God. This means that even if Israel stumbles, even if Israel fails, it doesn't necessarily end the relationship. In fact, some psalms suggest that any breakdown in the relationship between God and Israel should be considered God's fault—highlighting just how strong some believed Israel's covenantal status to be (see Pss. 44, 89). Simply put, Israel can rest securely in its special relationship with God, which dates back to God's loving choice of Abraham. You could call this divine entitlement.

For an alternative view, let's turn to Amos, that feisty arborist and shepherd from Tekoa. Despite his reluctance to be seen as a prophet (Amos 7:14), God called him to deliver a powerful message. Amos had a few choice words about Israel's chosenness, and we can start with what might be the core passage among all his judgments:

> Hear this word that YHWH has spoken to you, O people of Israel, to the whole family that I brought up out of the land of Egypt: "You alone I have known of all the families of the earth." (Amos 3:1-2a)

The prophet captures the essence of God's special relationship with Israel using the language of "knowing," which suggests an intimate connection similar to sexual "knowledge." The Common English Bible (CEB) translates this as, "You only have I loved so deeply," highlighting the idea that God's relationship with Israel is monogamous. However, there is another way to translate this line: "Surely, you I have known *more than* all the families of the earth." This is a perfectly acceptable translation given the ambiguities of Hebrew grammar. While God knows all the nations, Israel is the most intimate partner in that relationship. Depending on the translation, Israel's special status can be seen as either absolutely unique or relatively distinct—a difference in degree rather than a complete separation. Either way, Israel stands out among the nations, with that distinction tracing back to the exodus event when God brought Israel out of Egypt, or in God's words, "brought you to myself" (Exod. 19:4).

After summarizing Israel's election and deliverance from Egyptian slavery, the prophet drops a "therefore." What will Amos say next about the consequences of Israel's election? His audience would likely have expected him to say something about Israel's privilege of being known most intimately by God. Instead, Amos delivers a surprising—and no doubt scandalous—message to his listeners: "Therefore, I will punish you for all your wrongdoings" (Amos 3:2b). Rather than proclaiming a special blessing, God announces Israel's special punishment. But for what? What are the reasons behind this? Amos makes clear elsewhere that Israel is oppressing its own people socially and economically (Amos 2:6-7). His language is damning from the beginning to (almost) the end. So, what does Israel deserve for being chosen by God? Punishment! And as for the exodus as a demonstration of God's special treatment, Amos has something pointed to say to his fellow Israelites:

> Are you not like the Cushites to me, people of Israel? says YHWH. Have I not brought Israel up from the land of Egypt, and the Philistines from Caphtor and the Arameans from Kir? (Amos 9:7)

Amos boldly claims that the exodus isn't a unique event in the international realm. God has also brought up the Philistines and the Arameans from their own places of departure; they've experienced their own exoduses too. By challenging the alleged uniqueness of the exodus, Amos makes clear that Israel can't use it as a basis for entitlement. God is actively working not only with Israel but also with other nations, including those with whom Israel has had conflicts in the past. While it's true that God has a special relationship with Israel (Amos 3:1-2), this relationship is defined by great expectations and specific responsibilities, such as dismantling economic oppression within their own community. A beloved community must also be a just community. Unfortunately, Israel hasn't fulfilled its part of the equation.

ISRAEL FOR THE WORLD

Moving from punishment to self-sacrifice, Israel's election by God takes on another dimension in relation to the nations—one of self-suffering service. In the famous "suffering servant" poem from Isaiah, the nations express what Israel, through its suffering (as noted in Chapter 6), has done for them:

> Surely, he has borne our infirmities and carried our diseases; yet we accounted him stricken, struck down by God, and afflicted. But he was wounded for our transgressions, crushed for our iniquities; upon him was the punishment that made us whole, and by his bruises we are healed. All we like sheep have gone astray; we have all turned to our own way, and YHWH has laid on him the iniquity of us all. (Isaiah 53:4-6)

> Out of his anguish he shall see light; he shall find satisfaction through his knowledge. The righteous one, my servant, shall make many righteous, and he shall bear their iniquities. Therefore, I will allot him a portion with the great, and he shall divide the spoil with the strong; because he poured out himself to death, and was numbered with the transgressors; yet he bore the sin of many, and made intercession for the transgressors. (Isaiah 53:11-12)

Through the suffering of the servant, who represents Israel, the nations are "made . . . whole." Ordained by God to "bear" the "infirmities," "iniquities," and "sins" of the nations, even unto death—the righteous servant ultimately receives vindication, leading to his exaltation.

One might think, based on Isaiah, that Israel's suffering service to the nations defines its election from the outset. Indeed, Israel is elected to serve the nations with justice, as expressed in another passage from Isaiah:

> Here is my servant, whom I uphold, my chosen, in whom I delight. I have put my spirit upon him; he will bring forth justice to the nations. (Isaiah 42:1)

It's important, however, to note that the passage doesn't say that Israel is specifically chosen *in order to* "bring forth justice to the nations." Rather, this is a consequence of Israel's election—part of its calling. Additionally, God's choice of Israel is fundamentally rooted in divine "delight"; God is lovingly committed to God's people. If the servant's election were *solely* about serving the nations, there would be no need for his exaltation in the end. The servant-representative of Israel remains the object of God's special love, a love that ultimately has no explanation and is therefore inviolable.

Isaiah continues this exploration of the servant in the following lavish and evocative passage:

> Thus says YHWH, your maker, who formed you in the womb and will help you: Do not fear, my servant Jacob, Jeshurun, whom I have chosen. As I will pour water on the thirsty land, and streams on the dry ground, so I will pour my spirit upon your descendants, and my blessing on your offspring. They shall spring up among the reeds like willows by flowing streams. This one will say, "I am YHWH's," another will be named after Jacob, yet another will write on the hand, "YHWH's," and adopt the name of Israel. (Isaiah 44:2-5)

God's choice of Jacob is accompanied with images of a lush, well-watered garden. The luxurious trees symbolize the individuals who comprise God's people, each declaring that they belong to YHWH. This description is meant to evoke blessings of sustenance and prosperity, not just for the present but for future generations as well (see also Isa. 65:23). Chosen by God, Israel is meant to thrive forever. No mention is made of Israel's service to the nations, let alone bearing their sins. Instead, the focus is exclusively on Israel's election as an act of covenantal love—a love that is entirely undeserved:

> It was not because you were more numerous than all the peoples that YHWH loved you and chose you—for you were the fewest of all the peoples. It was because YHWH loved you and kept the oath that he swore to your ancestors that YHWH has brought you out with a mighty hand and redeemed you from the house of slavery, from the hand of Pharaoh king of Egypt. (Deuteronomy 7:7-8)

However, if we take another look at Isaiah, we can see that there's also a vocational dimension to being God's specially loved people:

> I am YHWH; I have called you in righteousness. I will grasp you by the hand and keep you; I will give you as a covenant to the people, a light to the nations, to open the eyes that are blind, to bring out the prisoners from the dungeon, from the prison those who sit in darkness. (Isa. 42:6-7; see also 49:6)

This is Israel's purpose-driven calling, which flows from its election—a calling focused on liberation. In Isaiah, election and calling are inseparably linked. That calling is further emphasized in a later verse from Isaiah, which becomes even more familiar through Jesus' use of it in his very first (and nearly only) sermon:

> The spirit of the Lord YHWH is upon me, because he has anointed me; he has sent me to bring good news to the impoverished, to bind up the brokenhearted, to proclaim release for the captives and liberation to the imprisoned; to proclaim the year of YHWH's favor and the day of vindication of our God; to comfort all who mourn. (Isaiah 61:1-2; see Luke 4:18-19)

From election comes calling. It's possible that this calling was embedded in Israel's election from the very beginning. Let's go back to Abraham and revisit the calling that started this journey of election:

> Go from your country, from your kindred, and from your father's house to the land that I will show you. I will make of you a great nation, and I will bless you, and make your name great, so that you will be a blessing. I will bless those who bless you, but the one who belittles you I will curse; and in you all the families of the earth will gain a blessing. (Gen. 12:1-3)

In the middle of Abraham's call, there's what looks like a purpose statement: Abraham's status as a "great nation" and "great name" will lead him to become a blessing for the "families" of nations. However, there's another way of translating Genesis 12:2 from the Hebrew that's just as compelling—if not more so: "I will make of you a great nation, and I will bless you, and make your name great. *So be a blessing*!" (the Hebrew reflects an imperative form). This raises the question: could it be that built into Abraham's blessing from God is the expectation that he, in turn, *be* a blessing to others? In this case, blessing becomes both a gift and a task, or as the Germans poetically put it, *Gabe und Aufgabe.*

THE ELECT AND THE NON-ELECT

The Old Testament presents a range of perspectives regarding the status of non-Israelite peoples. While many of these viewpoints can seem antagonistic—especially passages that advocate acts of genocide like in following passage from Joshua—it's important to recognize the diversity of thought throughout these texts:

> So Joshua conquered the whole land, the hill country and the Negeb and the lowland and the slopes, and all their kings. He left no one remaining, but utterly destroyed all that breathed, as YHWH, the God of Israel, had commanded. (Joshua 10:40)

In his conquest of the land, Joshua is said to have wiped out all the inhabitants of the land of Canaan, the Canaanites, who were condemned to destruction, as "YHWH . . . had commanded." This divine command was the *ḥerem* or "ban," which required devoting everything to God "for destruction" (Josh. 6:17). The destruction of Jericho marked the first episode of this practice of ethnic cleansing, whereby every man, woman, child, and domestic animal was devoted to destruction (Josh. 6:17, 21). Motivating such destruction was the fear that the Canaanites would compromise Israel's worship of YHWH by introducing idolatry (Exod. 23:23-25; Deut. 7:1-5).

The question is whether these traditions of conquest and cleansing provide a model for how Israel should treat foreigners. It's undeniable that some texts in the Bible call for genocide. However, even here, there are notable exceptions granted to certain Canaanites. For instance, Rahab and her family are spared from destruction in Jericho for helping out Israelite spies (Josh. 2:1-21; 6:17, 23-25). The Gibeonites are also spared, albeit through their own deception, and they are later defended by Joshua and his army (Josh. 9:3-27; 10:1-15). Still, these exceptions are just that—exceptions within the larger narrative of conquest.

One group in particular is universally deemed worthy of annihilation: the Amalekites.

> Remember what Amalek did to you on your departure from Egypt—how he attacked you on the way when you were weak and tired, striking down all who were lagging behind you. He did not fear God. Therefore, when YHWH your God has given you rest from all your enemies on every hand, in the land that YHWH your God is giving you as an inheritance to possess, you must wipe out the remembrance of Amalek from under heaven. Do not forget! (Deuteronomy 25:17-19, see also Exodus 17:8-16)

But much later, Saul forgot this command. When he spared King Agag of the Amalekites after defeating him, King Saul was rejected by

Samuel (1 Sam. 15:1-33), paving the way for a new king, David (1 Sam. 16:1-13). Yes, the Old Testament has it in for the Amalekites, but not because of their way of worship; it's due to a brutal, unprovoked attack that goes back to the Exodus—what turns out to be an eternal grudge (Exod. 17:14-16). One should note that the nation of Amalek no longer exists.

Is that, then, the ultimate fate for the non-elect—consignment to genocidal destruction? Far from it. Nowhere in the Bible does Israel's election imply that every non-Israelite (man, woman, and child) is doomed to destruction. Exceptions, like the Amalekites, can be more accurately described as the "anti-elect" rather than the "non-elect."[2] The Old Testament portrays the vast majority of foreigners as benign. For example, the immigrant or alien (*gēr*) who "resides with you in your land" is someone you are commanded to "love . . . as yourself" (Lev. 19:33-34), just as you would your neighbor (Lev. 19:18). For all the emphasis on holy war (Deut. 20:1-20), Deuteronomy instructs the Israelites to respect the borders of neighboring nations, even those that were often Israel's enemies, like Edom, Moab, and Ammon (Deut. 2:1-13, 19). Even the Egyptians, who once enslaved the Israelites, warrant some modicum of respect, according to Deuteronomy (Deut. 23:8-9).

When it comes to commendable non-Israelites in the Old Testament, there are quite a few. We have the heroic Jael (Judg. 4) and the wise Queen of Sheba (1 Kings 10). Then there's the long-suffering Job, an Uzzite, and the Persian king Cyrus, who is referred to as God's anointed and "shepherd" (Isa. 44:28; 45:1). Let us not forget the non-Israelite sailors who sacrificed to YHWH and were reluctant to throw Jonah overboard (Jon. 1:14-16), or Ruth the Moabite, who remained devoted to Naomi, or Jethro, Moses' Midianite father-in-law who offered his own testimony of faith along with some sage advice on how to govern (Exod 18:10-23). We should not overlook Naaman, the Aramean general who worshiped

2. Joel S. Kaminsky, *Yet I Loved Jacob: Reclaiming the Biblical Concept of Election* (Nashville, TN: Abingdon, 2007), 111-119.

YHWH (2 Kings 5), or Balaam, the foreign prophet hired to curse Israel but who instead blessed Israel by God's command (Num. 22-24).[3] Not one of these individuals is looked down upon or held in contempt within the biblical narrative.

ORACLES AGAINST THE NATION

As for the non-elect nations, the accounts vary. On the one hand, there are numerous "oracles against the nations," which appear in almost every prophetic book of the Bible, including Amos 1-2, Isaiah 13-23, Jeremiah 46-51, and Ezekiel 25-31. These oracles announce the defeat of enemy nations during times of warfare, whether that warfare is actual or simply anticipated. Many construe God as a divine warrior trouncing foreign armies or stirring up conflict against other nations (for instance Isa. 13:1-5, 14:24-27, 19:1; Jer 50:25). Israel is portrayed as YHWH's "war club" and "weapon" to "smash" nations and kingdoms (Jer. 51:20-23).

Babylon is laid low, and all of creation rejoices—including the cedars of Lebanon, which will no longer be cut down (Isa. 14:7-8). Damascus, the capital of Syria, is destined to "become a heap of ruins" (Isa. 17:1). Often, the defeated nations are depicted as bringing tribute to God on Zion, acknowledging their subservience to Israel (Isa. 18:7). Several nations or city-states, like Moab (Jer. 48:29), Edom (Jer. 49:16), Babylon (Jer. 50:31-32), Egypt (Ezek. 29:3, 9), and Tyre (Ezek. 27:3-4), are condemned for their pride. Tyre even boasts, "I am a god!" (Ezek. 28:2). Victory over these nations is portrayed as the result of God's vengeance and as Israel's vindication, particularly in the case of Babylon's defeat (Jer. 51:34-37). "Babylon must fall for the slain of Israel" (Jer. 51:49a), serving as a form of repayment for Israel's suffering (Jere. 51:56b; see also Ps. 137:8-9). Israel, in turn, will have nothing to fear and will "have quiet and ease" (Jer. 46:27). Yet, despite all the harsh language surrounding their defeat, God

3. For a complete list, see Kaminsky, *Yet I Loved Jacob*, 124-125.

promises to restore certain nations, like Moab (Jer. 48:47), Ammon (Jer. 49:6), and Elam (Jer. 49:39).

A more positive view of the nations can also be found in certain psalms. On one end of the spectrum, the nations are condemned for their rebellious uproar (Pss. 2:1, 46:6), and are destined to face God's "vengeance" (Ps. 149:7) and discipline (Ps. 94:10), with their "counsels" nullified (Ps. 33:10). God views them with derision (Pss. 2:4, 59:8), and they deserve the full measure of divine anger poured out on them (Ps. 79:6).

This divine wrath against the nations is not unjustified, but it doesn't necessarily stem from their non-elect status. It arises because these nations have violently attacked God's people. Psalm 79 recalls the horror of the Babylonian invasion, which led to the wholesale destruction of both the Temple and the city, as well as the slaughter of YHWH's "servants" (Ps. 79:1-4; see also Ps. 74:3-8). As the nations mercilessly "poured out" the blood of the faithful, leaving the land littered with corpses, the psalm implores YHWH to "pour out . . . wrath upon the nations" (Ps. 79:6)

On the other end of the spectrum, some psalms view the nations as bona fide recipients of God's blessing, making them vehicles of praise and thanksgiving. For example, Psalm 67 features a petition for blessings and a testimony of praise that embraces all nations:

> May God grant us grace and bless us;
>   may he shine his face on us, *Selah*
> so that your way be made known throughout the earth,
>   (so that) your salvation (be made known) among all the nations.
> Let the peoples give you thanks, O God;
>   let the peoples give you thanks, all of them.
> Let the nations be glad and shout with joy,
>   for you judge the peoples equitably,
>   and guide the nations on the earth. *Selah*
> Let the peoples give you thanks, O God;
>   let the peoples give you thanks, all of them.

The earth has yielded its produce.
God, our God, does bless us!
May God (continue to) bless us,
so that all the ends of the earth will revere him.
(Psalm 67:1-7)

Psalm 67 opens with an indirect request that God's blessings be made known "among all the nations." While this blessing is specifically petitioned for Israel ("us"), the nations are also encouraged to acknowledge God's saving "way" with gratitude. They are to understand that the God of justice is also the God of blessing, and vice versa. Instead of pronouncing punitive judgment against the nations, the psalm declares justice (Ps. 67:3-4). The nations are called to give thanks for this justice, and rightly so—God's guidance is given on their behalf to benefit them rather than harm them. God's salutary ways extend beyond Israel to all nations, offering to adjudicate for them and "guide" them, just as God once guided the Israelites in the wilderness (Exod. 13:21, Ps. 78:14, Neh. 9:12). God's dealings with Israel serves as a sign for how God will deal with the nations: with equity and guidance. In return, the nations are expected to acknowledge the God of justice with thanksgiving for the earth's abundant harvest. Such reverence is driven by gratitude, not fear.

Distinguished by its brevity, Psalm 117 does the theologically unthinkable, at least in comparison to other psalms:

Praise YHWH, all you nations!
Acclaim him, all you peoples!
For mighty indeed is his benevolence toward us;
YHWH's faithfulness endures forever.
Praise YH! [Hallelujah!] (Psalm 117:1-2)

The psalm begins with a command to praise Israel's God, YHWH, and the second verse explains why: praise is given on behalf of what is central to YHWH's character in relation to Israel—YHWH's "benevolence" or faithful love (*ḥesed*). This love is most often directed toward Israel through the covenant, but here "benevolence" emphasizes God's enduring and steadfast care in the face of human need. Integral to God's nature, "benevolence," along with "compassion," has existed "from of old" (Ps. 25:6). The psalm's description of divine character may very well draw from YHWH's self-declaration at Sinai (Exod. 34:6-7).

However, the verb used in Psalm 117 stands out. Instead of using a common descriptor like "great" or "abounding" (*rab*) to describe "benevolence" (see Exod. 34:6b), the psalmist deploys the forceful verb *gābar* ("be mighty"). This word can refer to everything from swelling floodwaters (Gen. 7:18-19) to achieving military victory, as in the sense of "prevail" (for example Exod. 17:11, 2 Sam. 11:23). It's a strong verb, suggesting that God's "benevolence" has a forceful, victorious quality. One alternate translation for Psalm 117:2a is "For his benevolence has prevailed against us," as if the "us" in question is God's enemy! While that interpretation may make little sense, it nevertheless underscores the militant power of God's "benevolence," which can bring about deliverance in times of distress.

In Psalm 117, the "prevailing" power of God's "benevolence" is directed against but "toward us," which includes both Israel *and* the nations, linked together in common praise. This psalm invites the nations to join in worship, and to do that the nations too must experience something of the same "benevolence" and "faithfulness" that Israel has enjoyed from YHWH. For the nations to be true partners in praise, they must be beneficiaries of God's "benevolence." In this context, a good nation isn't a destroyed nation but a thankful one—grateful for God's ever-expanding "benevolence" in the world, extending beyond Israel.

OLD TESTAMENT CONCLUSION

In this brief survey of views in the Old Testament—a mere scratch on the canonical surface—we've encountered a wide range of perspectives. Some see Israel's chosenness by God as problematic, while others view it as a blessing. The family stories in Genesis record the challenges faced by those who are not chosen in relation to the chosen, and vice versa. Moreover, God's special love for Israel can elicit a sense of entitlement, leading to a prideful or provincial attitude. Other nations be damned! However, the prophet Amos was a fierce critic of this mindset. While his audience, the northern Israelites, eagerly anticipated the "day of YHWH" as a day of victory and vindication, he preached a different message: it would instead be a day of disaster because of the people's waywardness (Amos 5:18-20). Israel's special election came with the special responsibility of being a just community, and failure was not an option. So much for privilege!

On the other end of the spectrum, Israel's election comes with a strong sense of responsibility for the nations, serving as an instrument of blessing that started with Abraham (Gen. 12:3). But the journey is not easy. God's choice of the particular lineage that runs from Abraham to Joseph leads to (often violent) conflicts, as among brothers. We see this with Cain and Abel. Throughout this trajectory, election includes a calling—one that can even lead to Israel's near demise—as witnessed in the "suffering servant" being chosen to bear the sins of the world. By divine decree, the nations receive some measure of restoration through Israel's sacrifice. Finally, the ethos of praise in the Psalms leans toward achieving parity, or eventual parity, between the nations and Israel. Both are genuine partners in praise, united by God's benevolence.

ISRAEL AND THE GENTILES: PAUL'S STRUGGLE

In the New Testament, Israel's election is seen through a different lens, specifically that of Jesus Christ—a Galilean Jew whose followers launched a movement that ultimately became a new religion. Many of the early Christians were devout Jews, with some retaining their Jewish identity. However, from the very beginning, self-identified Christians also included non-Jews, or Gentiles, making the early church a diverse community. One prominent figure within this movement was Paul, a Pharisee-turned-Christian, who struggled mightily to discern the meaning of Israel's election in light of the Christ's ministry, death, and resurrection.

You can imagine that Paul could have taken the easy route by claiming that since Jewish religious authorities rejected Jesus as their Messiah, God has rejected Judaism. In fact, he comes quite close to this in Galatians 4:22–5:1, where he interprets the story of Hagar and Ishmael versus Sarah and Isaac as an allegory. In this interpretation, the "children of slavery" represent the Jewish people (linked with the "present Jerusalem"), while the "children of the promise" refer to the emerging church (connected to the "Jerusalem above"). According to Paul, this enslavement comes from following the "law," which he describes as a harsh "disciplinarian" that is now rendered obsolete in Christ (Gal. 3:24-25). In his view, faith supersedes the law, and as a result, Christianity supersedes Judaism.

It seems, however, that Paul forgot about the relative openness conveyed in this story from Genesis, which is framed by the constraints of Israel's election through the line of Isaac. Isaac and Ishmael do not cancel each other out; one does not supersede the other. Rather, they coexist and thrive, even if they are apart. As Abraham's child, Ishmael receives his share of blessing and protection from God (Gen. 16:10; 21:13, 18, 20). He is even promised to become a "great nation" and is circumcised as required by the covenant (Gen. 17:26), despite the fact that he and his descendants remain outside of God's covenant with Abraham. Ishmael, the non-chosen, remains an "*inside* outsider," as mentioned earlier. What's truly puzzling in Galatians is how Paul connects the lineage of Hagar and Ishmael with Judaism, while associating Sarah and Isaac with Christianity. This is something of a head-scratcher in light of the Genesis narrative.

In his later and more mature letter to the Romans, Paul lays out a more nuanced understanding of Israel's election in relation to the emerging Christian faith, but he starts on a sorrowful note:

> I am speaking the truth in Christ—I am not lying, as my conscience assures me by the Holy Spirit—I have great sorrow and constant anguish in my heart, for I wish that I could be cursed

> and cut off from Christ for the sake of my own people, my kindred according to the flesh. They are Israelites, and to them belong the adoption, the glory, the covenants, the giving of the law, the worship, and the promises; to them belong the ancestors, and from them, according to the flesh, comes the Christ, who is over all, God blessed forever. Amen. (Romans 9:1-5)

Paul, an Israelite himself, fully acknowledges the gifts and privileges that come with being God's chosen people. He highlights all that "belongs" to them, beginning with Israel's "adoption" by God and culminating with the coming of the sovereign Messiah. Like the authors of the Old Testament, Paul doesn't try to give any reason why Israel was chosen; that remains a mystery rooted in God's freedom to "show mercy" on whomever God chooses (Rom. 9:14-15). Paul also contends that none of these gifts and privileges are taken away by Christ. In fact, he writes, "as regards election, [the Israelites] are beloved, for the sake of their ancestors; for the gifts and the calling of God are irrevocable" (Rom. 11:28-29). It cannot be overstated that the Messiah, Jesus Christ, comes "from" Israel ("according to the flesh," Rom. 9:5); the arrival of the Messiah is the ultimate expression of Israel's special relationship with God. Paul could have stopped there, but his sorrow over his people's rejection of Christ compels him to comment further.

In view of Jesus' rejection by the Jewish religious authorities, Paul makes clear that this does not reflect any failure on God's part. On the contrary, God works in mysterious ways by choosing the "children of the promise" not because they deserve it, but because God exercises sovereign freedom and mercy, calling both Jews and Gentiles (Rom. 9:24). According to Paul, the major distinction between these two groups is that the Jews sought "righteousness" through the "law" and through "works," while the Gentiles attained "righteousness through faith" (Rom. 9:30). Christ himself "is the end of the law so that there may be righteousness for all who believe" (Rom. 10:4), including both Jews and Gentiles. In God, "there is no distinction between Jew and Greek; the same Lord is Lord of all and is generous to all who call on him" (Rom. 11:12).

Nevertheless, Paul continues to make distinctions. He contends that Israel's failure to believe was necessary for allowing the inclusion of Gentiles; in effect, this "stumbling" leads to salvation for the Gentiles. "Their defeat means riches for Gentiles" (Rom. 10:12). In fact, it was providentially ordained that Israel would become "jealous" of the Gentiles enough to believe (Rom. 10:19; 11:11, 14), with the hope that full inclusion of Jews into the ever-expanding circle of God's grace could still be achieved. Israel's "failure" does not necessitate God's rejection (Rom. 11:1, 11), which would have voided God's special covenant with the Jewish people. Instead, Israel's refusal will ultimately lead to "full inclusion" (Rom. 10:12; see Gal. 3:28). The apostle Paul turns out to be a prophet of hope for his people.

If you asked a practicing Jew today about their alleged "jealousy" of Christians, I suspect most would respond with, "What are you talking about?" Clearly, Paul's argument hasn't played out as he had hoped. However, one important takeaway is this: Paul's argument ultimately leads him to warn Gentile Christians against boasting (Rom. 11:17-22). He drives this home by employing a familiar metaphorical image: a tree. The tree represents Israel, while the Gentiles are like a "wild olive shoot" grafted onto the tree in place of some "broken branches" (Rom. 11:17). But the tree and its roots remain; "if the root is holy, then the branches also are holy" (Rom. 11:16). Paul cautions his Gentile audience not to gloat over the "broken branches." He reminds them, "If you do boast, remember that it is not you that support the root, but the root that supports you" (Rom. 11:18). To put it more pointedly, whether a branch is native to the tree or grafted onto it, it does not make the trunk and its roots holy (see Rom. 11:16). It's just the opposite! Instead, Gentiles should "stand in awe" (Rom. 11:20) and, I would add, in gratitude. The mystery of God's election of Israel, paired with the mystery of God's inclusion of the Gentiles through Christ, should merit no more than these four words: "Thanks be to God."

DISCUSSION QUESTIONS

1. Do you see "election" as more of a problem or a promise?
2. As a Christian, what do you think are the rights, privileges, and responsibilities that come with being chosen by God?
3. How do you connect the ideas of "election" and "holiness"?
4. Can you relate to Paul's struggle with the issue of election? How do you feel about his perspective?
5. As chosen or elected of God, what do you think is the church's relationship with the world?
6. As a Christian, how do you view your relationship with your Jewish siblings?

CHAPTER 8

Whence Evil?

From genocide and sexual violence to economic oppression and bodily disease, the Bible does not shy away from depicting evil and human suffering. To the contrary, evil takes on many forms in scripture. The common Hebrew word for "evil" (*rāʿâ*) covers a wide range of meanings, including maliciousness, misfortune, chaos, and calamity. The responses to evil in the Bible are just as varied, ranging from stoic acceptance to rancorous protest. This leads us to ask a few central questions: Where does evil come from? What role does God play in evil? And how should we respond to evil?

THE GENESIS OF EVIL

Nearly every creation account in the Bible tries to make sense of evil one way or another. In Genesis 1, the creation narrative is presented in a way that seems to preclude the reality of evil. Everything is described as "good," repeated seven times throughout this account. Nothing that is created is called evil, including the "great sea monsters" (Gen. 1:21). Any hint of "evil," in this context referring to cosmic "chaos," is quickly brushed aside in verse 2.

> The earth was vacuum and void,
>   and darkness covered the face of the deep,

> while God's breath hovered over the face of the waters.
> (Genesis 1:2)

Such is the cosmic state of affairs before God's first act of creation: light (Gen. 1:3). There's nothing inherently hostile about the darkness or the deep in Genesis 1, even though elsewhere in the biblical tradition both are often associated with chaos and death—like during Noah's flood.[1] Elsewhere, the deep needs to be contained in order for life to flourish, as seen in passages like Psalm 104:6-7 and Proverbs 8:27-28. The monstrous creature Leviathan calls the deep its home (Job 41:32), but there's nothing intrinsically evil about the deep or its creatures, even if they can be life-threatening. In Genesis 1, the watery depths are just part of the primordial soup that God works with to create form and the fullness of life. All in all, creation seems to enjoy a perfect start in Genesis, launching life without any noticeable red flags.

Well, except for one. In Genesis 1:28, God blesses humankind not only to be "fruitful and multiply" but also to "subdue" the earth—a verb that has its share of violent connotations (see Chapter 2). At the very least, it suggests conflict and resistance. But for now, the threat of violence is nowhere to be found. In fact, even predation is absent; in Genesis 1, all animals, including humans, are vegetarian (Gen. 1:29-30).

Things take a dramatic turn, however, when we get to the flood story just five chapters later: "The earth was wasted in God's sight, filled with violence . . . for all flesh had laid waste its ways upon the earth" (Gen. 6:11-12). Violence has truly ravaged the earth. How could this happen? It looks like the idea of "subduing" has spiraled completely out of control. However, another perspective offers an alternative assessment:

> YHWH saw how great was humanity's wickedness on the earth,
> and that every impulse (*yēṣer*) of the thoughts of their hearts was

1. See the following examples: Gen. 7:11, 8:2; Ezek. 26:19; Jon. 2:6; Hab. 3:10; Ps. 139:11; Job 3:4; Isa. 5:20, 59:9.

> only evil continually. And YHWH was sorry for having made humankind on the earth; it grieved him to his heart. (Gen. 6:5-6)

This passage locates the root of the problem within the human heart and mind, which has become evil to its core (see also Gen. 8:21). According to this perspective, behind every human thought lurks something wicked. The Russian dissident Alexander Solzhenitsyn captures this view vividly:

> The line separating good and evil passes not through states, nor between classes, nor between political parties either—but right through every human heart . . . even within hearts overwhelmed by evil, one small bridgehead of good is retained. And even in the best of all hearts, there remains . . . an uprooted small corner of evil.[2]

Between creation and the flood, the pendulum of the human heart swings inexorably toward evil. It all starts with disobedience in the Garden (Gen. 3:6) and escalates to fratricide outside of it (Gen. 4:7-8), where Cain, unable to master the sin coiled within him, strikes and kills his brother out of jealousy. In fact, the word "sin" makes its first appearance in the Bible during the story of Cain and Abel, linking "original sin" with violence (Gen. 4:7). This violence begets further violence resulting in the ever-present threat of violence, creating in an ever-widening spiral (Gen. 4:23-24) until all of creation is engulfed in it, prompting God to take drastic action: a violent flood to cleanse the world of this brutality. Is this a horrific form of poetic justice? The height (or depth) of irony? A watery holocaust? Regardless of how one frames the flood story (and it's certainly not a children's tale), the mission ultimately failed.

As much as God was sorry for having made humankind (Gen. 6:6), God also regretted unleashing the flood:

---

2. Aleksandr I. Solzhenitsyn, *The Gulag Archieplago, 1918-1952: An Experiment in Literary Investigation Volume 2*, trans. Thomas P. Whitney (New York: Harper Perennial, 1974), 746.

> YHWH said in his heart, "I will never again curse the ground on account of humanity, for the impulse of the human heart is evil from youth. Nor will I ever again destroy every living creature as I have done." (Gen. 8:21)

God had hoped that with Noah—a "righteous" and "blameless" man (Gen. 6:9)—a new humanity would emerge. But that wasn't the case. Even Noah's family proves to be dysfunctional (Gen. 9:20-27), just ask Ham or Canaan. As a result, God concedes humanity's "fallen" nature, even allowing for the consumption of meat, although with limitations (Gen. 9:2-7). In short, evil is primarily, if not exclusively, identified with human character and conduct, rooted in the human "heart" or mind.

Another creation account confirms this, but in a different way. Consider Leviathan in Psalm 104—the quintessential chaos monster of the deep waters, whose destruction is considered necessary to maintain cosmic order (Ps. 74:14; Isa. 27:1). However, in Psalm 104, this chaotic creature poses no threat to God. To the contrary, Leviathan is portrayed as God's playmate: "There go the ships, and Leviathan with which you fashioned to play" (Ps. 104:26). If Leviathan isn't the source of chaos, then what is? The psalmist points out the real culprits at the end: the wicked (Ps. 104:35). They are the ones who bring chaos, and their elimination will make the world all the better: "Let sinners be wiped away from the earth, and the wicked be no more. Bless, YHWH, O my soul. Praise YHWH!" So ends the psalm with both praise and imprecation.

NATURAL DISASTERS

So far, we've explored creation texts that clearly place the blame for evil on human shoulders. With their God-given freedom, humans can choose between good and evil. However, the biblical witness suggests a tendency for people to choose the latter, often committing acts of evil that can even lead to worldwide destruction. Humanity is the unpredictable variable, a wildcard in creation that can easily spiral into chaos. Such is the nature of moral evil. But what about the kind of "evil" that transcends individual actions and even collective behavior—something that no one person or community can control? Think of natural disasters, for example, which are often referred to by insurance companies as "acts of God." What role does God actually play in such "evil"? Is God complicit? The Bible is filled with stories of disasters brought about *by* God, including famines, plagues, earthquakes, and diseases.

Often these events are regarded as divine punishment, but that's not always the case. Take famine, for instance. Sometimes it occurs without any rhyme or reason, not implicating God at all (see Gen. 12:10, 26:1, 47:13; Ps. 105:16; Jer. 14:12). However, when it comes to pestilence or plague, God more often uses these as instruments of punishment (Gen. 12:17; 2 Sam. 24:13; Lev. 26:25; Num. 14:12; Jer. 14:12). If you're looking for consistency in the Bible regarding whether these natural disasters are sent by God or not, you won't find it. However, there is one key text that often gets overlooked. It tightens the connection between human misconduct and natural disasters, which, in turn, rules out divine intervention:

> Hear the word of YHWH, people of Israel; for YHWH has a dispute with the inhabitants of the land. There is no faithful love or loyalty, and no knowledge of God in the land. Swearing, lying, murder, stealing, and adultery erupt; bloodshed strikes bloodshed. No wonder, then, the land languishes, and all who live in it grow weak. Together with the wild animals and the birds of the air, even the fish of the sea are dying. (Hosea 4:1-3)

More than any other passage in the Bible, this prophetic message from an eighth-century BCE northern prophet links the breakdown of community with the breakdown of creation. The last verse describes an ecological disaster, while the first two verses state why it's happening. The explanation is not divine punishment. Rather, it's the violence that has once again engulfed the community, fueled by various violations of the Decalogue (Exod. 20:13-17). "No wonder, then, the land languishes" (Hosea 4:3a). The state of the natural world mirrors the state of the human world. The prophet urges his listeners to stop and smell the dead fish and then to reflect on the root cause of such calamity: human violence and unfaithfulness, which go hand in hand. Here, God doesn't intervene to bring about disaster, nor is God even implicated. Everything is driven by human actions, from cause to consequence. God has designed the world so that every action has a consequence, whether for good or ill—even on a biblical scale. In this context, there's no need for God to intervene and bring about disaster because of human sin. No, humans manage that well enough on their own, punishing themselves and the world in the process.

NATIONAL DISASTER

All in all, whether "evil" calamities are sent by God is a matter of debate in the Bible. Another prominent "evil" discussed extensively is Israel's own national disaster—the Babylonian invasion and exile, which marked a significant turning point in its history and faith. This devastating invasion, which led to an exile lasting almost fifty years, was an onslaught of death and destruction, including the destruction of Jerusalem's Temple.[3] This left an indelible mark upon ancient Israel's collective identity and sparked a wide variety of responses and interpretations that are recorded as part of the biblical tradition. For instance, the Deuteronomistic historian offers a straightforward explanation: It was Israel's own fault! King Manasseh, the son of good King Hezekiah, "did what was evil in the sight of YHWH" (2 Kings 21:2). He led the people to worship other gods and adopt the abominable practices of the surrounding nations (2 Kings 21:3-7). The consequence for these actions was a dire judgment:

> YHWH spoke through his servants the prophets, "Because King Manasseh of Judah has committed these abominations, things more evil than all that the Amorites did, who were before him,

---

3. For a thorough going historical analysis of the Babylonian exile, see Rainer Albertz, *Israel in Exile: The History and Literature of the Sixth Century B.C.E*, trans. David Green (Studies in Biblical Literature 3; Atlanta: SBL Press, 2003), esp. 70-111.

> and has caused Judah also to sin with his idols; therefore thus says YHWH, the God of Israel, I am about to bring upon Jerusalem and Judah such evil that the ears of everyone who hears of it will ring. . . . I will wipe Jerusalem clean as one wipes a dish clean, wiping it and turning it over. I will cast off the remnant of my inheritance and deliver them into the hand of their enemies. They shall become a prey and a spoil to all their enemies, because they have done what is evil in my sight, provoking me to anger, since the day their ancestors came out of Egypt, even to this day." (2 Kings 21:10-15)

In short, Judah's destruction at the hands of the Babylonian Empire is justified by the evil reign of one king. The blame falls squarely on the shoulders of Manasseh and his people. This historical account fully accepts the national disaster, with only a slight hint of protest:

> Before him there was no king like [Josiah], who turned to YHWH with all his heart, with all his soul, and with all his might, according to the entire *tôrâ* of Moses. Nor did any like him arise after him. *Still* YHWH did not turn from the fierceness of his great anger, by which his anger burned against Judah, because of all the provocations with which Manasseh had provoked him. (2 Kings 23:25-26)

This is the ancient historian's assessment of King Josiah (640-609 BCE), who was Manasseh's grandson. Josiah was considered one of the greatest kings for his loyalty to YHWH, second only to David and Hezekiah (2 Kings 18:5; 22:2). He represented everything good in contrast to the bad of Manasseh's reign. But despite all of Josiah's goodness as a leader of God's people, disaster couldn't be avoided. This tragic inevitability is captured by a single, simple word: "still" (Hebrew *'ak*), which creates a strong contrast with the rest of the passage. A better translation would be, "*But alas*, YHWH did not turn from the fierceness of his great wrath." In other words, despite everything, despite Josiah's genuine repentance and reforms, God persisted in punishing the nation.

However, the Deuteronomist's overall response to this punishment—accepting the blame for it—represents only one of the responses to the trauma of destruction and exile found in the Bible. Some psalms offer a completely different response.

PSALM 74

Psalm 74 provides a detailed account of the destruction of the Jerusalem Temple, describing it in vivid, blow-by-blow fashion:

> Your foes roared in your own meeting place;
> (there) they set up their own banners as (victory) signs.
> It looked like axes raised
> against a thicket of trees.
> In short order all its carvings
> they hacked down with hatchets and pickaxes.
> They set your sanctuary on fire, (burning it) to the ground;
> they desecrated the dwelling place of your name.
> They said in their heart, "We will subdue them altogether!"
> So they burned all of God's meeting places in the land.
> We no longer see our own signs; there is no prophet left;
> no one among us knows how long. (Psalm 74:4-9)

It's a scene of utter devastation. But unlike the Deuteronomist, the psalmist doesn't accept this catastrophe as God's rightful punishment. Instead, the psalm expresses protest and calls for a reversal:

> Why, O God, have you rejected us forever?
> (Why does) your anger fume against the sheep of your pasture? (Psalm 74:1)

> Why do you withdraw your hand?
> Why is your right hand held close to your breast?
> (Psalm 74:11)

Do not let the downtrodden dwell in shame.
  Let the afflicted and the destitute praise your name.
Arise, O God! Make your case!
  Remember how fools insult you all day long!
Do not forget the voice of your foes,
  the racket of your adversaries that rises up relentlessly.
   (Psalm 74:21-23)

"Why, why, why?" the psalmist cries, pleading with God to turn things around ("arise!"). Far from stoic acceptance or self-blame, the psalmist instead delivers a stinging protest, holding God ultimately responsible for this catastrophe. For the psalmist, there is nothing to confess and no one to blame . . . except God.

The same goes for Psalm 44, which directs its outrage squarely at God. As one of the most anguished communal laments in the Psalter, this psalm is also a strong protest demanding action from God. It begins by affirming Israel's absolute trust in God, and rightly so: God is praised for liberating and settling Israel in the land (Ps. 44:1-8). "In God we glory always; we give thanks to your name forever" (Ps. 44:8). The speaker proclaims personal trust not in weapons of war, but in God as the divine warrior. While the first half of the psalm ends on a high note of praise and thanksgiving for all that God has done for Israel's ("Jacob's") freedom and security, the second half takes a sharp turn, ripping into God for everything that God has done *against* God's people:

But alas you have spurned and debased us;
  you do not go out with our armies.
You turn us back from the foe,
  and our enemies plunder us.
You hand us over as sheep for slaughter;
  you have scattered us among the nations.
You sell your people short;
  you have not increased their price.
You make us the butt of our neighbors,

> the scorn and derision of those around us.
> You make us a byword among the nations,
> a laughingstock (literally "head-shaker") among the peoples.
> All day long my disgrace is before me;
> and the shame of my face has covered me
> at the sound of the taunting despiser,
> at the sight of the enemy avenger. (Psalm 44:9-16)

That's the essence of the psalm's protest. Instead of God "delighting" (Ps. 44:3b), God "debases" (Ps. 44:9a). The evidence is clear: the people suffer defeat, diaspora, dispossession, and disgrace—all because of God's unconscionable rejection. God refuses to join them on the battlefield. As a result, enemies "plunder," and the people are slaughtered like "sheep" (Ps 44:10; see also Ps. 44:22). They are devalued in God's sight (Ps. 44:12) and suffer utter disgrace among the nations (Ps. 44:14-15).

God has completely reversed course and has seemingly done so for no reason. The next section drives home this point, as the community proclaims its unwavering faithfulness in the face of divine rejection (Ps. 44:17-22): Israel has "not forgotten," "not broken" the covenant, "not turned back," and "not strayed." The people have remained devoted to God, refusing to worship any foreign deities. They've kept up their end of the covenant. The fact that God knows about Israel's faithfulness makes the shock of suffering at God's hands even more painful: the community is "crushed" in darkness (Ps. 44:19) and "slaughtered" like "sheep" (Ps. 44:22), all without cause. The fault lies not with the sheep but with the Shepherd (Ps. 44:23a). In short, the psalmist reminds God that "Israelite lives matter!" This is the community's protest against God, demanding decisive action, while accusing God of being "asleep" through it all. The psalm's strategy is clear. Israel's testimony of trust as counter-testimony to God's betrayal and Israel's persistent faithfulness all build up to pointed calls to action: "wake up," "awaken," "arise," and "redeem." In other words, God needs to get up! God needs to do something!

When it comes to the greatest "evil" that ancient Israel ever faced, the Old Testament presents two contrasting responses: self-blame and overall acceptance, on the one hand, and protest along with blaming God, on the other. The question of who is responsible for this "evil" remains an open question, and it's a question that's posed with a vengeance in the book of Job. The main character in Job suffers unimaginable hardships on a personal level, much like Israel did on a national scale.

THE CASE OF JOB

The book of Job is the most dialogical book in the Bible, filled with strong perspectives vying for attention. You have Job and his friends arguing about what it means to be righteous and how to show proper reverence. Then there's God, who responds to Job with an entirely new way of looking at the world. Plus, you can see Job himself wrestling with differing views within his own mind. Overall, the book of Job is a polyphonic text, making it ideal for the kind of dialogical reflection we've been discussing.[4]

Job the Stoic

Job's story is legendary (see Ezek. 14:14, 20; James 5:11). He's the most righteous person in the land, yet he suffers more than anyone could ever bear: he loses all his possession, experiences the violent death of his children, endures bodily disease, and, to add insult to literal injury, faces betrayal by his friends. Devastated and alienated, Job accepts all of this without question (Job 1:21). When he's afflicted with a painful disease, Job responds to his wife, who urges him to "curse God and die," with, "Are we to receive the good at God's hand, and not receive the bad?" (Job 2:10).

And where is God amid Job's suffering? The reader knows more than Job does because the narrator reveals everything, while Job is left in the

4. For a whole study on this, see Carol A. Newsom, *The Book of Job: A Contest of Moral Imaginations* (Oxford: Oxford University Press, 2003).

dark, knowing only that he is in pain. We see God bragging about Job's righteousness to the heavenly council (the "sons of God"), which is what leads to Job's troubles. This boast prompts a professional skeptic in the divine assembly, known as "the *satan*" (from now on referred to as "the accuser"), to question Job's integrity. The accuser, a member of the heavenly council, asks a simple yet profound question: "Does Job fear God for nothing?" (Job 1:9). In other words, does Job genuinely revere God without any strings attached, or is there an ulterior motive behind his devotion?

The accuser, acting like a prosecuting attorney, continues to accuse God: "Have you not fenced him in, including his house and all that he has, on every side? You have blessed the work of his hands, and his possessions have spread out in the land" (Job 1:10). Essentially, he argues that it's easy for Job to honor God when he has wealth and success, but if all that were taken away, would Job still bless God? It's a compelling question, but it leads to a tragic and horrific test. God consents to the accuser's plan, allowing Job to lose all his possessions and even his children. This is where we find Job's well-known response: "Naked I came from my mother's womb, and naked I will return there. YHWH has given and YHWH has taken away; blessed be YHWH's name" (Job 1:21). No cursing here—Job passes the test.

But the accuser isn't satisfied: what if Job's health is affected? God agrees once more, despite some push back this time (Job 2:3), but sets a limit on the accuser, preventing him from taking Job's life (Job 2:6). Now suffering from "loathsome sores" all over his body, Job responds again with stoic acceptance while also admonishing his wife (Job 2:9-10). Despite everything, Job "persists in his integrity" in the face of such "evil." Yes, evil. As the narrator makes clear at the end of the story, "evil" is precisely what "YHWH had brought upon him" (Job 42:11)—evil that destroyed much of what Job held dear, from his children to his possessions to his health. Now, as we see in Job 3, he yearns for death. Who can blame him?

This introduction to Job reflects a biblical perspective that God is the author of both good and evil, a theme echoed also in Isaiah:

I form light and create darkness,
I make shalom and create doom (*ra'*);
I am YHWH who does all these things. (Isaiah 45:7)

This passage emphasizes God's complete control over everything, including both the good and the bad, prosperity and "doom"—the same word in Hebrew for "evil." In the context of Isaiah, this evil refers to Israel's suffering at the hands of the Babylonians, from Jerusalem's destruction to the people's exile. However, the prophet assures us that shalom is on the way.

In Job's case, God's involvement with "evil" or "doom" is more complicated. The drama that unfolds in the heavenly realm shows that while God was not directly responsible for Job's suffering, God was still complicit. It was the accuser's initiative that put Job through this horrific test. All God did was boast about Job, but God also consented to the accuser's "evil" plan: a test of suffering. This arrangement doesn't excuse God from Job's pain; to the contrary, it places ultimate responsibility on God—the buck stops with God, since the accuser's actions take place under God's watch. A student once told me that, "God seems to be a betting man." God is betting that Job's integrity will hold up against this "evil," and God's willing to go to great lengths to be vindicated, even at Job's expense. To put it mildly, God does not come off well in these first two chapters. This is not the God who is "abounding in benevolence" and "forgiving iniquity" (see Exod. 34:6-7). God may have won the bet because Job ultimately passes the test of faith, but in Job's eyes, God fails the test of justice.

A Psalmic Detour

As a sidenote, another example of God being removed from direct involvement in the world's suffering can be found in Psalm 82. In this unique passage, the curtain rises to reveal a courtroom drama unfolding in heaven:

God takes his stand in the divine council;
  amid the gods he gives judgment.
"How long will you keep judging unjustly,
  showing favor to the wicked? *Selah*
Give justice to the vulnerable and the orphaned!
  Maintain the rights of the afflicted and the impoverished!
Rescue the vulnerable and the destitute!
  Deliver them from the hand of the wicked!"

They do not know, nor do they understand;
  they wander about in darkness.
  All the earth's foundations are shaking.
I hereby declare, 'Gods you are,
  sons of *Elyon*, all of you;
Nevertheless, you shall die like mortals;
  like any prince you shall fall.' "

Rise up, O God! Judge the earth,
  for you retain possession of all the nations! (Psalm 82)

Psalm 82 recounts God's judgment against the gods, referred to as the "sons of *Elyon*" (often translated as "Most High"), through a process of interrogation, indictment, and sentencing. The scene takes place in a heavenly courtroom, where God issues a death sentence to these gods for their failure to deliver justice on earth, especially for the most vulnerable. The "shaking" of the "earth's foundations" isn't due to God's negligence but rather to the negligence of these gods. Since this cosmic chaos occurs on the gods' watch, the gods must be held accountable. However, like God in the book of Job, God in Psalm 82 is ultimately held responsible. This is underscored in the final verse, where the community implores God to judge the nations as God has judged the gods. The burden of justice now rests upon God alone. So, whether it's the clueless "gods" in Psalm 82 or the wily "accuser" in the first two chapters of Job, we see God relatively removed from direct involvement in evil, yet still ultimately responsible.

Job the Protester

Back to Job. Beginning in Job 3, when Job speaks again, we encounter a very different man and, ultimately, a very different view of God in this journey of theodicy. No longer do we see the stoic Job, who accepts all things—both good and bad. Instead, we find Job as a protester, complaining about all the misfortunes that have befallen him. Job is no longer the stoic who calmly accepts his suffering. The Job we see now is filled with bitter lament and indignation, even cursing. It is as if Job is protesting against his former self. Why the sudden turnaround? Perhaps with the passage of time, Job has decided to be more honest with God.

He first expresses a death wish filled with anguish and yearning (Job 3:3-26), begging God to "crush" him and "cut" him "off" (Job 6:8) to end his misery. Elsewhere, Job accuses God of being a terrorist (Job 6:4), stating that God has set him up for target practice. "Why have you made me your target? Why have I become a burden to you?" he exclaims (7:20).

At other times, Job simply wants God to leave him alone, to look away so he can have at least one moment of peace (Job 7:16, 19). Yet, even as he seeks comfort on his bed, he finds God terrifying him with nightmares to the point of contemplating suicide (Job 7:15). In a fit of furious despair, Job spins the psalmist's praise of God's benevolence toward humanity into a complaint: "What are human beings, that you make so much of them, that you set your mind on them, visiting them every morning, testing them every moment?" (Job 7:17-18; Ps. 8:3-4).

To Job, God's attention toward humanity feels far from loving; it seems downright sadistic, indiscriminately so. Job contends, "[God] destroys both the blameless and the wicked" (Job 9:22). How does Job reach such a conclusion—that God has turned "evil"? Because Job knows that he is innocent of any wickedness. In his mind, this innocence leaves him no other choice except to condemn God for committing a travesty of justice.

Job's friends think otherwise, and they don't take kindly to his words. Bildad asks, "How long will you say these things, and the words of your mouth be a great wind? Does God pervert justice?" (Job 8:3). They fail to recognize the God that Job now sees. In their eyes, Job's understanding of God is a perversion of the God they believe in, and Job himself has become a stranger instead of the friend they once knew. But they think they have a solution: if only Job would confess his wrongdoings, then God would "restore to you your rightful place" (Job 8:6).

However, Job insists that he has no sin to confess, while his friends are convinced that he must have committed some truly heinous acts. "Is not your wickedness great? There is no end to your iniquities!" exclaims Eliphaz, accusing Job of extortion, stripping the naked, refusing water to the weary, withholding food from the hungry, and sending widows away empty-handed—the list goes on and on (Job 22:6-9).

Though Job's friends charge him with wrongdoing, Job turns the tables and accuses God of the same. He wants to know why God has it in for him, and he holds God to account, as if he's calling God to court:

> Oh, that I knew where I might find him, to come even to his dwelling place. I would lay my case before him and fill my mouth with arguments. I would learn what answers he would give me and know what he would say to me. Would he contend with me his great power? No, but he would listen to me. There an upright person could argue with him, and I would be acquitted forever by my judge. (Job 23:3-7)

In other words, Job wants God to be held accountable. He cries, "O that I had the indictment written by my adversary! Surely, I would carry it on my shoulder; I would bind it on me like a wreath; I would give him an account of all my steps; like a prince I would approach him" (Job 31:35b-37). "I will defend my ways to his face," he boldly declares (Job 13:15). But Job also knows he needs help. Early on, he laments, "There is no arbiter between us, who might lay his hand on us both" (Job 9:33). A judge above God to hold God to account? Unthinkable!

Later, though, Job is convinced that he has at least one advocate in heaven: "O earth, do not cover my blood; let my outcry find no resting place. Surely now my witness is in heaven, my advocate is on high" (Job 16:18-19). Job becomes even bolder with his most famous words: "For I know that my Redeemer lives, and that at the last he will rise upon the dust; and after my skin has been torn apart, then from my flesh I will see God" (Job 19:25-27). Job pins his hope on his "Redeemer," but his boldness stems from the fact that, in his eyes, the Redeemer is not God but another heavenly being. For Job, God is not a redeemer but a tyrant, declaring, "God has wronged me and closed his net around me" (Job 19:6). He adds, "[God] has uprooted my hope like a tree" (Job 19:10b).

In response to Job's demand for answers and accountability, God remains silent and distant. Job's concerns aren't just about his own suffering; he has a lot of questions about how the world is governed. "Why do the wicked live on, reach old age, and grow mighty in power?" he asks (Job 21:7; see also 21:30). He wonders, "Why are times for judgment not kept by the Almighty, and why do those who know him never see his days?" (Job 24:1).

Job's conclusion? "It is all one . . . [God] destroys the blameless and the wicked. When suddenly disaster brings death, he mocks at the slaying of innocents. The earth is handed over to the wicked; [God] covers the eyes of its judges—if it is not he, then who is it?" (Job 9:22-24). In his frustration, Job accuses God of being biased in favor of the wicked.

God's Answer

Does God address these questions, these accusations? Disappointingly, no, at least not directly. However, we can perhaps give God some credit for showing up—not in a courtroom as Job had hoped, but in a whirlwind (Job 38:1), echoing the horror of when Job lost his children by a "great wind" back at the beginning of the story (Job 1:19). God doesn't show up as Job's friend or advocate or redeemer. Instead, God confronts Job as an adversary. God challenges Job to "gird up your loins like a combatant," demanding answers from him, thus turning the tables on Job. But Job hardly gets a chance to respond. Just as Job dominated the conversation with his friends, now God dominates the conversation with Job, engaging in a monologue that explores the vastness and wildness of creation.

God takes Job on a wild ride powered by divine poetry, showcasing the wonders of creation, from cosmic light to hungry lions and the fearsome Leviathan—a breathtaking panorama of creation described both cosmically and, in the end, zoologically. But for what purpose? God aims to instruct Job on what he has missed amid all his tirades, complaints, prayers, questions, and laments: a sense of God's governance of the world and Job's place in it. At one point, God asks Job, "Would you violate my justice and deem me guilty to justify yourself?" (Job 40:8). From Job's perspective, his innocence would prove God's guilt. But from God's perspective, Job is demanding God to prove Job's innocence. Either way, God begins to sever this correspondence between one's guilt and another's innocence.

God first dares Job to take a shot at running the world. Go ahead and be God for a day!

> Adorn yourself with majesty and splendor; clothe yourself with glory and honor. . . . Look on all who are proud and bring them low; tread down the wicked in their place. Hide them all in the dust together; bind their faces in obscurity. Then even I will praise you that your own right hand has delivered you. (Job 40:10-14)

This is exactly what Job (and his friends) would have wanted God to do. But Job doesn't have the power to create such order, and it seems God has no intention of doing so either. Sure, there is some degree of order in the world; for instance, God describes the dawn "shaking" the wicked "out of" "the skirts of the earth" (Job 38:13). So, the world isn't entirely chaotic, contrary to how Job perceives it. However, God's sense of justice goes beyond Job's understanding and that of his friends. God points out that amidst all the wonders of creation, there is no all-encompassing moral order that ensures the wicked are punished and the righteous prosper. In fact, Job himself stands as a paradigmatic exception to this kind of moralistic governance; an example that doesn't prove the desired rule but instead contradicts it.

God shows off creation to Job, highlighting everything from the heights and depths to specific wild animals, capturing both the vastness of the world and its various lively details. It's a world bursting with life and filled with wonder. Yet, throughout this grand display, there's never a word about God intervening to fix anything. Clearly, God loves a world that is full of life and takes pride in having created it that way. But when it comes to conflict and violence—like lions hunting and eating their prey or vultures "sucking up blood" on the battlefield—God simply allows it to be. Creation is given the freedom to live as it will. This includes the mighty monster of chaos, Leviathan. While Leviathan is seen as evil and destructive elsewhere in the biblical tradition (as in Psalm 74:14 and Isaiah 27:1), that's not the case in Job. Just as God boasted about Job at the beginning of the book, God takes a moment to boast about Leviathan at the end:

> I will not keep silent concerning its limbs, or its mighty strength, or its impressive form. Who can remove its outer garment? Who can penetrate its double coat of mail? Who can pry open the doors of its face? There is terror all around its teeth. . . . Its sneezes flash forth light, and its eyes are like the eyelids of the dawn. From its mouth shoot forth flaming torches; sparks of fire leap out. Its breath ignites coals, and a flame shoots out of its mouth. . . . When it rears up, the gods are afraid; at its crashing down, they withdraw. (Job 41:12-14, 18-19, 21, 25)

And then we get these final words: "On earth it has no equal, made to be fearless. It surveys everything that is high and mighty; it is king over all that are proud" (Job 41:33-34). Leviathan is the king! Job once fancied himself as something like a king in his community (Job 29:25), but now he realizes who the real king on earth is—a sea monster. Rather than being typecast as a purveyor of chaos, Leviathan has a constructive role to play, a positive purpose in creation: to check human pride and ensure humility.

In God's world, all life has its place. If conflict and violence erupt among God's creatures, then God seems to say, "So be it." If war breaks out between nations, so be it; the vultures await to clean up the battlefield. If Leviathan wields its destructive power, so be it. Human beings should take note of their smallness amid the rich panoply of life and act accordingly with humility. And that's exactly what Job does; he responds with a sense of humble awe and wonder, echoing some of God's own words (Job 42:2-4). Most importantly, Job concedes by dropping his case against God and finds resolution—even comfort—"on dust and ashes" (Job 42:6, CEB). In the end, God succeeds where Job's friends have miserably failed: extending comfort to Job in his distress (see Job 16:2).

But it is not just God who steps in to "comfort" Job; Job's community also rallies around him to offer material support for "all the evil that YHWH had brought upon him":

> All his brothers and sisters and all who had known him before came to him, and they ate bread with him in his house. They consoled and comforted him for all the evil that YHWH had brought upon him; and each of them gave him a piece of money and a gold ring. (Job 42:11)

Job's community provides the kind of restorative comfort that counters YHWH's "evil"—that is, the disasters that YHWH allowed to be unleashed upon Job to settle a dispute with "the accuser" about the genuineness of Job's faith. In this context, YHWH is deemed directly responsible for Job's suffering, while the accuser is not mentioned at all. Regardless, it was all a test of Job's faith, with or without the accuser's involvement.

So we return to Job's initial responses: "YHWH has given, and YHWH has taken away; blessed be YHWH's name" (Job 1:21) and "Are we to receive the good at the hand of God, and not receive the bad?" (Job 2:10). But the later Job does not merely "receive the bad"; he resisted and protested! He is a different man now. In chapters 38-41, we encounter a different God as well—one who does not inflict harm, much less evil, on anyone. God is not a "tester" in the end. Instead, God grants creation freedom, admiring the manifold ways its diverse creatures develop, conflict and suffering notwithstanding (Ps. 104:24). The world as God sees it is de-moralized.[5] In other words, there is no moral arc to the universe, especially one bending toward justice, according to the book of Job. Nevertheless, the world brims with the wonders of life; it pulses with vitality. Life in all its diversity is of great value to God. Still, the problem of theodicy remains unresolved, the problem of how to square the prevalence of evil in the world with God's goodness. Job leaves us wondering.

THE WICKED AS GOD'S BAD DREAM

Why is evil so rampant in the world? Why do the wicked prosper? The God of the whirlwind in Job is silent on these issues. The same questions troubled not only Job but also the psalmist:

> As for me, my feet nearly stumbled;
>   my steps almost slipped,
> for I envied the arrogant;
>   I looked favorably upon the wellbeing of the wicked,
> for they suffer no pangs;
>   their body is fit and fat.
> They are free from human misery;
>   they are not afflicted as others are. (Psalm 73:2-5)

Psalm 73 is a deeply personal testimony of doubt and resolution that tackles the problem of theodicy head-on. The central question is: How should we respond to the prosperity of the wicked? The psalm begins with feelings of personal envy but ends with a renewed assurance about the fate of the wicked. The answer lies in trusting God—the God who will bring down the wicked in due time. What makes this trust possible is the

---

5. See Matitiahu Tsevat. "The Meaning of the Book of Job," in *The Meaning of the Book of Job and Other Biblical Studies* (New York: Ktav, 1980), 1-38.

psalmist's experience in God's sanctuary or Temple, which serves as the turning point and theological resolution of the psalm:

> But when I pondered how to make sense of this,
>   it was too arduous for me,
> until I entered God's sanctuary,
>   and discerned their end.
> Indeed, you have set [the wicked] in slippery places,
>   causing them to fall in [their] ruinous deceptions.
> How quickly they have become a horrific devastation,
>   finished off completely by (their) calamities,
> like a dream when one awakes.
>   O Lord, upon awakening you despise their figment.
>   (Psalm 73:16-20)

In the sanctuary, the psalmist discerns the demise of the wicked. As a place of resolution—if not revelation—the sanctuary serves as the "temple of doom" (to borrow the title of an Indiana Jones movie) for those who do evil. The psalm vividly depicts the downfall of the wicked, as if it happened instantaneously. The reference to awakening from a dream likely reflects the practice of incubation in the Temple, where revelations are thought to be received through dreams. However, here this language is ascribed to God, the dreamer, who upon waking, views the wicked as merely a fleeting "figment" or image (*ṣelem*) that dissipates with the dawn. In this sense, the actions of the wicked constitute a bad dream just waiting to end. From the psalmist's perspective, the sanctuary becomes a place of awakening for both God and the speaker.

Job also experiences an awakening during his encounter with God in creation, but God doesn't directly address the issue of the wicked (Job 38:12-13). All in all, God allows life to unfold in manifold ways, both good and bad. God is the impartial God, showing a bias only for life in all its diversity. Creatures associated with evil and chaos are part of the mix; they aren't punished or even restrained by God—just ask Leviathan. The key takeaway from Job is that divine retribution doesn't operate in a world filled with beings who have the freedom to choose, whether for good or ill.

This message is so radical that one Jewish scholar has called Job the only book in the Bible that is against the Bible![6] Interestingly, Jesus makes a point similar to the one found in Job during his Sermon on the Mount: "[Your Father in heaven] makes his sun rise on the evil and on the good and sends rain on the righteous and on the unrighteous" (Matt. 5:45). God is indiscriminate in this regard. While rain is beneficial, too much of it can lead to problems; the same goes for the sun and its heat. Both the righteous and the wicked receive these gifts in equal measure. So, what's Jesus getting at? "I say to you, Love your enemies and pray for those who persecute you" (Matt. 5:44). That message is just as radical.

REDEMPTIVE SUFFERING

Finally, we conclude with a discussion of an entirely different take on suffering, one that is both promising and problematic, often referred to as "redemptive suffering." This is the kind of suffering borne for the sake of others—suffering that is, in a word, *sacrificial.* One of the most powerful expressions of this can be found in the final "suffering servant" poem in the book of Isaiah (Isa. 52:13–53:12; see also Isa. 42:1-4; 49:1-6; 50:4-11). Like Job, this servant figure suffers unjustly, but unlike Job, his suffering serves a greater purpose. As described in Isaiah, the suffering servant isn't just a single individual but represents the larger community—or some part of it—during the time of Babylonian exile. His suffering ultimately brings redemption to the nations:

> See, my servant will prosper.
> He will be exalted and lifted up very high.
> Just as there were many who were appalled at him—
> so disfigured was his appearance, inhuman,

6. Oral communication with Matitiahu Tsevat at the 1991 Society of Biblical Literature meeting in Kansas City.

and his form unlike that of mortals—
so he shall startle many nations;
kings shall shut their mouths because of him;
for they will see what has not been told them,
and they will ponder what they have not heard.

Who can believe what we have heard?
To whom has YHWH's arm been revealed?
For he grew up before us like a young plant,
and like a root out of dry ground.
He had no form or majesty for us to see,
nothing about his appearance that we would find desirable.
He was despised, shunned by others;
a man of suffering, familiar with infirmity;
like someone from whom others hide their faces,
he was despised;
we did not regard him.

Yet he surely bore our infirmities and carried our sufferings,
even as we accounted him stricken, struck down by God,
and afflicted.
But he was wounded for our wrongdoings,
crushed for our crimes;
upon him was the punishment that made us whole;
by his wounds we were healed.
We all are like sheep that have gone astray,
each going its own way,
but YHWH let fall on him
(the consequences of) all our crimes.

He was oppressed, and afflicted,
but he did not open his mouth;
like a lamb brought to the slaughter,
like a ewe silent before its shearers,

so he did not open his mouth.

By oppressive judgment he was taken away.
Who could have imagined his fate?
For he was eliminated from the land of the living,
stricken for the sins of my people.
They made his grave with the wicked
and his tomb with evildoers,
although he had committed no violence,
and there was no deceit in his mouth.

Yet YHWH chose to crush him with pain.
If his life is given as a reparation offering,
he shall see his offspring,
and shall prolong his days.
Through him YHWH's will succeed.
From his anguish he will see light and be satisfied;
through his knowledge the righteous one, my servant,
will make many righteous,
but their guilt he will bear.
Therefore I will give him a portion with the great;
he shall divide the spoil with the strong,
because he exposed himself to death,
and was numbered among sinners,
though he bore the sins of many,
and made intercession for the transgressors.
(Isaiah 52:13–53:12)

The poetry is strikingly visceral: this "servant" suffers physically, socially, and spiritually—and does so in silence. His appearance becomes so disfigured that he is barely recognizable as human, shocking the nations with his grotesque condition. He is not only sick with suffering but also suffers from sickness itself, leading to his rejection. Described as "wounded," punished, afflicted, oppressed, "eliminated from the land," associated with the wicked, and even stricken by God, this servant endures abuse on every level—from both people and God. Yet, like Job, the servant is entirely innocent. He has committed no violence and spoken no lies. The poem acknowledges that his suffering comes from an "oppressive judgment," a punishment that doesn't fit the crime—*because there is no crime*. But, also like Job, he is destined to be restored, even exalted, as a form of reparation for his unjust suffering. The poem is wrapped in a promise of divine vindication, opening and closing with the assurance that God will ultimately right these wrongs.

Here's the categorical difference between God's servant and Job: the servant suffers punishment on behalf of those who actually deserve it, taking on the consequences for the crimes others have committed. The language used here turns sacrificial—the servant bears the sins of the nations as their "guilt offering," a type of offering meant to make reparations (Isa. 53:10, see Lev. 5:6-25, 7:1-7). Through the servant's sacrifice, the sins of the nations are atoned for. His unjust punishment brings healing and wholeness to the nations, sparing them from the consequences they should have faced. Much of the poem, especially in Isaiah 53:1-6, is framed as a testimony given by the nations themselves, describing their moment of realization—the startling recognition that their crimes have been forgiven because their victim, God's servant, took the punishment on their behalf. The servant's suffering is ultimately rooted in God's will, just as it was in Job's story. But here, there's no "accuser" ("the *satan*") orchestrating the suffering. Instead, "YHWH chose to crush him with pain" (Isa. 53:10a) by allowing the consequences of the nations' sins to "fall on him" (Isa. 53:6b).

The servant's suffering serves a larger purpose: it transforms undeserved pain into something good for those who should rightly face the consequences of their actions. It becomes redemptive. The poem severs the usual legal connection between crime and punishment by shifting the burden from the perpetrators to the victim. And that is precisely what makes "redemptive suffering" so problematic—it walks a fine line between blaming the victim and using their suffering for a so-called "greater good."

In this case, the good is for the nations, for their healing, but it comes entirely at the servant's expense. Another troubling aspect is the servant's silence; his voice is completely absent. Nothing is ever said about whether the servant had a choice in making this sacrifice. From the perspective of the nations, he did not. He was "stricken" by God, a silent sheep led to the slaughter, a sacrifice for the sake of others.

For a people exiled in Babylon, the empire of the nations at the time, regarding their suffering as redemptive—and shocking the nations into recognizing their crimes—likely provided some measure of comfort and purpose. The idea that their suffering could serve a greater good likely made it more palatable, which gives this text a sense of resilient hope—or perhaps hopeless naïvety. To think that the nations would repent for their sins and acknowledge the suffering caused by their imperial crimes might be pure fantasy. But, for the moment, the poem extends the benefit of the doubt to the nations. What it doesn't do is give voice to the suffering victim, and that's where the real issue lies. On the one hand, the servant appears to be forced into this sacrificial role, without any say. On the other hand, the poem offers a resolution by focusing on the good such suffering can achieve. But can this really hold up without the servant's consent—without the *victim's* consent—which is notably absent from the poem?

For Christian readers, this final suffering servant poem points directly to Jesus Christ and his suffering on the cross, where he takes on the sins of the world. In fact, if we could have overheard Jesus talking with the two disciples on the road to Emmaus, as he "interpreted to them the things about himself in all the scriptures" (Luke 24:27), this passage from Isaiah would likely have been front and center. So much of what is said about the suffering servant in Isaiah seems to foreshadow Christ (see Matt. 8:17, 1 Pet. 2:22). Just ask the Ethiopian eunuch (Acts 8:27-35). However, there's a key difference between the silent suffering servant in Isaiah and Jesus: what happens in the Garden of Gethsemane. In that moment, just before his arrest and execution, Jesus isn't silent. He's with his disciples one last time, grappling with the weight of what's about to happen. This moment reveals something deeper about his experience of suffering, distinguishing it from the servant's silence:

> Then he said to them, "I am deeply grieved, to the point of death. Stay here and keep awake with me." Then he went a little farther and fell on his face and prayed, "My Father, if it is possible, let this cup pass me by—yet not what I want but what you want." (Matthew 26:38-39)

With these words, Jesus expresses both his deep desire to avoid crucifixion and his free choice to go through with it. It's this freedom of choice—made in the face of resistance to such a torturous death—that makes Christ's redemptive suffering so powerful and credible. His sacrifice was meant to ensure that no one else would ever need to suffer for the sake of the world. Redemptive suffering becomes a limited event: first with Israel, as described in Isaiah, and then with Jesus, according to the Gospels. But after Jesus, it never needs to happen again.

If we set aside the problematic aspects of redemptive suffering, the poem in Isaiah offers another important message: a call for empathy. The suffering servant's mission is to embrace his suffering—not in a masochistic way, but in a way that benefits others. For readers, his plight reflects the experience of all who suffer unjustly—innocent victims of the world.

The poem is meant to open the eyes of the nations, and by extension, all readers, to the atrocity of suffering. It aims to startle us, demanding that our gaze be focused upon those who suffer unjustly rather than looking away in denial. The suffering of the innocent is a painful reality throughout the world, but one defining moment in American history brings this need for the collective gaze into sharp focus. In 1955, Mamie Elizabeth Till-Mobley, the mother of fourteen-year-old Emmet Till, who was brutally murdered by a group of white men in Mississippi, made a bold decision. She insisted on an open casket at her son's funeral, declaring, "I wanted the world to see what they did to my baby." The sight of Emmett's body, beaten beyond recognition, shocked the nation and galvanized the

Civil Rights movement.[7] As the Rev. Wheeler Parker said when eulogizing his cousin fifty years later: "We're put on this earth to give back . . . His life meant far more because of the way he died, his sacrifice. His voice still cries out for justice."[8]

In Emmett Till's story, we see the power of innocent suffering to galvanize the demand for justice. The suffering servant and Christ stand in the background, reminding us of the enduring call to confront injustice and empathize with those who suffer from it.

CONCLUSIONS

This biblical journey of "evil" has been a rugged one. It has taken us from Genesis to Job to Jesus, including a slight detour into the Psalms, and that's only skimming the surface. "Evil" in the Bible covers a wide range of events, from "acts of God" to human-instigated atrocities, from personal distress to national disaster. Responses to evil, we have seen, are equally wide ranging, from stoic acceptance to righteous protest (both embodied by Job!) to finding redemptive hope. Recognizing that suffering, in its many forms, is endemic to the human condition, the Bible does not flinch when it comes to addressing the complexities of "evil." In the biblical tradition, "evil" (Hebrew *rāʿâ*) has a broader meaning than it does today. One could say that the Bible uses the term somewhat indiscriminately. But one thing is consistent, whenever "evil" is used in the Bible, it demands an accounting. Today we often use the term as an escape, allowing ourselves to avoid any action in response, as in the case of a mass shooting. It is "pure evil," we say. It is simply accepted, even normalized. Not so in Scripture. There is nothing "pure" about evil. Just ask the psalmist or Job.

---

7. For the photograph and the story, see https://medium.com/christ-school/the-uncivil-image-dafdbc278c7f. See also Devery Anderson, *Emmett Till: The Murder That Shocked the World and Propelled the Civil Rights Movement* (Jackson, MS: University Press of Mississippi, 2015).
8. Anderson, *Emmett Till*, xxix.

It is also worth noting a common assumption shared by many of our biblical authors: God is in control of everything; therefore, both good and evil come from God's hand. Other authors, however, find that divine sovereignty means that God does not micro-manage the world's affairs. Far from it, in fact. Ecclesiastes, for example, recognizes the prominent role of chance:

> I have also seen under the sun that the race is not to the swift, nor the battle to the mighty, nor food to the wise, nor riches to the intelligent, nor favor to the skillful; but time and chance happen to them all. No one can anticipate their time. Like fish caught in a cruel net, and like birds caught in a snare, so humans are snared in times of calamity (*rāʿâ*), which suddenly beset them. (Ecclesiastes 9:11-12)

God has given creation, including humanity, its freedom and it is, tragically, often exercised in ways that are evil. Such is the world in which we live. But it need not be. Like his siblings rallying around Job to lift him up from the ash heap (Job 42:11), so the Bible calls us to attend to the victims. We are to restore the brokenhearted and those crushed in spirit and body, and we are to call out unjust systems and policies that serve only to dehumanize and destroy people, often for profit. Therein lies the redemptive potential.

DISCUSSION QUESTIONS

1. What do you think is the worst kind of evil in America? In the world? How do you make sense of it, if you can?
2. Of all the types of suffering described in the Bible, which one feels most relevant to you?
3. How do you think "redemptive suffering" can be misused or abused? How can it be used positively?
4. Can you think of situations where the victim of a crime is often blamed?
5. Do you find God's response to Job's suffering satisfying?
6. How do you make sense of your own suffering?

CHAPTER 9

God

What are the defining qualities of God's character? Is God primarily a God of judgment or a God of grace and compassion? Ancient Israel and the early church experienced God in many different ways. For our final biblical dialogue, we turn to the biggest question of all: "Who is God, really?" This question is most directly addressed in the encounter between Moses and God at Mt. Sinai, the high point of Israel's journey from the Exodus to the Promised Land. After Moses calms God down over the Israelites worshiping the golden calf, he demands a clearer picture of who God is: "Show me your ways so that I may know you and find favor in your sight" (Exod. 33:13). In response, God promises to "go with" the people. But Moses pushes further: "Show me your glory" (Exod. 33:18). That's a significant leap from asking to know God's "ways" to asking to see God's "glory," which gets closer to God's very essence. God responds with the following:

> "I will make all my goodness pass in front of you and will proclaim before you the name, 'YHWH.' I will be gracious to whom I will be gracious and have compassion for whom I will have compassion. But," he said, "you cannot see my face; for no one can see me and live." And YHWH continued, "See, there is a place near me where you can stand on the rock. While my glory passes by I

> will put you in a cleft in the rock, and will cover you with my hand until I have passed by; then I will take away my hand, and you will see my back; but my face will not be seen." (Exodus 33:19-23)

God proves remarkably accommodating to Moses, but only to a point. Moses will get to hear God declare God's own name—a significant revelation in itself. Beyond that, Moses is given insight into God's very character: God "will be gracious" and "merciful" to whomever God chooses. In other words, God's primary attribute is the freedom to extend mercy—and judgment—at will. This divine freedom is foundational to what it means for God to be God.

But there's much more to the story. Regarding God's glory, Moses will be allowed a fleeting glimpse of God's "back," but not God's "face." A direct, face-to-face revelation of God is something that no human, even Moses it seems, could handle. This is what God offers, and the plan unfolds in the next chapter with a full verbal disclosure of YHWH's character—the most concise yet comprehensive description of God in all of scripture:

> YHWH passed before him and proclaimed,
> "YHWH, YHWH, a God compassionate and gracious,
> slow to anger,
> abounding in benevolence and faithfulness,
> preserving benevolence (*ḥesed*) for a thousand generations,
> forgiving iniquity, transgression, and sin,
> yet by no means clearing the guilty,
> but visiting the iniquity of the parents upon the children
> and the children's children,
> to the third and the fourth generation."
> (Exodus 34:6-7)

How many descriptors of God's character are given here? I count seven: 1) compassionate, 2) gracious, 3) slow to anger, 4) benevolent, 5) faithful, 6) forgiving, and 7) punishing. In the Old Testament, the number seven often signifies completeness, as in the case of the "seventh day" (the Sabbath).

Let's break them down one by one. First, "compassionate" (*raḥûm*) leads the list, a word that is related to the Hebrew word for "womb" (*reḥem*). This etymological connection gives "compassion" a distinctly maternal feel. To say God has "compassion" for a people is to say that God "wombs" them—surrounding them with intimate, nurturing love and protection. With compassion, God takes on a motherly role. Next is "gracious," which can also be translated as "merciful" (*ḥannûn*)—a fitting partner to "compassionate" on the list. God's grace is reflected, for example, in God's refusal to abandon the people, never turning God's "face" away (2 Chron. 30:9), and responding to the cries of the dispossessed (Exod. 22:27). "Slow to anger" is fairly straightforward but has an interesting twist in Hebrew, where it literally means "long in nostrils." The nose is often a symbol of anger—think of "burning nostrils" to indicate fury (for example Gen. 30:2, Exod. 4:14). The opposite, a "long nose," signifies patience—slow to ignite with anger and reluctant to punish.

Perhaps the most critically defining term found here is "benevolence," *ḥesed* in Hebrew, which lies at the heart of God's self-description. Just ask the psalmist, who frequently uses *ḥesed* to describe God (for example Pss. 6:4, 31:7, 36:7). It's the psalmist's one-word thesis about who God is. *Ḥesed* is such a rich word: it conveys both covenantal commitment and freely given grace. It connotes God's loving fidelity and faithfulness—reflecting God's trustworthy character and compassionate nature. In short, *ḥesed* encapsulates God's saving attentiveness, which is both accessible and reliable, freely given yet also fully expected, a love that overlooks the speaker's sins and tempers divine anger (Ps. 103:8-9).

According to the Psalms, if there's one constant about God's character, it's benevolence. It's the first and final source of appeal in many petitions and the foundational reason for praise (for example Pss. 5:7; 31:7, 21; 63:3). God responds with deliverance out of, and because of, this benevolence. The psalmist's most basic cry is, "Save me according to your *ḥesed*" (Pss. 109:26; 31:16). A typical expression of praise is, "I will exult and rejoice in your *ḥesed*" (Ps. 31:7). It's no wonder that *ḥesed* is considered God's most central quality. God's faithfulness serves to support God's benevolence, ensuring that it will last a "thousand generations," essentially forever. God is not just benevolent but faithfully so, and this benevolence is demonstrated in forgiveness. In the language of the Psalms, forgiveness literally means "taking away"—God "takes away" sin, leaving the person both liberated and cleansed.

So far, God's character has been described as nothing but positive—compassionate, forgiving, and benevolent. But there is a catch, as the last verse makes clear. While forgiveness marks the culmination of God's faithful benevolence and compassion, it has its limits. The final verse of YHWH's self-revelation introduces the flipside of God's character: judgment. God will not let the guilty go unpunished. Instead, God will "visit" the sins of the parents upon their descendants. The verb here implies a "transfer" or "carryover" of sins from one generation to the next. This concept of intergenerational guilt or punishment isn't a footnote or an afterthought in God's message to Moses. It's part of who God is. God's resolve to punish is even reflected in the Decalogue:

> You shall not bow down to them or worship them; for I YHWH your God am a zealous God, punishing children for the iniquity of parents, to the third and the fourth generation of those who hate me, but showing faithful benevolence (*ḥesed*) to the thousandth generation of those who love me and keep my commandments. (Exodus 20:5-6)[1]

And Moses' response to God's self-revelation? He "quickly bowed his head toward the ground and worshiped" (Exod. 34:8). How fitting! So much divine disclosure packed into just two verses! God's verbal density in this passage mirrors the weight of God's physical glory. You might even

---

1. It's worth noting that the version in the Decalogue reverses the order, since it follows a negative command or prohibition that requires punishment. (We'll circle back to this later.)

call it a "verbophany" to match the theophany! But what about the Bible's response? Here's where things get complicated—and perhaps more interesting, from a dialogical perspective.

VARIATIONS ON A THEME OF *ḤESED*

Mt. Sinai is not the only place where God reveals the divine self; God's "verbophany" shows up throughout the Old Testament—in narratives, prophetic writings, and the Psalms—but in different forms. Some are shorter, some altered, others expanded, all tailored for various reasons. In total, some version of God's self-disclosure can be found in Exodus 20:5-6, Numbers 14:18, Deuteronomy 5:9-10, Jeremiah 30:11, 32:18–19, 46:28, and 49:12, Joel 2:13, Jonah 4:2, Micah 7:18–20, Nahum 1:2, Psalms 103 and 145:8, Lamentations 3:32, Daniel 9:4, and Nehemiah 9:17. Whew! That's sixteen instances, in addition to the foundational one in Exodus 34. Each offers its own unique and nuanced take on God's character, setting up a dialogue of divine proportions about what is truly at the heart of God's nature. While we won't go through all of these passages in this chapter, let's explore a sampling of that dialogue.

Numbers 14: Mitigating Judgment

Back on the road, the wandering Israelites decide they'd rather return to Egypt, believing it's better than the land God promised them. God, in response, resolves to wipe them out and start over with Moses (Num. 14:11-12). But Moses pushes back, rejecting the offer and reminding God of God's own confession at this critical moment in the wilderness. It turns out to be Moses' ace-in-the-hole for changing God's mind. He starts by appealing to God's reputation among the nations:

> But Moses said to YHWH, "They have heard that you, YHWH, are in the midst of this people; for you, YHWH, appear face-to-face, and that your cloud stands over them and you go in front of them, in a pillar of cloud by day and in a pillar of fire by night.

> Now if you kill this people, every last one of them, then the nations who have heard about you will say, 'It is because YHWH was unable to bring this people into the land he swore to give them. So he slaughtered them in the wilderness.' And now, therefore, let YHWH's power be great in the way that you promised when you spoke . . . (Numbers 14:13-17)

At this point, Moses argues that if YHWH follows through and destroys the people, then the surrounding nations will believe that YHWH was *incapable* of leading the people into the Promised Land—essentially undermining God's power. But Moses doesn't stop there; he presses further, citing YHWH's own confession:

> "YHWH is slow to anger and abounding in faithful benevolence, forgiving iniquity and transgression, but by no means clearing the guilty, visiting the iniquity of the parents upon the children to the third and the fourth generation." Forgive the iniquity of this people according to the greatness of your faithful benevolence, just as you pardoned this people from Egypt even until now. (Numbers 14:18-19)

Moses argues that destroying the people wouldn't just damage YHWH's reputation for keeping promises—it would compromise YHWH's own character. In other words, if the people are wiped out, then what would happen to YHWH's abounding "benevolence"? Interestingly, Moses doesn't quote the full self-revelation from Exodus 34 (he leaves out the part about the "thousand generations" for instance), but he clearly emphasizes YHWH's *ḥesed,* which leads to forgiveness—exactly what Moses is seeking from God. So why would Moses mention YHWH's punishment to the "third and fourth generation"? Likely to anticipate that YHWH's forgiveness comes with limits.

> Then YHWH said, "I hereby forgive, just as you have asked. Nevertheless, as I live, and as all the earth shall be filled with YHWH's glory, none of the people who have seen my glory and

> the signs that I did in Egypt and in the wilderness, and yet have tested me these ten times and refused to obey my voice, will see the land that I swore to give to their ancestors; none of those who despised me shall see it. (Numbers 14:20-23)

Although YHWH forgives, YHWH condemns the first generation to death for their stubborn rejection of the land that was promised them. Their fate is to wander the desert for forty years, until the entire first generation has passed away. It's judgment paired with forgiveness—not destruction by pestilence, as initially threatened (Num. 14:12), but the slow punishment of wandering. What's remarkable, though, is that this judgment does *not* extend to the third and fourth generation, as YHWH's earlier statement might suggest. It's limited to only the first generation. The second generation, which had not witnessed YHWH's glory in Egypt, are the ones to gain entrance into the Promised Land. They are spared. This outcome shows how YHWH's *ḥesed* and judgment converge. While judgment is still carried out, it is also significantly mitigated.

Jonah: The Case of Runaway Mercy

The book of Jonah stands out as a sore thumb among the prophets. Here we have a prophet who starts by running away from his calling and by scolding God for being *too* merciful. Jonah is called by God to pronounce judgment against Nineveh, the capital of Assyria, for its "wickedness" (Jon. 1:2). The Assyrian Empire, known for its brutality in war and its harsh treatment of conquered peoples, had a notorious reputation. Assyria was responsible for the destruction of the Northern Kingdom in 722 BCE and for laying siege to Jerusalem in 701 BCE—hardly a friend of Israel. So, when God called Jonah to proclaim judgment at the very heart of this enemy, it's no surprise that Jonah fled in the opposite direction!

But it's no use—Jonah can't escape. After being swallowed up and spewed out by a "large fish," he's forced to head in the right direction: to Nineveh, "that great city," to deliver YHWH's message (Jon. 3:2-3). That message is a simple one: "Forty days more and Nineveh will be overthrown!" (Jon. 3:4). The verb translated as "overthrown" can mean many different things—it could signify destruction, as in the case of Sodom and Gomorrah (Gen. 19:21, 25, 29; Deut. 29:22), but it can also mean "have a change of heart" (Exod. 14:5, Hos. 11:8, 1 Sam. 10:6). To Jonah's dismay, everyone in Nineveh—from the king to the animals—does exactly that: they have a change of heart and repent fully, fasting and wearing sackcloth (Jon. 3:6-8) in the hope that "God may relent and change his mind; he may turn from his wrath, so that we do not perish" (Jon. 3:9). Much to Jonah's chagrin, God does relent, deciding not to destroy the city. So, what gets "overthrown" in the end? Not the city, but God's resolve to destroy it.

Jonah's reaction? Utter outrage! Imagine how this weary prophet must have felt when his message of judgment—that Nineveh be "overthrown"—ended up being about Nineveh's "turnaround" instead, along with God's turn of heart! Jonah claims that he sensed something was off all along: "YHWH, isn't this just what I suspected while I was back in my own land? That's why I fled to Tarshish in the first place!" It's at this point that Jonah recalls God's "verbophany":

> For I know that you are a gracious God and compassionate, slow to anger, and abounding in faithful benevolence, and ready to relent from punishing. (Jonah 4:2)

There it is: God's self-disclosure of mercy *without* the corresponding emphasis on judgment. Jonah learns the hard way, at the cost of his own prophetic identity, that God's *ḥesed* not only outweighs God's commitment to "not clear the guilty," but in this case completely displaces it. After all, who could be more guilty or wicked than Nineveh? Well, maybe Babylon—but that's a story for later. The book of Jonah is set before Babylon emerged on the historical stage to unleash its own brand of imperial destruction across the region.

Jonah insists he knew all along that God's compassion and *ḥesed* would always "overturn" any inclination to punish. But perhaps he still held onto some hope that Nineveh might prove to be an exception—that

God would reignite God's burning zeal for judgment. But God doesn't. And the reason is made clear at the end of the book:

> Should I not take pity on Nineveh, that great city, in which there are more than a hundred and twenty thousand people who can't tell their right hand from their left, and also many animals? (Jonah 4:11)

God is "gracious and compassionate," "slow to anger," "abounding in benevolence," and, drawing from God's last statement in Jonah, compassionate to the point of pity. Meanwhile, Jonah is left angry and disheartened, struggling to reconcile himself with this boundless mercy.

Nahum: Irrevocable Judgment

If you find Jonah's take on God's overwhelming compassion to be too scandalous (as Jonah himself did), then look no further than the book of Nahum. Jonah would've loved Nahum. We know almost nothing about "Nahum of Elkosh" aside from the fact that he was a seventh-century prophet. Unlike Jonah (who's also mentioned in 2 Kings 14:25), Nahum doesn't appear anywhere else in the Bible, and Elkosh—his hometown—is equally mysterious. Scholars surmise that it was somewhere in southwestern Judah, but who really knows? One thing is certain, though: Nahum had his eye on Nineveh, the capital of Assyria. He spoke up just as things were going south for the Assyrian Empire, with Babylonia, the next rising superpower, breathing down its neck. Assyria eventually fell in 612 BCE, its army crushed by the Babylonians and the Medes. If Nahum lived to see it, he'd have been the first to celebrate (Nah. 1:15, 3:19).

Nahum doesn't mince words. He uses his rhetoric to paint a vivid picture of God's wrath. God is described as "jealous," "avenging," "wrathful," "vengeful," and filled with "indignation" (Nah. 1:2-6a). God's anger breaks rocks and burns like fire (Nah. 1:6b). Nahum makes it crystal clear: God is unequivocally against Nineveh (Nah. 2:13, 3:5), leaving no room for mercy or pity. The prophet also has some sharp words for Nineveh itself, calling out the city and alleging that Nineveh "plots evil against YHWH" and "counsels wickedness" (Nah. 1:11). Nineveh is portrayed as an oppressive "yoke" that must be broken (Nah. 1:13), a ravenous lion who has filled its "caves with prey . . . with torn flesh" (Nah. 2:12). Assyria's king is known for his "endless cruelty" (Nah. 3:19), cruelty that spanned more than one hundred twenty-five years of brutal imperial domination. Unlike in Jonah, the people of Nineveh certainly know "their right hand from their left" (Jonah 4:11), for both hands have been engaged in slaughter; both hands are covered in blood.

The rest of Nahum revels in Nineveh's total destruction, with voyeuristic glee (Nah. 2:1-13). So, what does Nahum have to say about God's character? Like Jonah, he selectively draws from God's self-confession or "verbophany":

> YHWH is slow to anger but great in power,
> but YHWH will by no means clear the guilty.
> His way is in whirlwind and storm,
> and the clouds are the dust of his feet. (Nahum 1:3)

Nahum uses YHWH's words from Exodus 34:6-7 as a point of departure to emphasize YHWH's terrifying power to shake the earth and bring devastation (Nah. 1:4-5). But notice how Nahum filters and tweaks God's self-revelation. First, he leaves out everything related to God's *ḥesed*, essentially cutting the entire first half. There's no mention of extending compassion to third and fourth generations, let alone the thousandth. Nahum is solely focused on Nineveh's immediate fate. He also inserts a reference to YHWH's "great power," specifically the power to carry through on Nineveh's complete destruction. Nahum sums it up perfectly in just three words, delivered as a curse: "desolation and devastation and destruction!" (Nah. 2:10a). The Hebrew version—*bûqâ ûmĕbûqâ ûmĕbuqālâ*—is even more striking, with its powerful alliteration and the assonance—rhyming with a vengeance!

If Jonah and Nahum were to meet, they'd probably agree on how God should have acted. Jonah, the reluctant and satirized prophet, would likely clap with joy along with Nahum, the prophetic purveyor of destruction: Nineveh deserved what it got—divine punishment and total destruction. No quarrel there. Nahum perfectly illustrates what Jonah believed what *should* have happened over a century earlier.

The real issue, though, is with God, who spared Nineveh in Jonah's day. Jonah knows God can be merciful, even in the face of human cruelty, and he hates it. For both prophets, their versions of God's character resolve the tension between justice and mercy, but in completely opposite ways. Jonah sees God as indiscriminately merciful, much to his chagrin, while Nahum views God as relentlessly judgmental. However, Nahum does offer one bit of nuance: he admits that "YHWH is good, a stronghold in a day of trouble, protecting those who take refuge in him, even in a rushing flood" (Nah. 1:7-8a). While Nineveh deserved God's destruction, Judah, at least, deserves God's protection.

Palm 86: Benevolence in Vindication

Yahweh's self-confession continues its journey in other contexts beyond Exodus and the prophets (see also Joel 2:13). It shows up repeatedly in the Psalms, as in Psalm 86, a plea for salvation and vindication in the face of intense conflict. In the midst of this urgent cry for help, the psalm offers a testimony to God's incomparable sovereignty "among the gods" (Ps. 86:8-9). God is praised not only as the "worker of wonders" (Ps. 86:10a) but also as "compassionate and gracious, slow to anger and abounding in benevolence and faithfulness" (Ps. 86:15). These affirmations of God's character are woven into the context of dire conflict:

> O God, the arrogant rise up against me,
> and a violent gang seeks out my life,
> and they do not set you before them.
> But you, O Lord, are a God compassionate and gracious,
> slow to anger and abounding in benevolence and faithfulness.
> Turn to me and grant me grace!

Bestow your strength upon your servant;
save the son of your slave-girl!
Create in me a sign of your goodness,
so that those who hate me will be ashamed to see
that you, YHWH, have helped me and comforted me.
(Psalm 86:14-17)

Toward the end of the psalm, the speaker laments violent, arrogant enemies who are out to kill him. In this context of mortal conflict, you'd expect some mention of God's refusal to "clear the guilty," as in Nahum. But no, instead, the speaker lifts up God's abundant benevolence and compassion. You might assume the psalmist would want God to punish his enemies, to condemn them and even wipe them out. But that's not the case. By avoiding the language of punishment, the psalmist focuses exclusively on God's benevolence and grace, but with a particular aim. It's not about forgiveness here—that's absent in this version—but about vindication. The speaker asks God to be a sign of God's "goodness," God's help and comfort, so that his enemies will be "ashamed" (Ps. 86:17). The logic is that if only the arrogant and the violent saw clear evidence of God's favor toward their target, then they would feel ashamed of their violent ways and stop. And that's how the psalm ends.

The versatile nature of God's self-confession is clear in other psalms as well. In Psalm 103, the psalmist draws on God's qualities of "compassionate and gracious, slow to anger and abounding in faithful benevolence" (Ps. 103:8) to testify that YHWH won't "harbor his anger indefinitely" or "deal with us according to our sins." Instead, God removes the people's sins "as far as the east is from the west" (Ps. 103:9-12). This compassion is compared to a father's love for his children (Ps. 103:13). There's no punishment here. It's all about forgiveness as an expression of God's compassion, cast as parental love.

Joel 2: Repentance from Punishment

In Joel 2, the prophet appeals to YHWH's grace and mercy as a way to soften, or even prevent, the coming "day of YHWH"—a "terrible" day, filled with "darkness and gloom" (Joel 2:2). Joel warns of a mighty army coming to ravage the land (Joel 2:2-11), and it turns out that YHWH is leading the charge! But then Joel offers this surprising twist:

> Yet even now, says YHWH, return to me with all your heart,
> with fasting, weeping, and mourning!
> Rend your hearts rather than your clothing!
> Return to YHWH, your God,
> for he is compassionate and gracious, slow to anger,
> and abounding in faithful benevolence and relents from punishing! (Joel 2:12-13b)

"Even now," with the army fast approaching, YHWH seeks the people's repentance. Joel makes an addition to the divine self-confession: "and relents from punishing"—a new take that counters YHWH's earlier refusal "to clear the guilty." Here, necessity is the mother of invention. The inevitability of military catastrophe prompts an appeal to YHWH's abundant benevolence, but with a twist: benevolence is now interpreted as God's willingness to "relent from punishing," a phrase that can also mean "to regret" or "be sorry" (from Hebrew verb *nḥm*) for sending disaster. But there's one condition: complete repentance. Yet, even with repentance, is disaster truly avoidable? Joel offers this thought:

> Who knows whether he will turn and relent,
> and leave a blessing behind him,
> a grain offering and a drink offering for YHWH,
> your God? (Joel 2:14)

"Who knows?" Only God. Joel acknowledges YHWH's freedom to relent—or not. Repentance, while appealing to YHWH's benevolence, offers no guarantees, but it's worth trying. The prophet calls for a fast to sanctify the people, signaled by the blast of a trumpet and accompanied by weeping (Joel 2:15-17). Then, something remarkable happens: Joel recounts YHWH's "jealousy" for the land and its people, and instead of sending an invading army, God promises agricultural abundance (Joel 2:19). Crisis averted; the army is removed (Joel 2:20). Even the land and the animals are reassured (Joel 2:21-22). YHWH has indeed relented!

Psalm 145: Inclusive Benevolence

Speaking of God's creatures, Psalm 145 declares that YHWH's compassion, grace, and abundant benevolence extend to "all" (Ps. 145:8-9). The psalm references YHWH's self-confession, but with a subtle tweak:

> Gracious and compassionate is YHWH;
> slow to anger and great in faithful benevolence.
> YHWH is good to all;
> his tender compassion is over all his works. (Psalm 145:8-9)

While quoting the first half of YHWH's self-revelation, the psalmist makes a slight, almost unnoticeable, change by replacing "abounding in faithful benevolence" with "great in faithful benevolence." In what follows, the psalmist stresses the inclusive nature of YHWH's benevolence. In fact, the word "all" (a tiny word in both English and Hebrew) is repeated seventeen times in the psalm, underscoring the totality of God's care, as captured in the following passage:

> YHWH supports all who fall down,
> raising up all who are bowed down.
> The eyes of all look to you in hope,
> and you give to them their food in its season,
> opening your hand,
> and satisfying the desire of every living thing.
> Righteous is YHWH in all his ways,
> faithfully benevolent in all his deeds. (Psalm 145:14-17)

From lifting up the fallen to feeding every living creature, YHWH's "faithful benevolence" is truly "great"—universally wide-reaching and all-encompassing. "All" of God is devoted to "all" of God's creatures. The "allness" reflects the "greatness" of God's *ḥesed*.

But the psalm also introduces a dissonant note: "YHWH protects all who love him, but all the wicked he will destroy" (Ps. 145:20). The wicked be damned! Yet, this dissonance is minor compared to YHWH's earlier self-confession, which includes YHWH's refusal to "clear the guilty." On the one hand, YHWH fulfills "the desire of everything living thing," while on the other, YHWH promises to destroy "all the wicked." In this case, the word "all" cuts both ways, wielding a double-edged sword.

Nehemiah 9: Forbearing Abundance

In Nehemiah 9, we find the most extensive prayer set to prose in the Bible, and it includes a reference to YHWH's self-confession, but not in its entirety. Ezra offers a public prayer that recounts the vast sweep of YHWH's mighty acts throughout history, from the creation of the world to Israel's deliverance and the conquest of the land (Neh. 9:6-31). This is followed by a plea for God to preserve a people who are now enslaved in their own land (Neh. 9:32-37), referring to Israel under Persian rule. YHWH's confession is cited not once, but twice, though in an abbreviated form both times. The fullest version is squarely in the middle of Ezra's historical survey:

> But they—and our ancestors—acted arrogantly. They stiffened their necks and would not obey your commandments. They refused to obey and were not mindful of the wonders that you performed among them. Instead, they stiffened their necks and determined to return to their slavery in Egypt. But you are a God ready to forgive, compassionate and gracious, slow to anger and abounding in faithful benevolence. You did not forsake them. Even when they had cast an image of a calf for themselves and said, "This is your God who brought you up out of Egypt," and

> committed great blasphemies, you in your abundant mercy did not abandon them in the wilderness. The pillar of cloud that led them in the way did not leave them by day, nor the pillar of fire by night that gave them light on the way by which they should go. (Nehemiah 9:16-19)

In this section, Ezra recounts the Israelite's wilderness wanderings during the forty years between the Exodus and their settlement in the Promised Land, focusing on Israel's "fall" when they worshiped the golden calf—an act that could have warranted severe judgment or even annihilation (Exod. 32:10). However, because God "abounds in faithful benevolence," God resolved not to abandon them in the wilderness. Instead, God continued to guide them and sustain them, providing manna and water (Neh. 9:20-22).

The second, more concise reference to God's self-confession occurs during another similar crisis of disobedience. Due to Israel's stubborn and stiff-necked behavior, which had tested God's patience for many years, God chose to "hand them over to the peoples of the lands" (Neh. 9:30). Nevertheless, even in this moment of judgment, Ezra says of God, "In your abundant compassion you did not make an end of them or forsake them, for *you are a compassionate and gracious God*" (Neh. 9:31). Once again, God's compassion ensures that Israel is not utterly abandoned.

The message is clear: while there comes a point when God has had enough, God's compassion pushes the boundary even further, allowing compassion to outweigh ultimate punishment. God's judgment is never final. God's benevolence is all about forbearance—a literal "holding back" of wrath, a refusal to unleash deserved fury, no matter how deserved it might be. God's abundant benevolence tempers the scourge of judgment, and it is never depleted. Even when God is pushed to the precipice of abandoning God's people, God remains firmly grounded in grace. In short, thanks to God's *ḥesed*, judgment is never the end, according to Ezra's prayer.

Punishing Children

Having surveyed the many ways God's confession is used, adapted, and interpreted throughout scripture, one major point of contention remains: the issue of transgenerational punishment, which concludes YHWH's full confession in Exodus 34:

> "YHWH, YHWH, a God compassionate and gracious,
> slow to anger, abounding in benevolence and faithfulness,
> preserving faithful benevolence for a thousand generations,
> forgiving iniquity, transgression, and sin,
> yet by no means clearing the guilty,
> but visiting the iniquity of the parents upon the children
> and the children's children,
> to the third and the fourth generation."
> (Exodus 34:6-7)

This idea is also mirrored in the Decalogue as part of the second commandment:

> You shall not bow down to them or worship (other gods); for I YHWH your God am a zealous God, visiting the iniquity of parents upon the children, to the third and the fourth generation of those who hate me, but showing faithful benevolence for a thousand generations of those who love me and keep my commandments. (Exodus 20:5-6)

The commandment reverses the order, as noted earlier, but also includes a crucial difference: it introduces the language of "love" and "hate." Those who love God receive "faithful benevolence," covering a "thousand generations," while punishment is reserved for those who "hate" God, reaching only to the "fourth generation." This clarification in the second commandment helps define who receives *ḥesed* and who faces punishment. In doing so, it clears up some of the ambiguity present in God's self-confession from Exodus 34, which lacks this qualification.

But what about the case of wicked parents and righteous children? Do the children still get punished? According to God's self-confession in Exodus 34, the answer is yes. However, the second commandment offers a different perspective: no, unless the children, like their parents, also "hate" God. Furthermore, even if the descendants continue to "hate" God, the punishment is limited to four generations. In short, the second commandment makes God's punishment of subsequent generations more discriminating.

But there's still the proverbial "elephant in the room"—the concept of transgenerational punishment itself. Why should children suffer God's punishment for their parents' actions? It sounds deeply unfair, even inhumane. Yet the Bible contains several examples where children bear the consequences of their parents' wrongdoing. One such instance is when Noah curses not his son Ham, who violated his privacy while he was drunk, but Ham's son, Canaan (Gen. 9:25). This raises troubling questions about the justice of such punishment across generations.

However, before critiquing this belief, one clarification is needed: many, if not most, translations incorrectly use the word "punishment," as seen in the NRSV and CEB, for instance:

> I the LORD your God am a jealous God, punishing children for the iniquity of parents, to the third and the fourth generation of those who reject me. (Exodus 20:5, NRSV)

> I, the LORD your God, am a passionate God. I punish children for their parents' sins even to the third and fourth generations of those who hate me. (Exodus 20:5, CEB)

The same goes for the translation of Exodus 34:7, where the NRSV moves away from the word "punishing" and instead uses the word "visiting": "Yet by no means clearing the guilty, but visiting the iniquity of the parents upon the children" (Exod. 34:7, NRSV). The Hebrew verb in question is *pqd*, which carries a whole host of meanings, from "inspect" and "muster" to "seek out" and "appoint." However, when used in the context of accountability, *pqd* carries a more nuanced meaning—not one of punishment in the lightning-bolt sense of divine wrath, but rather the idea of guilt being passed down or transferred from one generation to the next. In fact, the Septuagint (the Greek translation of the Old Testament) translates the verb as "bring upon": "And he will not clear the guilty, *bringing* the iniquity of the fathers *upon* the children" (Exod. 34:7).

This translation suggests a movement of sin from parents to children, from one generation to the next. Yes, God facilitates this process, but it's a far cry from the idea of God directly punishing children for something their parents did. It's more about consequences than punishment. Think of it like an inheritance—though an unwanted one—of accumulated guilt passed down through generations. The best modern example would be climate change: my generation (and those that came before) have so damaged the planet by pumping greenhouse gases into the atmosphere that future generations will inevitably suffer the consequences—severe storms, massive flooding, and withering heat waves that may last centuries. In this case, the "visiting" of iniquity from one generation to the next is painfully real, and God isn't stepping in to miraculously reverse it. It's up to us, though much of the damage may already be irreversible. The sin of building an economy dependent on burning fossil fuels will affect far more than just four generations.

Breaking the Cycle of Sin

An oft-repeated proverb in the Bible illustrates this idea of transgenerational guilt: "The parents have eaten sour grapes, and the children's teeth are blunted." The "sourness" of sin passes down through generations—the consequences of the parents' misdeeds are felt all the more by their children. However, two prophets in particular take issue with this proverb. Take Jeremiah, for example:

> Voilà! The days are coming, says YHWH, when I will sow the house of Israel and the house of Judah with the seed of humans and the seed of animals. And just as I have watched over them to uproot and break down, to overthrow, destroy, and bring evil, so I

> will watch over them to build and to plant, declares YHWH. In those days they shall no longer say: "The parents have eaten sour grapes, and the children's teeth are blunted." But all shall die for their own sins; (only) the teeth of everyone who eats sour grapes will be blunted. The days are surely coming, says YHWH, when I will make a new covenant with the house of Israel and the house of Judah. (Jeremiah 31:27-31)

In the time of exile, Jeremiah witnessed the collapse of Israel and now proclaims YHWH's promise to rebuild the community through a new covenant. As part of this restoration, Jeremiah says, the cycle of transgenerational consequences will be broken. No longer will children suffer for their parents' sins—only the parents' teeth "will be blunted" when they eat sour grapes. In other words, when it comes to iniquity, only the parents will bear the consequences.

Ezekiel, another prophet (and priest) of the exile, agrees but takes it a step further with an additional admonition:

> What do you mean by repeating this proverb concerning the land of Israel, "The parents have eaten sour grapes, and the children's teeth are blunted"? As I live, says the Lord YHWH, this proverb will no longer be used by you in Israel. Know that all lives are mine; the life of the parent as well as the life of the child is mine: it is only the person who sins that will die. (Ezekiel 18:2-4)

In other words, only the individual who sins will face the consequences. However, even those consequences don't have to be permanent, as Ezekiel makes clear later in the same chapter:

> Only the person who sins will die. A child will not suffer for the parent's iniquity; neither will a parent suffer for the child's iniquity. The righteousness of the righteous will be his own, and the wickedness of the wicked will be his own. But if the wicked one turns away from all his sins that he has committed and keeps all my statutes and does what is lawful and right, he will surely live;

> he will not die. None of the transgressions that he has committed will be remembered against him. Because of the righteousness that he has done, he will live. (Ezekiel 18:20-22)

In a word: repentance. "Turning away" from sin is the key to overturning the "suffering" caused by one's own wrongdoing. While righteousness and wickedness are "owned" solely by the individual, Ezekiel makes it clear that things can change when the wicked repent—their "transgressions" will no longer "be remembered." Curiously, Ezekiel never uses the word "punishment" and avoids any reference to direct divine intervention. Instead, he talks about transgressions being "remembered" or not, but doesn't specify by whom. God is almost absent as an active agent here; God simply declares that the consequences of sins are contained, limited to the individual and their wickedness, which can be renounced. As Ezekiel puts it, "When the wicked one turns away from the wickedness he has committed and does what is lawful and right, he will preserve his life. When he realized and turned away from all the transgressions he had committed, he will surely live; he will not die" (Ezek. 18:27-28).

An example of sin's containment and the overturning of its transgenerational effects is found in the wilderness stories of the wandering Israelites in Numbers 14, as previously discussed. A strict transgenerational doctrine of sin would have condemned not only the next generation, but at least two more generations to wander in the wilderness. Instead, God permits the children to enter the Promised Land. Even this sweeping narrative doesn't fully adhere to the tenet found in God's own self-confession. While God does not clear the guilty, God does clear their children. In the end, divine forgiveness transcends generations and wins the day.

Conclusion

We've traced many variations of YHWH's self-confession to Moses on the mountaintop, suggesting that this confession provides more of a spectrum than a single, rigid direction concerning God's response to God's people. Sin happens—but how will God react? With forgiveness and compassion, or with judgment? God is both gracious and just. Is there a tension between these two aspects of God's character? Do love and justice pull against each other in a divine tug of war?

The prophets and psalmists wrestle with these questions, sometimes leaning toward one side, sometimes the other, or finding a balance in between, as we've seen. Even Jeremiah and Ezekiel seem to adjust God's self-confession, preferring a version that might say: "By no means clearing the guilty, but letting them suffer for their own iniquity until they repent, while sparing their children and their children's children."

I wonder, though, if the full version of the divine confession featured in Exodus 34 actually regards love and justice as being in tension, as opposing polarities. While God is ready to forgive, God also ensures that the unjust don't get away with injustice. That seems more like a coherent statement rather than a perplexing paradox. It's not as if God is pulled in opposite directions by some internal struggle. The difference between love and justice, for God, is perhaps more about scale than category: love covers a "thousand generations," while punishment lasts only to the "third and fourth generation," or less. Love endures. And what is justice? Love made manifest in the public arena.[2] Perhaps punishment reframed by love becomes restorative rather than punitive in God's heart. In any case, the dialogue continues, perhaps even in God's own heart.

DOES GOD CHANGE?

Our discussion has skirted around another big question about God: does God change? Not surprisingly, there are conflicting views in biblical tradition, ranging from a hard "NO!" to a resounding "YES!" The majority of classic Christian theology, it must be said, leans heavily toward the negative response. God is described as omniscient, omnipotent, omnipresent, and *impassible*. "Impassible" is different from the similar-sounding word

---

2. Based on Cornel West's famous quote: "Justice is what love looks like in public." https://x.com/CornelWest/status/1052585306916974592.

that we're more familiar with—that's "impassable"—as in a blocked road. This more archaic term refers to God being without passions, meaning God doesn't experience emotional change and is, therefore, unchangeable or "immutable." In fact, the Westminster Confession of Faith (1648), a foundational document for many Protestant churches, lists the following attributes of God:

> There is but one only living and true God, who is infinite in being and perfection, a most pure spirit, invisible, without body, parts, or passions, immutable, immense, eternal, incomprehensible, almighty, most wise, most holy, most free, most absolute . . .[3]

Among these attributes, two are phrased in the negative: "without . . . passions" and "immutable."

So, how does the Bible address this issue? Balaam offers a few words that seem quite definitive:

> Then Balaam uttered his oracle, saying: "Arise, Balak, and hear; listen to me, O son of Zippor: God is not a man that he would lie, or a human being, that he would change his mind. Has he ever spoken and not done it, or promised and not fulfilled it? See, I received a command to bless; he has blessed. I cannot revoke it. (Numbers 23:18-20)

Fearing that Israel would defeat him, Balak, king of Moab, hired the prophet Balaam to curse the Israelites as they traveled through his territory on their way to the Promised Land. However, every time Balaam opened his mouth, God compelled him to bless the wandering Israelites instead. In one of his declarations to Balak, Balaam professes that God does not change or go back on what God has promised or commanded. In this context, a "change of mind" refers specifically to God not reneging on what God has promised. Unlike fickle human beings, God always follows through on God's promises.

3. Westminster Confession of Faith, Chapter 2.1.

The same idea is echoed in Samuel's declaration to Saul, after Saul failed to fulfill his duty as king to utterly destroy the Amalekites:

> And Samuel said to him, "YHWH has ripped the kingdom of Israel from you this very day, and has given it to an associate of yours, one who is better than you. What's more, the Glory of Israel will not deceive or change his mind; for he is not a human being who would change his mind." (1 Samuel 15:28-29)

Here, YHWH's decision to reject Saul (and favor David) is the central issue (see 1 Sam. 15:26; 16:1). God will not change course no matter how remorseful Saul is (1 Sam. 15:24-25). Consequently, Saul becomes a tragic figure. Similarly, the psalmist declares, "YHWH has sworn and will not change his mind, 'You are a priest forever according to the order of Melchizedek" (Ps. 110:4). These passages about God's unchangeability focus on God's unwavering commitment to what God has promised and commanded. Simply put, God does not lie. God means what God says (see Num. 23:19).

Other passages address the issue of God's "immutability" more generally, such as in the book of Malachi:

> I will draw near to you for judgment. . . . For I YHWH do not change; therefore you, O children of Jacob, have not perished. (Malachi 3:5-6)

YHWH's self-declaration here is clear: God does not change, period. However, there's a reason and context for this divine immutability—God's judgment is irrevocable. Yet, even in judgment, God's unchanging nature ensures Israel's survival. If God were to change, Israel would "perish." The most general statement of this is found in Psalm 102:

> Long ago you established the earth;
>   your handiwork is the heavens.
> They will perish, but you endure;
>   all of them will wear out like a garment.
> You change them like clothing,

and they pass on.
But you are the one!
    Your years have no end!
Let the children of your servants be settled securely,
    and their offspring established before you.
        (Psalm 102:25-28)

This evocative passage contrasts the fleeting nature of creation with God's enduring presence. Creation is like clothing that can be changed, but God is not. God remains constant. Most translations of Psalm 102:27, including the NRSV and KJV, translate this phrase as, "But you are the same . . .", but that is not entirely accurate. The Hebrew says, "But you are the one," meaning the one who *endures* and does not wear out like clothing or creation. God's unchangeability here is tied to God's everlasting nature in contrast to the transience of creation. While creation may be like clothing that God wears, God never becomes worn out and discarded.

These affirmations of God's "immutability" are tied to their specific contexts. Not one of them talks about divine unchangeability in a metaphysical or philosophical way. Instead, the language is used to emphasize that when God promises something—whether in salvation or judgment—God never wavers. God does not change course when God resolves to act; and God never goes back on God's word.

But there are exceptions, you might even call them loopholes. The prophet Jeremiah recounts two instances where God is open to change:

> At any time I may declare regarding a nation or a kingdom that I will uproot, pull down, and destroy it, but if that nation, about which I have spoken, turns from its evil, I will change my mind about the disaster that I intended to bring on it. And at the same time I may declare regarding a nation or a kingdom that I will build and plant it, but if it does evil in my sight, not listening to my voice, then I will change my mind about the good that I had intended for it. (Jeremiah 18:7-10)

Interestingly, from God's very mouth, no less, we find an admission that God *does* have a change of mind, depending on how a "nation or a kingdom" responds to God's declaration of destruction or restoration. Such outcomes are not set in stone. God is open to change if the nation in question changes—whether by turning toward good or evil. A dramatic example of this is found in the book of Jonah, as we discussed earlier:

> Then [the king] made a proclamation in Nineveh: "By the decree of the king and his officials: Neither human nor animal, cattle nor flock, will taste anything. They shall not feed, nor shall they drink water. Human beings and animals shall be covered with sackcloth, and they shall cry mightily to God. Let all turn from their evil ways and from the violence that is in their hands. Who knows? God may relent and change his mind; he may turn from his fierce anger, so that we do not perish." God saw what they did, how they turned from their evil ways. So God changed his mind about the "evil" that he had said he would bring upon them; and he did not do it. (Jonah 3:7-10)

God "changed" by not carrying out the judgment announced by Jonah: "Forty days more, and Nineveh will be overthrown!" (Jon. 3:4). Why? Because the Ninevites repented—from the king all the way down to the animals. As they "turned from their evil ways," so God turned from delivering punishment against Israel's most hated enemy. God was moved from wrath to pity in response to *their* response. But Jonah was furious. He had hoped God would follow through on what he was sent to announce, assuming that God's word was final. To Jonah's dismay, that wasn't the case.

While Jonah didn't welcome God's change of mind, another prophet certainly did—Moses. After discovering the Israelites worshiping their golden calf, God was ready to destroy them. But Moses intervened with these words:

> Why should the Egyptians say, "It was with evil intent that he brought them out, only to kill them in the mountains and

> annihilate them from the face of the earth"? Turn from your burning wrath! Change your mind regarding the "evil" (you have planned) against your people. Remember Abraham, Isaac, and Israel, your servants, how you personally swore to them by your own self, saying to them, "I will multiply your descendants like the stars of heaven, and all this land that I have promised I will give to your descendants; they will inherit it forever." And YHWH changed his mind regarding the "evil" he planned against his people. (Exodus 32:12-14)

God relented from unleashing "burning wrath" on the Israelites for being so "stiff-necked" (Exod. 32:9), all due to Moses' intervention. Moses reminded God of the ancient promise made to Israel's ancestors, assuring them land and descendants. Destroying Israel in the wilderness would have effectively broken that covenant. This is one instance when both Moses and the Israelites could breathe a sigh of relief, grateful that God *can* change!

As for the idea that God is supposed to be devoid of emotions, Hosea challenges that by revealing the depths of a passionate and deeply emotional deity:

> My people persist in turning away from me.
> Although they call to the Most High,
> he will not raise them up.
> How can I give you up, O Ephraim?
> How can I hand you over, O Israel? . . .
> My heart stirs within me;
> my compassion grows warm and tender.
> I will not execute my burning anger;
> I will not again destroy Ephraim;
> for I am God and no human being,
> the Holy One in your midst,
> and I will not come in harshness. (Hosea 11:7-9)

In this anguished lament, mixed with strong resolve, God refuses to unleash wrath against Israel. Instead, God's "warm and tender" compassion wells up from within, leading God to resolve never again to "destroy Ephraim." Ironically, God declares a categorical distinction between the human and the divine. Back in the case of Saul and Samuel, God is said to be resolute in God's judgment of Saul, proving that God is "no human being." Unlike humans, God does not waver in judgment.

But in Hosea, the opposite is true! God is moved from "burning anger" to tender compassion, and that flexibility is what distinguishes God from mortals. Hosea celebrates the divine capacity for change. Here, the implication is that humans are the ones more inclined to act in anger and remain wrathful. Hosea's God, on the other hand, feels remorse for past actions, like Ephraim's destruction, and resolves to "never again" bring such "evil." In fact, moments of regret or sorrow seem to plague God at several points in the biblical narrative:

> YHWH was sorry for having made humankind on the earth;
> it grieved him to his heart. (Genesis 6:6)

> Samuel did not see Saul again until the day of his death, but Samuel grieved over Saul. And YHWH was sorry for having made Saul king over Israel. (1 Samuel 15:35)

> Thus says YHWH, the God of Israel . . . if you would only remain in this land, then I will build you up and not pull you down. I will plant you, and not uproot you; for I am sorry for the "evil" that I have brought upon you. (Jeremiah 42:9-10)

In each instance, God expresses remorse over past actions, whether in creation or judgment. One can imagine other moments, including those initiated by God, that may have brought sorrow to God's heart.

So what shall we say about God's supposedly "immutable" nature? It seems far more dynamic than fixed. God is not the "unmoved mover" of

Aristotle's physics-oriented definition.[4] Instead, scripture often portrays God as both the source of all creation and the one who is moved *by* it: the "moved mover." Yet, there are other things God doesn't budge on. Even Jonah recognized this, much to his disappointment. This resistant prophet discerned a divine constancy behind God's willingness to change course on prophetic judgments. Jonah saw that God is "gracious" and "compassionate, slow to anger, and abounding in benevolence, *ready to relent from punishing*" (Jon. 4:2). For Jonah, God's *ḥesed* is the constant that drives God's changeability. Jonah suspected it, feared it, and God proved him right.

God was moved by Nineveh's repentance, by Moses' prayer, and by the suffering of God's people. With the notable exception of Saul, God's merciful constancy is reflected in God's willingness to shift from judgment to mercy. God is always open to be moved by grief. The same is true of Jesus, the "image of the invisible God" (Col. 1:15), who was "deeply moved" and wept over the death of his friend Lazarus before raising him from the dead (John 11:33, 35).

The God of the Bible is paradoxically both dynamic and constant, impassioned yet resolute. This is an embodied God for an embodied people, one who prefers *ḥesed* over raising hell and love over destruction—a love that is hard-won and often painful, even for God. God, it seems, will seize any opportunity—especially through prayer and repentance—to move toward love, forgiveness, deliverance, and restoration, working toward "making all things new" (Rev. 21:5). As the letter of James says, "Every good and perfect gift is from above, coming down from the Father of the heavenly lights, who does not change like shifting shadows" (James 1:17). Yet, scripture shows that God does change—though more like the steady rising of the sun than the flicker of a shadow.

---

4. *Metaphysics*, Chapter 6, Book L.

DISCUSSION QUESTIONS

1. Does the idea of a God who can change feel threatening to your faith? Liberating? Somewhere in between? Why?
2. Has your understanding of God shifted after reading this discussion? What qualities or attributes define God for you?
3. What biblical account or tradition do you find most revealing about God?
4. In Genesis, God asks a lot of questions, beginning with "Where are you?" (Gen. 3:9; see also 3:11, 13; 4:9-10; 16:8). How does that fit with your view of God as omniscient? If God already knows the answers, why does God ask the questions?
5. How do you think God's sovereignty squares with human freedom—if at all?
6. What do you think of the stereotypical notion that the God of the Old Testament is about wrath, while the God of the New Testament is about love?

POSTSCRIPT

I hope you've found this journey through the dialogues of the Old Testament worth your time, offering a fresh perspective that the Bible is more like a library than a single book. The Bible is a sprawling anthology, crafted over a millennium, featuring a diverse collection of authors, editors, redactors, interpreters, and readers, including you and me. Regardless of where you stand on the topic of divine inspiration, the Bible's diversity is undeniable—and, I'd argue, intentional. This variety itself is inspired: a purposeful, canonical multiplicity designed to spark dialogue on issues you may have thought were long settled. But leave it to the Bible to reopen and complicate our understanding of long-held views about God, creation, human purpose, and so much more. And believe me, we've only scratched the surface.

Reading the Bible as dialogue may feel like an entirely new approach for many people. It demands a kind of deep reading, far removed from the quick scans we're used to on social media. This type of reading calls for diving deeply into each and every passage, understanding its background and historical context, and exploring what it contributes to the dialogue with other texts within the Bible's vast conversation.

Often, we read the Bible seeking a single, definitive answer to our questions. But the Bible's richness lies in its polyphony—it resists simplistic, soundbite interpretations. Proof-texting, the practice of ripping texts from their broader contexts, flattens the Bible's complexity. On the flip side, reading scripture in this dialogical way can enrich our appreciation for its wondrous diversity of perspectives and literary genres, encouraging a more attentive and thoughtful engagement.

The Bible was born out of multiplicity—from its numerous "original" texts and authors to the varied viewpoints they express and the various contexts from which they emerge. This inherent variety invites a multiplicity of readers, beckoning each one to find their own way through scripture's multiverse of voices. It's perfectly okay to be critical of some of these voices because engaging with the Bible's plurality naturally fosters critical thinking—and that's a good thing. Contrary to what some may believe, the Bible doesn't demand blind faith or naïve acceptance. Instead, it invites a posture of expectant, reverential, yet critical engagement.

Take, for example, the ethical challenges posed by the atrocity of America's historical involvement in the trans-Atlantic slave trade. While the Bible, in its historical context, accepts slavery (albeit in limited ways), we rightly reject it outright today. Similarly, many of us strive to make worship more inclusive, even though passages like Leviticus 21:18-19 exclude people with disabilities. And who among us would consider wearing polyester an abomination, as suggested in Leviticus 19:19?

The Bible thrives under dialogical engagement; it is crafted for transformation. It invites us into a process of wonder, questioning, and critical discernment. It was never meant to be static or simplistic—it was designed for exploration, challenging us to grow and rethink as we interact with scripture's dynamic, multivoiced character.

The Bible's rich diversity offers a kind of *dialogic* truth[1]—truth that emerges through critical engagement with differing perspectives, rather than the kind of truth that's accepted without question and considered beyond further investigation. This dialogic truth is often open-ended, inviting reflection, engagement, and even revision. It's truth on the move. This truth is certainly not something we arrive at through proof-texting—after all, even the devil can quote scripture (Matt. 4:6, referencing Ps. 91:12).

---

1. The most accessible and compelling discussion of the Bible's dialogic truth is found in Carol A. Newsom's essay, "Bakhtin, the Bible, and Dialogic Truth," *Journal of Religion* 76, 2 (1996): 290-306.

Biblical truths are often more timely than timeless, shaped by the context in which they are read and understood. The more we engage with scripture, the more it challenges us to sit with unresolved tensions on deeply pressing issues—abortion, war, the death penalty, sexual orientation, gender identity, creation care and more. The Bible has been, and continues to be, used to support arguments on both sides of these debates among people of faith. Unfortunately, such arguments often lack the mutual respect and careful listening needed for true dialogue. In today's polarized climate, it's even rarer for such debates to lead to mutual understanding and transformation.

Given its diversity, the Bible invites us into a kind of dialogue that isn't driven by an attitude of "winner takes all" or defeating the other side. Instead, genuine dialogue resembles a dance more than a battle. In a dance of equal partners, there's give and take, push and pull, balance and mutual guidance—creating something greater than what either partner could ever achieve alone. Dialogue is collaborative, not combative, and it reflects the kind of engagement the Bible itself calls for. Such is the Bible's gift: to promote rather than clamp down dialogue.

Reading the Bible with an eye toward its diversity—and exploring its own internal disagreements and tensions—cultivates a critical consciousness that can guide us in navigating contentious issues. It encourages us to approach these matters with a listening ear, a receptive heart, and genuine respect for others. This perspective is grounded in the conviction that God is actively at work in the world, calling us to pursue justice and peace for the sake of human flourishing—and for all creation—so that the whole world may join in the dance of life!

I end with a reflection from Katherine Johnson, a former student, on the dialogical nature of scripture—words that, honestly, I couldn't have said better myself:

> Perhaps a Bible that makes room for tension between divergent perspectives—a Bible that models a brave refusal to delete the voices that disagree, a Bible that is comfortable with leaving

questions open and unanswered, a Bible that invites dialogue, a Bible that compels us to take an active role in wrestling with its ideas in our own hearts and in community with other people who interpret it differently than we do—is precisely the kind of Bible that God intended for us to have.

Amen! And may the dialogues continue!

ACKNOWLEDGMENTS

This book has been a long time in coming, but patience, I can attest, does bear fruit, particularly the patience of others. First, this is the book that Gail, my partner in life, has wanted me to write for some time, a book that is easily accessible for a large readership, including folks who simply want "more Bible" and are not satisfied with scriptural soundbites or proof texts. It is also the book that David C. Teel, director of Laity in Leadership at Discipleship Ministries of The United Methodist Church, has wanted me to write for years. I thank David for generating the idea at its inception and being patiently encouraging for so long as I have bounced from one project to another over the years finally to arrive at this one. An immense thanks also to Benjamin Howard and Michael Stephens of Upper Room Books for helping to shepherd this project to its publication. I am honored and grateful that Upper Room deemed this project to be a worthy undertaking.

My gratitude also extends to Dana AbuGhazaleh, Columbia Theological Seminary student extraordinaire, for her research and helpful editorial suggestions throughout much of the book's development. Last and most importantly, my thanks to Gail, who diligently read every draft chapter and filled it with question marks and suggestions for clarity. This book is "Gail-approved," which means it is already a resounding success. Indeed, it is the most I could hope for. I dedicate this book to her in deep gratitude for our partnership of thirty-four years.

BIBLIOGRAPHY

Adichie, Chimamanda Ngozi. "The Danger of a Single Story." *TED Talk* (October 7, 2009) at https://www.youtube.com/watch?v=D9Ihs241 zeg.

Albertz, Rainer. *Israel in Exile: The History and Literature of the Sixth Century B.C.E.* Translated by David Green. Studies in Biblical Literature 3; Atlanta: SBL Press, 2003.

Ariarajah, S. Wesley. "Creation of a 'Culture of Dialogue' in a Multicultural and Pluralist Society." *Communication and Reconciliation: Challenges Facing the 21st Century.* Edited by Philip Lee. Geneva, Switzerland: WCC Publications, 2001, 1-9.

Auerbach, Erich. *Mimesis: The Representation of Reality in Western Literature.* Translated by Willard R. Trask. Princeton, NJ: Princeton University, 1974[1953].

Bohm, David. *On Dialogue.* London: Routledge Classics, 2004.

Brown, William P. *Deep Calls to Deep: The Psalms in Dialogue amid Disruption.* Nashville, TN: Abingdon, 2021.

Brown, William P. *The Seven Pillars of Creation: The Bible, Science, and the Ecology of Wonder.* New York: Oxford University Press, 2010.

Brown, William P. "When Wisdom Fails." *"When the Morning Stars Sang": Essays in Honor of Choon Leong Seow on the Occasion of His Sixty-Fifth Birthday*. Edited by Scott C. Jones and Christine Roy Yoder. BZAW 500; Berlin: Walter de Gruyter, 2018, 209-23.

Callahan, Allen Dwight. *The Talking Book: African Americans and the Bible*. New Haven: Yale University Press, 2006.

Crawford, Sidnie White. "41. 4QDeut^{n}." *Qumran Cave 4.IX: Deuteronomy, Joshua, Judges, Kings*. Edited by Eugene Ulrich et al. DJD 14; Oxford: Clarendon, 1995, 117-28.

Ellison III, Gregory. *Fearless Dialogues*. Louisville, KY: Westminster John Knox, 2017.

Fackenheim, Emil L. *God's Presence in History: Jewish Affirmations and Philosophical Reflections*. New York: Harper & Row, 1972.

Feenstra, Ernest S. "Christian Impact on Ecology." *Science* 156, 3776 (May 1967): 737.

Fox, Michael V. *Proverbs 1-9: A New Translation with Introduction and Commentary*. The Anchor Bible 18A; New York: Doubleday, 2000.

Gammie, John G. *Holiness in Israel*. Overtures to Biblical Theology; Minneapolis: Fortress, 1989.

Gates Jr., Henry Louis, and William L. Andrews, eds. *Pioneers of the Black Atlantic: Five Slave Narratives from the Enlightenment, 1772-1815*. Washington, DC: Civitas, 1998.

Kaminsky, Joel S. "Humor and the Theology of Hope: Isaac as a Humorous Figure." *Interpretation: A Journal of Bible and Theology* 54, 4 (2000): 363-75.

Kaminsky, Joel S. *Yet I Loved Jacob: Reclaiming the Biblical Concept of Election*. Nashville, TN: Abingdon, 2007.

LeFebvre, Michael. *Collections, Codes, and Torah: The Re-Characterization of Israel's Written Law*. LHB/OTS 451; London/New York: T&T Clark, 2016.

Lewis, C. S. *Reflections on the Psalms*. New York: Harcourt, Brace, Jovanovich, 1958.

McLaren, Brian. "I'd Like To Give You the Benefit of the Doubt, But . . ." (May 12, 2011), https://brianmclaren.net/q-r-id-like-to-give-you-the-benefit-of-the-doubt-but..

Newsom, Carol A. *The Book of Job: A Contest of Moral Imaginations*. Oxford: Oxford University Press, 2003.

Newsom, Carol A. "Bakhtin, the Bible, and Dialogic Truth." *Journal of Religion* 76, 2 (1996): 290-306.

Propp, Willam H. C. *Exodus 19-40: A New Translation with Introduction and Commentary*. Volume 2A. The Anchor Yale Bible Commentary; New Haven & London: Yale University Press, 2006.

Sanders, Seth L. "What If There Aren't Any Empirical Models for Pentateuchal Criticism?" *Contextualizing Israel's Sacred Writings: Ancient Literacy, Orality, and Literary Production*. Edited by Brian B. Schmidt. Ancient Israel and Its Literature 22; Atlanta: SBL Press, 2015, 281-304.

Schirsch, Lisa, and David Campt. *The Little Book of Dialogue for Difficult Subjects: A Practical, Hands-On Guide*. The Little Books of Justice and Peacebuilding; New York: Good Books, 2007.

Solzhenitsyn, Aleksandr I. *The Gulag Archieplago, 1918-1952: An Experiment in Literary Investigation Volume 2*. Translated by Thomas P. Whitney. New York: Harper Perennial, 1974.

Tsevat, Matitiahu. "The Meaning of the Book of Job." *The Meaning of the Book of Job and Other Biblical Studies*. New York: Ktav, 1981, 1-37.

Webster, John. *Holiness*. Grand Rapids, MI: Eerdmans, 2003.

White Jr., Lynn. "The Historical Roots of Our Ecological Crisis." *Science* 155, 3767 (10 March 1967): 1203-1207.

Yadin, Azzan. "Qôl as Hypostasis in the Hebrew Bible," JBL 122, 4 (2003): 601-26.

ABBREVIATIONS

BZAW	Beihefte zur Zeitschrift für die altestamentliche Wissenschaft
CEB	Common English Bible
DJD	Discoveries in the Judean Desert
KJV	Kings James Version
JBL	*Journal of Biblical Literature*
LHB/OTS	Library of Hebrew Bible/Old Testament Studies
NRSV	New Revised Standard Version
SBL	Society of Biblical Literature